THE OPEN UNIVERSITY

Arts: A Third Level Course

Modern Art 1848 to the Present:
Styles and Social Implications

Unit 10
FROM EASEL TO MACHINE

Prepared by Charlotte Benton for the Course Team

Unit 11
DE STIJL: THE RECONSTRUCTION OF LIFE THROUGH ART AND TECHNOLOGY

Unit 12
ARTISTS OF THE BAUHAUS

Prepared by Stephen Bayley for the Course Team

The Open University Press

The Open University Press
Walton Hall Milton Keynes MK7 6AA

First published 1976

Designed by the Media Development Group of the Open University.

Printed in Great Britain by
COES THE PRINTERS LIMITED
RUSTINGTON, SUSSEX

ISBN 0 335 05154 5

This text forms part of an Open University course. The complete list of units in the course appears at the end of this text.

For general availability of supporting material referred to in this text please write to the Director of Marketing, The Open University, P.O. Box 81, Walton Hall, Milton Keynes, MK7 6AT.

Further information on Open University courses may be obtained from the Admissions Office, The Open University, P.O. Box 48, Walton Hall, Milton Keynes, MK7 6AB.

1.1

Unit 10 From Easel to Machine

Introduction 4

Part I ***West versus East*** 8

Channels of Artistic Communication with the West 8

Primitivism and Other Movements 12

Suprematism 23

The Beginnings of Constructivism 27

'0.10: The Last Futurist Exhibition' 30

Part II ***Artists and the Revolution*** 32

A Policy for Art? 33

Russo-German Links 39

Art Education after the Revolution 42

Metaphors of Construction 51

1922 and After 59

Conclusion 61

Introduction

The subject matter of this unit cannot be classified under a style label—there is no single equivalent of the 'movements' which have provided the focus for the preceding three units. But you will be able to recognize many elements that are common to (and sometimes drawn directly from) Cubism, Expressionism and Futurism. And when you have read the other two units in this block, on *De Stijl* and the Bauhaus, you should be able to relate contemporary developments in Europe to those in Russia during the latter part of the period covered by this unit.

Considered in purely formal terms it is possible to view developments in Russian art *c.*1908–14 as a series of more or less quantifiable responses to more 'central' movements in European art—Fauvism, Cubism and Futurism especially. But to measure the 'success' or significance of Russian art only against its sources tends to lead to the conclusion that most Russian artists 'misunderstood' the sources on which they drew, crudely misappropriating formal devices to produce nothing much more than 'provincial' variants. Seen in this light the development of a powerfully radical abstract art between *c.*1914–16 must be, at best, fortuitous.

In the context of this course there are two main reasons for looking at Russian avant-garde art of the period covered by the unit, one of which has been outlined above. The names of a handful of Russian artists (Gabo, Kandinsky, Lissitsky, Malevich and Tatlin) will be found in any general history of modern art of the first quarter of the century, as 'pioneers' of abstraction in an 'heroic' age. Although some of these artists spent much of their working lives outside Russia, they maintained links which were important for the development of their own work as well as that of artists working in Russia. Another reason is for the more or less unique spectacle of avant-garde artists appearing to enjoy, for a few years after the Revolution of October 1917, the more or less exclusive patronage of the state.

The timespan covered by the unit (*c.*1908–22) is intended to reflect the points at which, at one end, current European art became of particular importance to Russian artists and, at the other, the point at which Russian art, in turn, made its major impact on Europe, partly through the emigration (or return) to Europe in or around 1922 of a number of Russian avant-garde artists, but more spectacularly through the huge exhibition of Russian post-Revolution art held at the Van Diemen Gallery in Berlin, and later in Amsterdam, in that year.

In a unit of this length it would obviously be unrealistic to attempt to include a survey of the various groupings and tendencies. I have chosen to concentrate on a handful of themes which can be expressed in the following aims:

1 To comment on, and in some cases amplify, Hamilton's narrative;

2 To indicate the context in which Russian avant-garde artists were working in the years before and immediately after the Revolution;

3 To suggest ways in which the relationship between Russian and European avant-garde art during these years might be considered and to suggest the particular contribution of Russian art to the development of European art from *c.*1922.

The text takes the form of a set of linked and parallel studies rather than that of a continuous narrative.

A NOTE ON THE SET TEXTS

Hamilton

Hamilton provides a basic outline of the period and you should read all the extracts listed below, if you have not already done so, *before* reading the rest of the unit. They will give you the general framework against which to set the material in the unit. You may find it useful to make brief notes on the various groups and artists, and I suggest that as you read the extracts you make some attempt to see what position Hamilton takes. (Why, for example, does he separate Chagall, and Gabo and Pevsner from the main discussion of the period—pp. 306–19?)

pp. 136–40: 'Symbolist Art in Russia: The Slavic Revival and Mir Iskusstva'. (Pay particular attention to the composition of the *Mir Iskusstva* group and its aims, the influence of Symbolism and the nature of the 'Slavic revival'.)

pp. 205–14: 'Kandinsky in Munich: 1896–1914'. (See also Unit 8, pp. 98–101.)

pp. 303–19: Introduction to Chapter 6 and 'Abstract and Non-Objective Art in Russia: 1904–22'. (Note particularly Hamilton's view of the reasons for the evolution of abstraction.)

pp. 352–56: Part of the section entitled 'Later Constructivist Sculpture: Gabo and Pevsner'.

pp. 435–39: 'Marc Chagall'.

Haftmann

You will need Haftmann for reference. Haftmann's selection of illustrations of Russian art of the period covered by the unit is fairly limited. Use the index to check how Haftmann's illustrations supplement those in Hamilton and in the unit, as they are distributed in different sections of his book.

The timespan of this unit covers the twin social upheavals of the First World War and the Russian Revolution. (Russia was heavily involved in the war, losing over one million men at the front and suffering casualties many times that figure. At least another 1.5 million lives were lost during the Civil War, 1918–21.) That these events are likely to have affected the work of artists, not least in their ability to practise their *métier*, must be obvious. But the ways in which the war affected Russian artists are not those we might be led to expect by reference to the effects elsewhere.

Exercise

On the basis of your reading of Hamilton, what would you note in particular about developments in art in Russia during the years of the First War? (Make sure that you are familiar with the illustrations in Haftmann as well before you answer this. I am not assuming that you have necessarily read already those sections of Hamilton which cover contemporary developments in Europe such as *De Stijl* in Holland and Dada in Switzerland but it is all to the good if you have.)

Discussion

You may have been surprised to note that some 'key' developments (e.g. Malevich's Suprematism and Tatlin's 'culture of materials') take place against this background. In other words, that it was precisely during these years that a powerful and formally radical abstract art can be seen to have developed in Russia (see, for example, Hamilton pp. 310–13 and 316–17 and Haftmann 353–54 and 360). There also seems to have been an intensification of artistic polemics (e.g. among the Russian 'Futurists' exhibiting at '0.10').

We tend to view this period as one in which, throughout Europe, radical artistic activity virtually ceased as artists were dispersed or isolated (e.g. in France, Germany and, to some extent, Italy) and in which there was a hiatus both in the lives of 'movements' or groups (e.g. the Cubists) as well as in the work of particular artists (e.g.

Picasso, Juan Gris). To some extent, also, we identify the development and transformation of pre-war avant-garde artistic ideas predominantly with those *neutral* countries (e.g. Holland, Switzerland particularly) which, during the war years, saw the coming together of new groupings (sometimes international in character) of avant-garde artists, e.g. in Dada and *De Stijl*. Clearly such tendencies need qualification in the light of developments in Russia.

That artistic activity should seem to have intensified in this period is, in many ways, surprising; one would tend to assume that artists would have found it *more* difficult not only to find the materials for their work, but more difficult to find opportunities to work (unless employed as official war artists). Yet Malevich's main period of intense activity on the development of his Suprematist paintings (see Haftmann 359–61) seems to have been during 1915. And it is surprisingly difficult to get any clear idea of the way in which many of the artists we shall consider spent the war years. Mikhail Larionov was involved in active service and invalided out of the army. But of many of the others, including the many artists who returned from Europe after the outbreak of war, it is difficult to be certain. Perhaps, like Marc Chagall—of whom we do have an account—they pulled strings to get desk jobs in agencies directing war supplies in Moscow or St Petersburg. Whatever their circumstances it was an extremely prolific period in terms of artistic output. Since many of the artists we shall discuss assumed positions of prominence in the years immediately after the Revolution we might also wonder about their involvement in politics. But it is difficult to be certain of the precise political sympathies, if any, of particular artists. During the years between the 1905 Revolution and the war, we can find signs of some of the future members of the avant garde actively involved in liberal and left-wing politics, but this was not unusual for the period. It was almost impossible for intellectuals not to be anti-Tsarist. And in some cases such involvement was short-lived.

Exercise

Now reread Hamilton pp. 303–19, 352–56 and 435–39.

1 What observations would you make about Hamilton's general approach (what are his particular emphases)?

2 What sort of questions do you think his approach avoids?

Discussion

1 It seems to me that Hamilton takes a typically broad view (partly conditioned, of course, by the scope and format of the book), tending to stress those formal and stylistic characteristics which will allow him to assimilate Russian developments with contemporary avant-garde developments in Europe. Thus the extent to which Russian artists were influenced by, or borrowed directly from, their European contemporaries is central to the discussion; Moscow and St Petersburg tend to be seen as artistic outposts, with artists practising predominantly in the *style* of Paris, with a dash of the styles of Munich and Milan. It is certainly true that we can identify to a number of close parallels and direct influences: for example the phenomenon of 'neo-primitivism' in Russian art (Hamilton, pp. 306–7) is more or less exactly contemporaneous with the primitivist phase of German Expressionist art (and, you may have noted, with Picasso's interest in African sculpture).

2 Hamilton has rather little to say about either the 'why?' of question 1 or the *differences* between parallel manifestations. For example, although he notes in passing that Russian neo-primitivism embodies the stylistic characteristics of Fauvism but is more like German Expressionist work in its 'emphasis on theme and content', he does not really indicate in what ways this may be shown. You may have noted also that the approach outlined in (1) results in the complete separation of Gabo and Pevsner on the one hand and Chagall on the other from the main discussion of Russian art on pp. 303–19, and that Kandinsky is slotted into the German sections on either side. In

other words Hamilton discusses them in their more familiar European contexts and, although he mentions changes in their work during their 'Russian' periods, does not discuss these changes in any detail.

I would also comment on the fact that Hamilton does not anywhere really explore the possibility of associational or symbolic qualities in the work discussed; in other words, *content* is more or less ignored.

Throughout this unit I hope you will bear in mind the idea that formal resemblances between works of different origins may need to be considered in a variety of ways, and that you will remember what has been stressed already elsewhere in this course—that 'influences' are not always transmitted in conveniently recognizable formal and visual terms.

Part I *West versus East*

The history of Russian art from the time of Peter the Great to the beginning of the twentieth century shows a predominance of European styles in Russian courtly and later bourgeois art, countered by recurrent attempts to inject a purely national character either through topical subject matter or through the revival of national styles (see, for example, Hamilton, pp. 136–40). Russian artists of the first decade of the twentieth century were no exception to tradition in looking towards the contemporary art of the west.

Channels of Artistic Communication with the West

Broadly speaking we should consider three main channels of communication of Western artistic ideas in the early twentieth century and their effect. They are (not necessarily in order of significance): personal travel, illustrated magazines, private collectors and patrons.

TRAVEL

As Hamilton points out, a large number of Russian painters visited or worked in Paris during the years before the First World War, but Munich was a powerful rival to Paris for Russian artists' attentions from the 1890s until the First World War. In addition to Kandinsky who had lived in Munich since 1896, there were also a number of other Russian émigré artists in the Munich *Neue Künstlervereinigung* (*NKV*: 'New Artists' Association') and *Blaue Reiter* circles, of whom Marianna Verefkina and Alexei Yavlensky are two of the best known[1]. Naum Gabo also lived in Munich from *c.*1910 when he was studying engineering but also attending Heinrich Wölfflin's art history lectures and mixing with artists.

MAGAZINES

The technical perfection and growth of the means of dissemination of photo-mechanical reproductions in the later nineteenth century gave artists access to a vastly enlarged repertoire of the history of European art, as well as to more sophisticated knowledge of the art and artefacts of non-European cultures. By the end of the nineteenth century it was possible to disseminate widely and rapidly good half-tone illustrations of recent work, and there was also a style—Art Nouveau—whose characteristics were particularly suitable to transmission through graphic means. It is an acknowledgement of the effectiveness of such means of communication that the last decade of the nineteenth century and the first decade of the twentieth saw the growth of a number of specialist art magazines, sometimes privately financed and luxuriously produced[2], which were aimed deliberately at an international market amongst artists, dealers and collectors. In a very real sense the 'museum without walls' had come into existence, and the 'global village' was growing with the rapid development of new means of transport and of telecommunications. Consciousness of these changes and the way in which they impinged on the artist's traditional procedures and thus gave him acute reason to question his social role, was one of the key ingredients affecting attitudes to, and the appearance of, avant-garde art.

COLLECTORS AND PATRONS

(See Hamilton, pp. 305–6.)

One characteristic which appears to distinguish the Moscow and St Petersburg avant garde, in the years before the Revolution, from their contemporaries in Paris or Berlin is their greater reliance on a small handful of private collectors and patrons, both for support for their own activities and for access to examples of contemporary European art[3]. (There seems to have been no equivalent of professional dealers like D.-H. Kahnweiler in Paris or Herwarth Walden in Berlin.)

To list some examples: Chagall was dependent on a patron in St Petersburg for help with his studies there and for a small subsidy on which he was able to travel to and work in Paris before the war. Nikolay Ryabushinsky, a member of a well established Moscow merchant family, financed as well as edited *Zolotoye Rune* (*The Golden Fleece*), the magazine of the *Golubaya Rosa* ('Blue Rose') group (see Hamilton, p. 306), founded in 1906 'to propagate Russian art beyond the country of its birth, to represent it in Europe in a whole and integrated fashion in the very process of its development'[4] and printed in Russian and French. Ryabushinsky also supported the primitivist painters (e.g. Larionov and Goncharova) and financed a series of exhibitions between 1907 and 1910. Vladimir Izdebsky, a friend of Kandinsky, himself a painter and a founder member of the *Neue Künstlervereinigung* (founded 1909) and exhibitor with the *Blaue Reiter* group, organized two major exhibitions in 1909–10 and 1910–11, which included the work of the Munich artists as well as of the Fauves and Cubists and were shown in Odessa and Kiev. A Moscow businessman offered exhibiting space to young artists, although he did not buy their work; and so on.

Collectors were important to artists in other ways as well. From the late 1880s and the 1890s a number of Russian collectors began to be interested in the work of the French Impressionists and Post-Impressionists, and it was partly through such collections that Russian artists became more knowledgeable about recent French art. Most important from the point of view of the period with which we are concerned were two collections, amassed by the Moscow merchants Ivan Morozov and Sergey Shchukin (see Hamilton, p. 305–6) which besides including examples of Impressionist and Neo-Impressionist painters' work also included Fauve and Cubist work. Note, also, that from *c.*1909 work by some of the key figures of the European avant garde could be seen in group exhibitions in Moscow, Leningrad and elsewhere.

IVAN MOROZOV (1871–1921)

Morozov began his collection in the late 1890s with paintings by the Russian *Peredvizhniki* ('The Wanderers') and *Mir Iskusstva* ('World of Art') artists, later moving on (probably after 1900) to collect the work of French Impressionist and Post-Impressionist artists. His collection included examples of work by all the major Impressionist painters. Post-Impressionist painters represented included Bonnard, Vuillard, Gauguin, Van Gogh, Signac and Maurice Denis. In 1907 he commissioned Denis to paint a cycle of paintings for his Moscow house on the theme of the story of Psyche. Morozov acquired a number of paintings by Fauve painters, and work by Matisse from between 1909–14, but, unlike Shchukin he never made the step from Fauvism to Cubism. Morozov's collection was less accessible than Shchukin's—only close friends and a handful of connoisseurs appear to have had access to it. Even so, the collection was well known in artistic circles through loans to exhibitions and certainly through publications[5].

SERGEY SHCHUKIN (1854–1936)

Shchukin began buying paintings from the Paris salons during the early 1890s, but it was only from *c.*1897 that he began to collect the kind of paintings for which his collection is now remembered. Either by luck or good judgement he acquired a fairly representative collection of work by Impressionist, Post-Impressionist and Fauve painters over the next few years (although it is possible that he was simply operating on the 'one of each' principle). Before he began to collect work by Matisse and Picasso, to the exclusion of all others, by far the best represented painters in his collection were Monet and Gauguin. Although he appears usually to have bought paintings he liked, it is likely that there was an element of *épater le bourgeois* in his choices[6]. Writing an appreciation of Shchukin in 1936, shortly after his death, Alexander Benois noted:

> .... some thirty years ago I visited his beautiful home for the first time.... Immediately on crossing the threshold one felt transported to Paris, the avant-garde Paris, where the visitor met the paintings of Monet, Renoir, Cézanne, and the others. My God! How Sergei Ivanonovich was made to suffer for his 'sins' at the hands of those 'aesthetes' among the Moscow money-bags. His collecting was not a whim, but a genuine feat of courage, for in addition to attacks by others he had to fight against his own doubts.... He emerged from all these conflicts with renewed daring, retaining his good humour and never spiteful....
> (Quoted in Ginsburg, 1973, pp. 484–85.)

Matisse introduced Shchukin to Picasso at just the time when the latter was working on the series of figure studies which followed the *Demoiselles*. Before 1914 Shchukin acquired fifty paintings by Picasso (apparently mainly Cubist works). Kahnweiler, Picasso's Paris dealer, later claimed that whenever he telegraphed that he had new paintings in stock Shchukin would travel at once to Paris to see them. Yet Gertrude Stein reported Shchukin as being shocked when he first saw the *Demoiselles*:

> I remember Tschoukine [*sic*], who had so much admired the painting of Picasso, was at my home and he said, almost in tears, what a loss for French art.
> (Stein, 1938, p. 18.)

Was Shchukin quickly converted to the work that followed the *Demoiselles*? Or should we read Gertrude Stein's 'evidence' as that of one collector vying with another for the 'most advanced' taste? Certainly the Steins may have encouraged Shchukin's interest in Picasso's work since one of the paintings in the Shchukin collection (*Three Women*, 1908/9, now in the Hermitage, Leningrad) appears to have been acquired from the Steins[7].

Whatever the circumstances in which Shchukin began to collect Picasso's work, he acquired a substantial number of precisely those paintings which explore the formal and expressive possibilities hinted at in the *Demoiselles*. These included a number of the figure paintings of 1908–9 which explore a variety of techniques of modelling form, from the kinds of striations and faceting Picasso had observed in African sculpture, and massively simplified form (Fig. 1) to the simplified classicism of *Three Women* (Unit 7, Fig. 15). Shchukin's taste for strong colour (he owned a number of the more hotly coloured of Gauguin's paintings as well as those by Matisse) is also reflected in some of the paintings by Picasso which he acquired. We tend to think of even the early phase of Cubism as dominated by a tendency to use muted colour but some of the figure paintings of 1908–9 used bright colour and Shchukin also owned later Cubist paintings of uncharacteristically varied colour. Both Picasso and Matisse were allotted special rooms of their own in Shchukin's Moscow house; Shchukin meticulously accumulated a collection of Congolese and Madagascan sculpture to display alongside Picasso's Cubist paintings.

By 1912 the quality of the collection as a whole was widely known to specialists; progressive museum directors[8] and private collectors whose opinion Shchukin valued visited Moscow to inspect the collection. Shchukin had hesitated initially over accepting *Dance* and *Music* but he can hardly have sustained his inhibitions for long

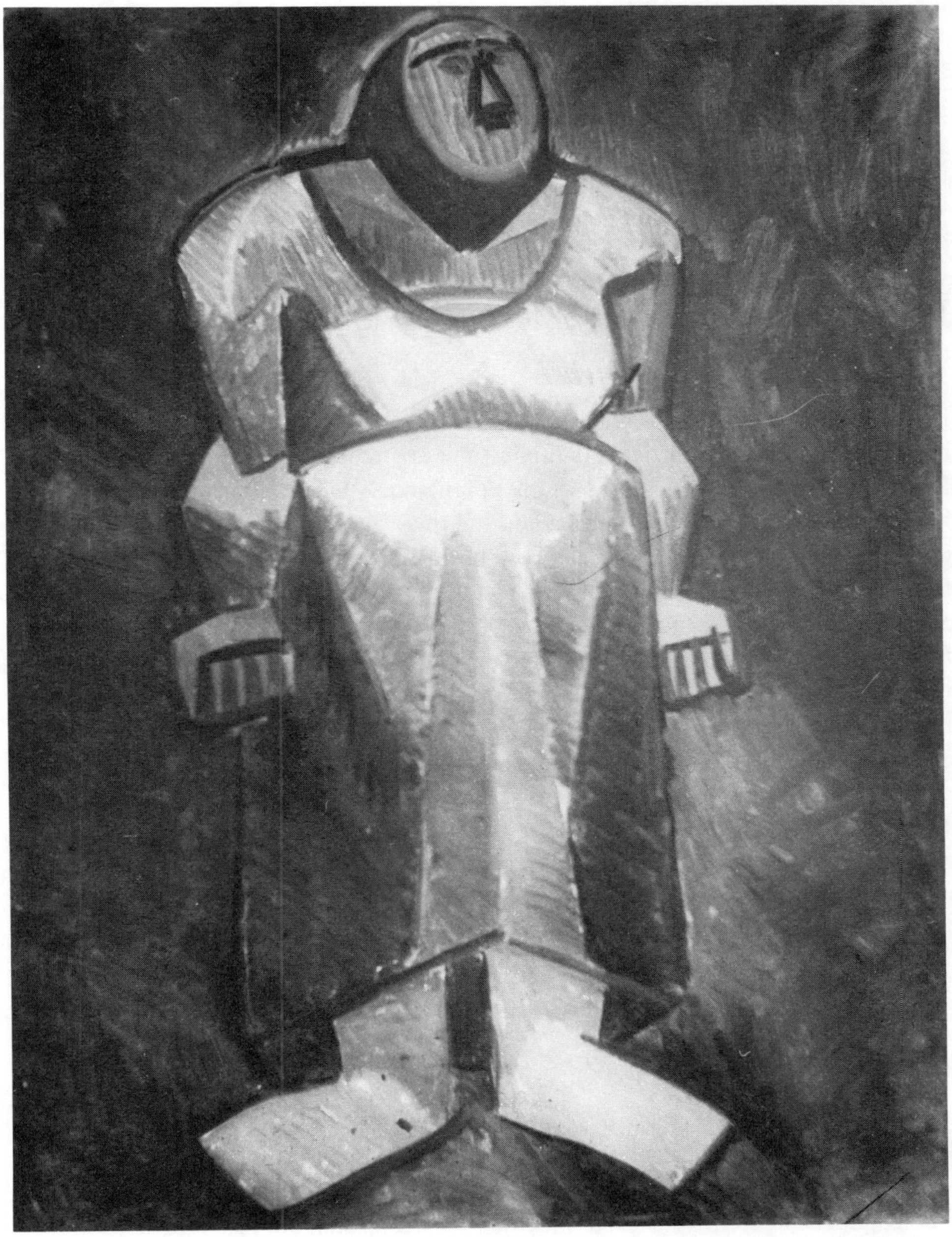

Figure 1 Pablo Picasso, *La Paysanne* (or *La Fermière*), 1908, oil, 32×26 ins (Formerly Shchukin collection, Hermitage, Leningrad; photo: Galerie Louise Leiris © SPADEM 1976).

after that. He now had an incentive to maintain a particular kind of 'standard' in his collection.

In the years before the war Shchukin's collection was open to visitors every Sunday when Shchukin was in Moscow and Shchukin would personally guide the visitors—who included artists, students and journalists—around the collection. The Shchukin collection was important both for the kinds of painting it contained and its rather pedantic, concentrated manner of display (e.g. African sculpture alongside Picasso's Cubist paintings)[9]. Its impact was widely felt in quite obvious ways. Leonid Pasternak, who taught at the Moscow School of Painting, Sculpture and Architecture, complained of its effect on his students:

> You can do nothing with them; the model is a pale skinny girl and the student's painting shows a dark African woman. 'Is this an Ethiopian?' I ask. 'Don't you see that she's white?' The reply is: 'This is how I see her, and I paint what I see.' 'Are you a frequent visitor at Shchukin's?' The enthusiastic answer is: 'Oh yes. Shchukin invites us all the time.'
> (Quoted in Ginsburg, 1973, p. 484.)

Primitivism and Other Movements

(See Hamilton, pp. 305–6.)

Hamilton notes that the phenomenon of primitivism in Russian painting parallels the *Blaue Reiter* artists' interest in non-European art at exactly this time. Incidentally, you may remember that David Burliuk contributed a companion essay ('The "Savages" of Russia') to one of Franz Marc's ('The "Savages" of Germany') in the *Blaue Reiter* almanac. In this section I shall attempt both to indicate some of the sources and to discuss further its relationship with European primitivism.

Primitivism as an identifiable visual phenomenon in Russian art lasts from *c.*1908–12, but traces of its characteristics and implications are to be found in later work (e.g. in Russian Futurism and in Tatlin's 'culture of materials'). Russian primitivism was not, however, a cohesive *stylistic* phenomenon and this is one characteristic which distinguishes it most clearly from, for example, the 'primitivism' of the *Brücke* artists or the Cubists; it drew on a vast range of sources and its significance is diffuse. As far as we are concerned here, the main importance of the primitivist movement in Russia is that it brought together certain formal characteristics borrowed or adapted from recent European painting with an indigenous interest in particular kinds of subject matter and in semantic issues[10]. In general terms Russian primitivism coincides with a renewed interest in Slavic and oriental (as opposed to Western) traditions as well as representing the assimilation of anti-naturalistic tendencies from recent French art. In his essay for the *Blaue Reiter* almanac Burliuk reviewed the significance of French painting of the last thirty years for his generation, in crystallizing the perception that paintings could be liberated from their traditional representational role:

> What we first thought to be the 'clumsiness' of Cézanne and the frantic 'handwriting' of Van Gogh is something greater after all: it is the revelation of new truths and new means...
> (Translated in Lankheit, 1974.)

Primitivism in Russian art certainly implied a polemical position in relation to the values of both traditional academic art and the Symbolist aesthetics (and aristocratic, Francophile, and literary tastes) of the *Mir Iskusstva* group, but to some extent the primitivist artists (e.g. Goncharova, Larionov, Malevich) retained an interest in semantic issues which can be related to the concerns of the Symbolists.

The emergence of primitivism corresponds with a period of social unrest in the years following the abortive Revolution of 1905 and of renewed concern with the 'peasant problem', as well as a period of national introspection following the Russian defeat in the Russo–Japanese war. And primitivist painters stressed that their works took subjects of social concern. But the rise of the primitivist movement must be seen also in the context of parallel interests in contemporary European art of changing attitudes to the historiography of art and to the growing interest in, and scholarly knowledge of, Russian art in Europe and Russia.

The enormously expanded comparative visual material available by the end of the nineteenth century saw European art historians gradually becoming conscious of the need to expand their critical/theoretical framework to account for not only the relationship between European and non-European art but also (for example) that between Italian 'primitive' painting and the art of the Renaissance. Wilhelm Worringer's *Abstraktion und Einfühlung* (*Abstraction and Empathy*, first published in 1908) is a good example, from the period, of this shift. Worringer himself points to the significance of these changes, citing the contemporary interest in Byzantine art as an example, and he uses Byzantine art as a prime example of one side of the dialectic implied by the title of his book. Russian artists, whether or not they had direct access to Worringer's book, were conscious of the expansion of the critical/theoretical frontiers of art history and perhaps because they had never had a secure place within established Western tradition were all the more prepared to jettison it. In this process the growth of interest in the *Slavic* art of the past among scholars and collectors provided a catalyst.

Although Russian Primitivism *c.*1908–12—unlike, in most respects, the parallel 'primitivist' manifestations in France and Germany (in the work of Cubist and Expressionist painters)—drew on a very wide range of predominantly *national* sources in both technique and subject matter, it was very far from being an 'archaeological' movement. Its sources included peasant art (carved and painted designs); Russian mediaeval and religious imagery (icons); folk imagery (*lubki*, playing cards, etc.); and, in addition, 'naive' sources such as sign-painting and graffiti (Plate 1).

Lubki were popular broadsheets which developed in the seventeenth century as secular counterparts to religious prints. Usually their subjects were proverbs, moralizing tales and satirical observations on social behaviour. In format the *lubok* usually consists of a graphic illustration with a caption or, more usually, a group of related illustrations and captions. Figure 2 shows an example in which image and caption are formally separated from one another, although frequently the caption would be arranged in the spaces around the figures. Typically they are bold line drawings with eccentric relationships in scale between the images in the picture. The captions frequently have words omitted or misspelt, or show signs of correction. These images are known to have been of considerable interest to primitivist artists. Mikhail Larionov made a considerable collection of *lubki*; in 1913 he exhibited *lubki* alongside oriental prints, folk and child art, icons and shop signs, and paintings by himself and his friends.

But Primitivist painters' interests extended also to pre-history, to 'primitive' art from non-Slavic sources, mediaeval manuscripts, pictographs and the speech of small children. This very wide variety of interests should in itself suggest the possibility of a variety of allusive content in Russian primitivist art; it also reflects an interest in the image as a means of direct communication. And it is these characteristics, as much as anything which differentiate Russian primitivism from its European counterparts. The deliberate crudity of technique and subject matter to be found in many paintings of this period was intended to express both a polemic against the traditions of Western art and an attempt to find a means of direct communication with a wider public. David Burliuk identified primitivism as:

> Not a restriction but an expansion of a programme—a protest against formal art—art for art's sake—because art is for the people, art is for the masses.
> (Quoted in Gray, 1962.)

and Malevich stated that:

> Goncharova and I worked more on the peasant level. Every work of ours had a content which, although expressed in primitive form, revealed a social concern.
> (Quoted in Gray, 1962, pp. 134–35.)

This social awareness is sometimes expressed in 'social' themes (e.g. peasant and religious subjects), but it is also expressed through the use of scatological and satirical imagery in, for example, the work of Mikhail Larionov (Plate 1) and to some extent in that of Marc Chagall. The paintings in Larionov's 'hairdresser' series are a good

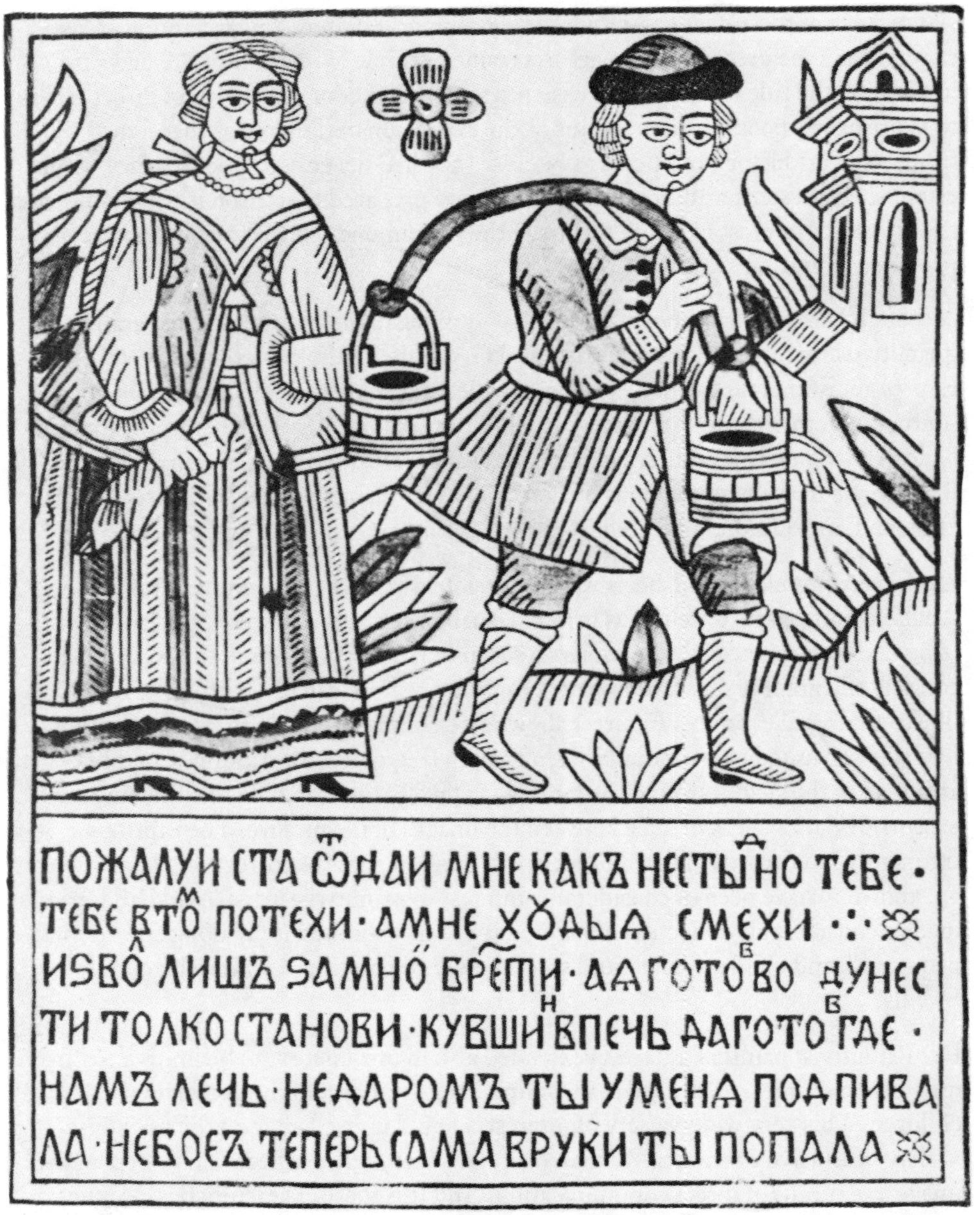

Figure 2 *Lubok*, Moscow, mid eighteenth century, 'Give me the pails': the man accuses the woman of being drunk and carries the pails, which should be her job (From Bakhtin, V. and Moiduvskiy, D. (1962) *Russkiy Lubok*, Izogiz, Moscow; courtesy Mary Chamot).

example. Figure 3 shows one of these—a scene in which a foppish officer and sycophantic barber are seen as co-conspirators, or as actors in a scene whose artificiality is stressed by the device of a framing curtain. Incidentally the subject of this series can be related to a theme found in *lubki* (a reference to which was probably deliberately intended by Larionov) in which a barber threatens to cut off the beard of an Old Believer[11].

Peasant subjects recur in Russian primitivist painting. While Natalia Goncharova's paintings often seem to express a kind of naive or natural social vitality (Plate 2), other paintings of peasant subjects are conspicuously free of the nostalgic utopianism or sensual themes to be found in much late nineteenth-century painting of such subjects (e.g. in the work of the Pont-Aven school). Peasant life is not seen, in the work of Chagall (Haftmann 214) or Malevich (Fig. 4), to represent surviving remnants of a stable and idyllic past.

The phenomenon of primitivism was not confined to painting; it can be found also in Russian literature and music of this period (e.g. in Igor Stravinsky's score for *The Rite of Spring*, first performed in 1913) and in dance (e.g. in some of the ballets performed by Diaghilev's *Ballets Russes*).

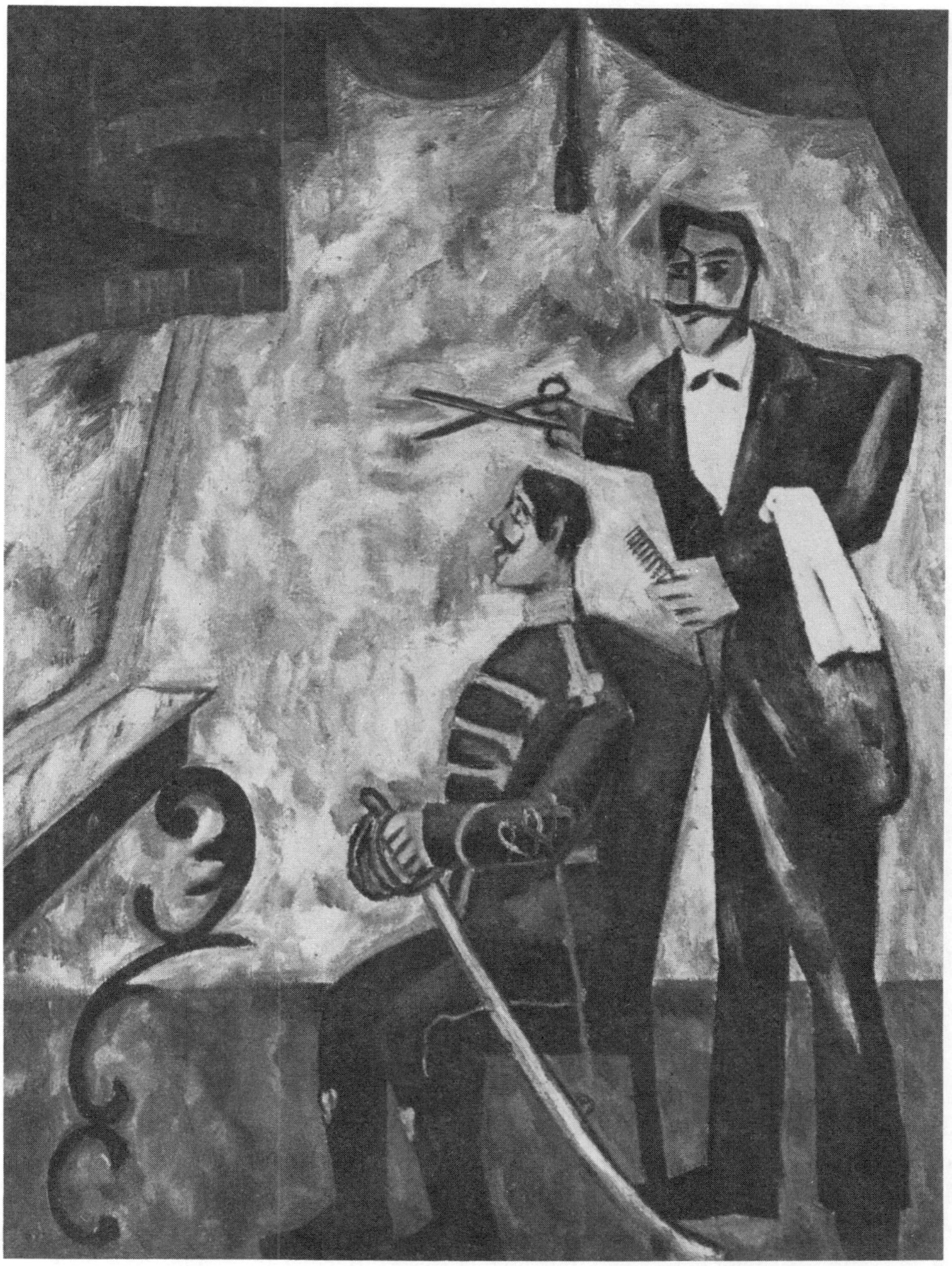

Figure 3 Mikhail Larionov, *Officer at the Hairdresser*, 1907, oil, 46×35 ins (Collection Madame Larionov; photo: La Bibliothèque des Arts, Lausanne, from W. George, *Larionov*, 1966).

Exercise

So far I have stressed the nationalist side of Russian primitivism: but there are ways in which work of this period can be fairly directly related to recent Western art as well. Looking at Plate 4 and Figure 5, can you suggest how?

Discussion

Both of these paintings make identifiable references to Western art of the kind which Larionov and Malevich might have seen at recent exhibitions or known through the Shchukin collection. Even without knowing that the Larionov painting is in bright colours (red, yellow, orange, predominantly), I am sure that you will have observed that the treatment of the figures, and probably the composition and the subject as well, reminded you of Gauguin. But you may also have noted that the composition is less static (and stylized) than is typical in Gauguin's later work.

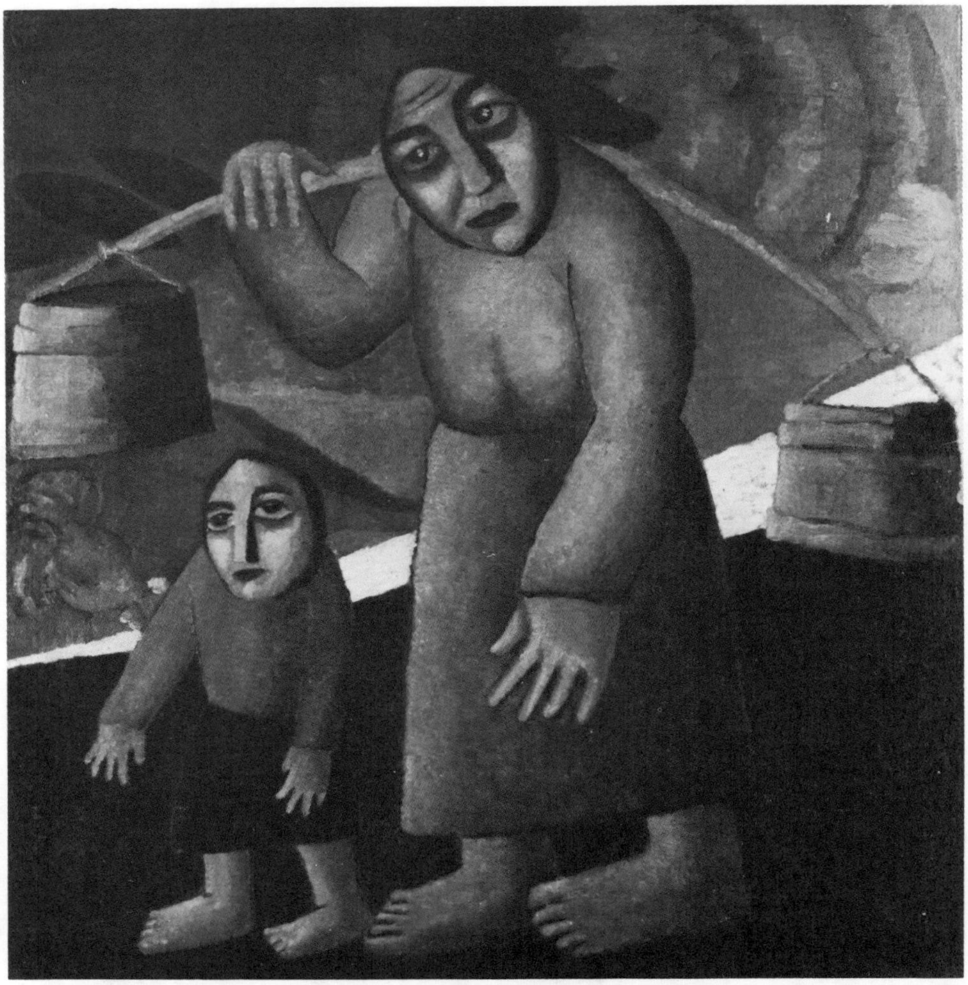

Figure 4 Kazimir Malevich, *Peasant Woman with Buckets*, 1912, oil, 29×29 ins (Stedelijk Museum, Amsterdam).

The compressed pictorial space and tubular, mechanical-looking forms in Malevich's painting may have suggested Léger. The comparison that is frequently made is with Léger's *Nudes in the Forest* (Haftmann 215). But the resemblances are rather superficial: there are considerable differences in the modelling of forms, in colour, handling of light and treatment of space in the two pictures. You may have suggested as well some connection between the peasant subject and the very simplified forms of the figures in the Malevich painting and the heavily simplified forms in Picasso's *La Paysanne* (Fig. 1, p. 11) in Shchukin's collection.

However, Léger's *Nudes in the Forest* is not a painting that Malevich is likely to have seen (although he may have seen other work by Léger exhibited in Russia at around this time) but he may well have known it in black and white reproduction. Monochrome illustration gives the Léger painting a character which it lacks in colour: the space looks more compressed, figures and landscape less clearly distinct from one another, and the forms of figures, trees and tropical fronds have a metallic, mechanized look.

In colour it is clear that Léger's figures and landscape are modelled by a kind of Cubist faceting (as well as by tone) or striation which is strongly suggestive of carved surfaces, characteristics which are conspicuously absent from the Malevich picture. The colours of the Léger are also the limited colours typical of Cubism of this period, greens, browns, greys, whereas Malevich's painting is in bright primary colours and the figures—much more regular than in the Léger—are modelled by a sort of spectral gradation of colour, highlighted by white.

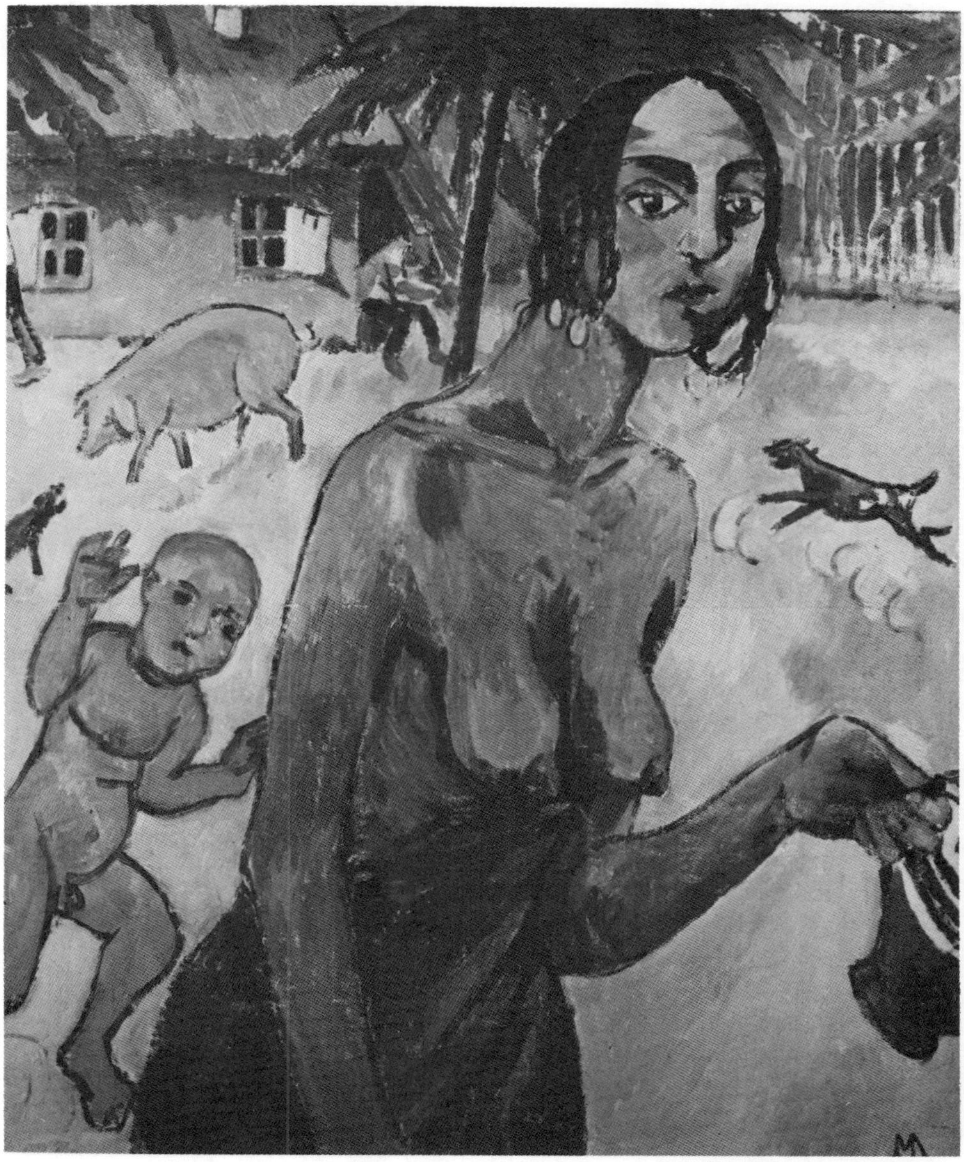

Figure 5 Mikhail Larionov, *Gypsies in Tiraspol*, 1903, oil, 38 × 32 ins (Collection Madame Larionov, Paris; photo: La Bibliothèque des Arts, Lausanne, from W. George, *Larionov*, 1966).

If Malevich was interested by this stage in early Cubist painting he brought to it an interest in bright colour, stimulated perhaps by his interest in icons and perhaps by first hand experience of the Matisses and the 'coloured' Cubist paintings in the Shchukin collection, which gives his work a very different character to its French counterparts.

Like the Expressionists and the Futurists, Russian artists' interests and activities were not confined to their 'own' medium, they also experimented with book design, poetry and design for the theatre. The kinds of characteristics evident in primitivist painting—especially the exploitation of authentically Slavonic and demotic imagery—are to be found in richer and more varied form in some of the books produced collaboratively by artists and writers. The medium of the book allowed inherently greater latitude for the exploitation of polemical and semantic issues. Many of these books were produced in a deliberately crude manner; printed on packing paper, they were given an amateurish and handmade appearance. In almost every respect they were the exact antithesis of the *de luxe* publications typical of the *Mir Iskusstva* circle, with the exception that they too had a small circulation.

Igra v adu (*A Game in Hell*) with texts by the poets Alexey Kruchenykh and Viktor Khlebnikov (1885–1922) and illustrations by Natalia Goncharova was first published in 1912 (Fig. 6). It was printed lithographically on wrapping paper, using the archaic Slavonic characters[12] typical of early Russian books and *lubki* (and thus conveying authentic Slavonic associations in opposition to westernized traditions). The style of the text and its subject (a satirical poem about a card game between devils and sinners in hell) are similar to those to be found in *lubki*. And the relationship between illustration and text, although not identical to that shown in the *lubok* illustrated on p. 14, is similar.

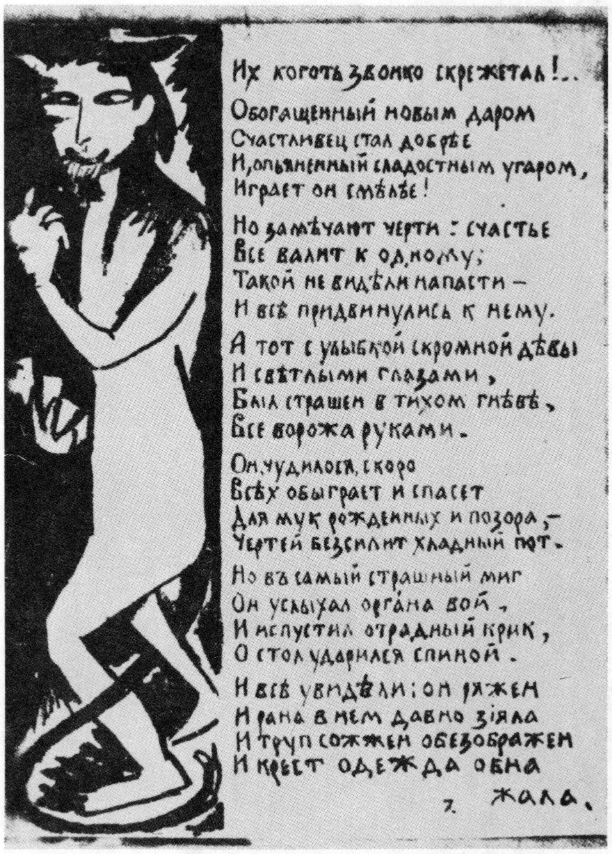

Figure 6 Natalia Goncharova, illustration for *Igra v adu*, 1912 (Courtesy Mary Chamot and *Apollo* magazine).

The deliberate play on the *lubok* genre is taken further in the 'second edition' of *Igra v adu*, published in 1913. In the same way as the *lubok* tradition included numerous variants on a single theme, so the second edition of *Igra v adu* was a modification of the first. The text was altered and added to; the illustrations were by Malevich and Olga Rozanova, and the presentation was made more informal with handwritten texts.

Mirskontsa (*The World Backwards*), published in 1912, like *Igra v adu* had texts by Kruchenykh and Khlebnikov and illustrations by Goncharova and employs many of the same kind of features, including a theme drawn from popular sources. In the case of *Mirskontsa* the title itself is drawn from a theme common not only to the Russian *lubok* but to be found in popular prints in many parts of Europe—the 'world upside down'. These kinds of representations (in which the Surrealists were later interested) usually take the form of linked episodes illustrating satirically the dislocation of 'natural' order (e.g. the seasons changing out of order and their consequences) and, more important, the involution or revolution of the 'normal' social order. In Kruchenykh and Khlebnikov's text the idea of the dislocation of accepted order is expressed as much in the visual presentation of the text as in its literal meaning. Some of the text is handwritten, and typefaces of different kinds and sizes are mixed in, letters printed in reverse, and so on (Fig. 7).

This interest in dissociation and discontinuity of means and meaning can be seen to link a number of Russian artists whose work is visually very different in character, such as Chagall and Malevich.

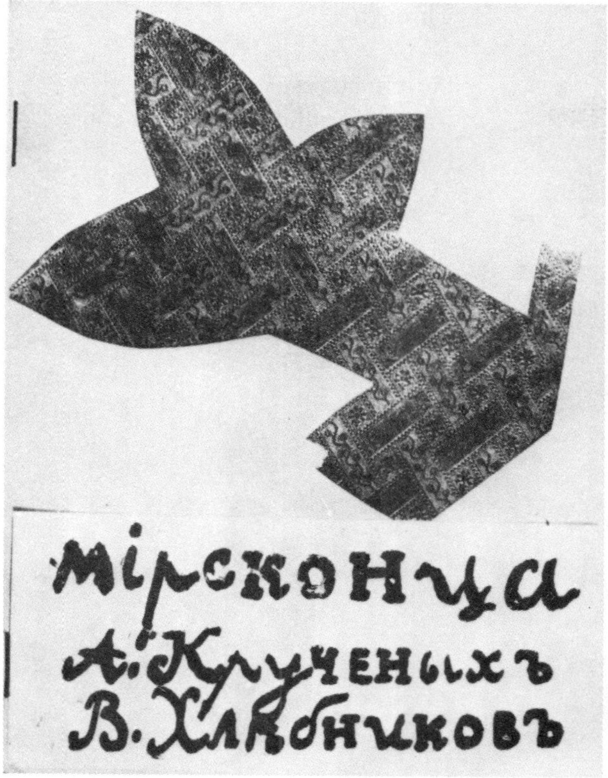

Figure 7 Natalia Goncharova, illustration for *Mirskontsa*, 1912 (Photo: Galerie Gmurzynska, Cologne).

KAZIMIR MALEVICH

Malevich's *Musical Instrument/Lamp* (Fig. 8) is ostensibly one of the most 'authentic' of his Cubist paintings. Its colour is fairly low-key (although brighter and more varied than the colour we would usually associate with Analytical Cubism). There are references to the kind of subject matter we can find in the work of Picasso and Braque: a musical stave, the neck of an instrument, a plaited rope or table-edge moulding. And there is the familiar centralized, oval composition. But that is about as far as the similarities go. The Malevich painting can be linked quite closely in visual terms with a painting by Picasso in Shchukin's collection, but the resemblances are entirely superficial; it is difficult to read the Malevich as an Analytical Cubist painting.

Whether or not Malevich read Cubism as object-based and naturalistic in intention, what seems to have interested him most were the possibilities which Cubist techniques of fragmentation suggested for breaking away from the representation of objects altogether. Malevich was also interested in the possibilities Cubist technique offered for the exploration of semantic issues. (The kind of visual paradox he perceived in Cubist work is perhaps most apparent to us in an example like Picasso's *Still Life with Chair Caning* (Unit 7, Plate 4) and in other Cubist collages, but its potential is clear in earlier paintings which use stencilled lettering, 'false' wood graining, and so on.) As with the examples of book design we have considered already, Malevich was interested in introducing an infinity of associations into his painting through dislocation, dissociation, or translocation of objects. He singled out an example of this dislocation in a poem by Mayakovsky:

U–	Street
Litsa	—
Litsa	Faces
u	of
dogov	the dogs
godov	of the years
rez–	sharper
che.	—

Che–	Through
rez	—
zheleznykh kovey	the iron horses
s okon begushchikh domov	from the windows of running houses
prynuli pervye kuby . . .	jumped the first cubes . . .
(Quoted in Andersen, 1970.)	

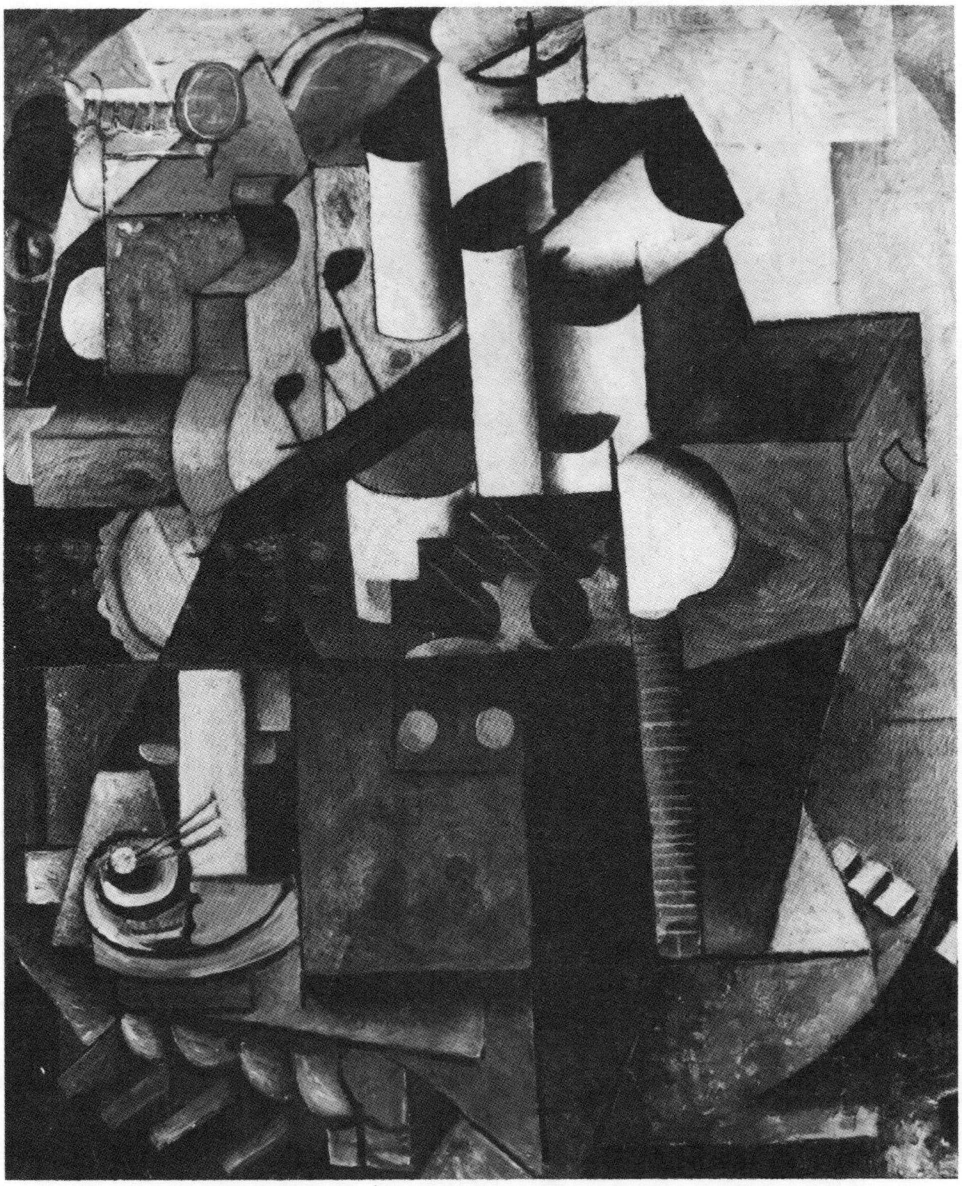

Figure 8 Kazimir Malevich, *Musical Instrument/Lamp*, 1913, oil, 33 × 27 ins (Stedelijk Museum, Amsterdam).

In the original, in both appearance and sound, this poem illustrates very well the idea of linguistic correspondences and paradoxes: in the use of words which sound the same but have different meanings; words which are the mirror image of one another in spelling but quite remote from one another in meaning; words which contain syllables which correspond to complete words but do not have the same sense. What the Mayakovsky poem emphasizes, in the same way as Picasso's *Still Life with Chair Caning* (Unit 7, Plate 4), is the relativity of meaning—that we recognize the meaning of words from their context and through familiarity with convention. When a word, or in painting the image, is displaced, the accepted meaning *may* be completely lost so that the word becomes unintelligible and we are left only with its form or sound; but it *may* carry echoes of its usual associations into its new context, setting up strange resonances of meaning or irrational meanings. The same goes for the displacement of formal conventions in painting.

Malevich stated that:

> We have come to reject reason, but we have rejected reason because a different kind of reason has arisen within us, one which might be called transrational if compared with the one which we have rejected; it also has its own law, construction and meaning, and only when we have cognized it will our works be founded on the truly new law of transrationalism. . . .
> (Quoted in E. Kovtun, 'The Beginning of Suprematism', in Galerie Gmurzynska, 1974.)

It is essential to understand Malevich's 'cubist' painting in the light of this interest in 'transrationalism' as well as for its visual adaptations of Cubist conventions. Cubist fragmentation gave Malevich the means to present representational images synoptically (Fig. 9). *An Englishman in Moscow* employs representational images which are dislocated (visually and associationally) through unexpected juxtapositions rather than through their method of representation. Malevich also employed lettering in a manner that is visually reminiscent of Cubist lettering but is used for semantic purposes in a way which reminds one simultaneously of the contemporary interest in *lubki*. He frequently uses complete words or phrases which can be seen to have an oblique reference to what is happening in the picture. In *Woman at a Poster Column* (Plate 3), a collaged phrase is used ironically to identify what has become of the notional 'subject' of the picture: 'it has come apart'.

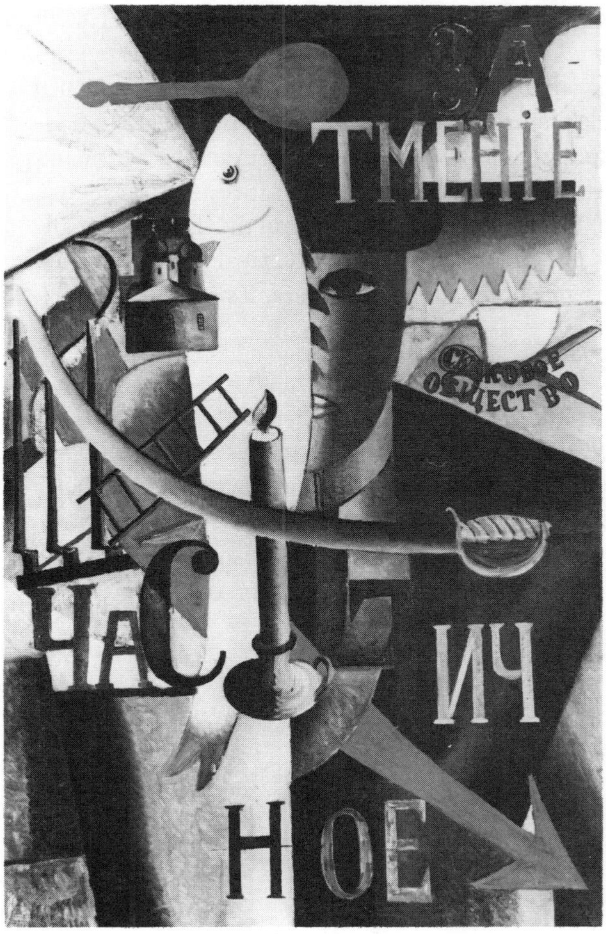

Figure 9 Kazimir Malevich, *An Englishman in Moscow*, 1913/14, oil, 35 × 22 ins (Stedelijk Museum, Amsterdam).

In *Woman at a Poster Column*, despite the title, representational images have all but disappeared. Malevich uses collaged fragments (newsprint, ribbon, photographs), stencilled lettering, a cubist type of drawing, suggestions of shadow, modelled areas of colour, and bold areas of dense colour, to build up a composition in which suggestions of limited depth are played off against assertive identifications of the surface of the picture. There is a constant tension and ambiguity; while the bold pink rectangle (upper right of the picture) appears as a dominant form 'in front of' other forms (an impression cunningly reinforced by the use of collaged photograph of two dancers which is cut-off or blocked out by the pink rectangle and on which Malevich has painted a perspective line), its position in pictorial space is complicated by the superimposition of a soft brushed black line on the left-hand side which anchors it firmly in the same plane as those elements which appear to be behind it. Malevich has taken in the title of this picture a notional subject (the poster column) which conjures up the idea of random associations and incongruous juxtapositions of colour, imagery and words, which should perhaps be seen not to identify the *subject* of this picture (it is really very difficult to interpret this as a cubist approximation of an observed subject) but the intention and the process of the picture.

MARC CHAGALL

(See Hamilton, pp. 435–37.)

Like Malevich, Chagall was primarily interested in the free association of images which he perceived in Cubism, but he developed this interest in a different direction. Chagall disliked what he described as 'realistic Cubism', by which he meant the object-based Cubism of Picasso and Braque. He preferred the work of those Cubist painters like Robert Delaunay who seemed to him to use fragmentation primarily for expressive and imaginative effects, and we can find echoes of Delaunay's technique in several of the pictures Chagall painted when he was in Paris before the war (compare Haftmann 203 and 209). Hamilton rightly points out (p. 436) that Chagall was interested in Delaunay's concept of *simultanéité* as confirmation of his own interest in the synoptic presentation of time. Chagall extended the concept by using simultaneously different techniques within a single picture, to indicate the qualitative and temporal differences between different images within the picture (see, for example, Haftmann 210 and 214). Chagall also shared the primitivists' interests in satire and in crudely painted and irrational images (e.g. Haftmann 214), exhibiting in the 'Donkey's Tail' exhibition organized by Larionov and Goncharova in 1912. (Chagall was, in fact, a primitivist *par excellence*, since he had worked for a short time as a sign painter.)

RUSSIAN FUTURISM

(See Hamilton, pp. 310–11.)

Russian Futurism is a complicated affair, which overlaps, in many respects, with primitivism, and I do not wish to discuss it here. Vladimir Markov's book (see the Recommended Reading list on p. 65), although primarily concerned with literature, documents the Futurist movement as a whole and gives details of some of the many collective ventures in which artists, writers and musicians collaborated.

Suprematism

Woman at a Poster Column (Plate 3) showed Malevich moving away from representation towards the use of shapes and colours as independent, non-referential, pictorial elements. With hindsight it is possible to see that these characteristics are related to those of the *Black Square* (Fig. 10), a painting which has assumed in recent times a canonical status in the history of modern painting as

> . . . the most uncompromisingly abstract, non-referential painting that the twentieth century had yet produced. It helped to usher in a new and dazzling phase in which Russia undisputedly took her place at the forefront of the avant-garde. And it was to launch its creator on a path of exploration that lasted one brief but meteoric decade . . . during which he posed and faced some of the most burning issues of twentieth-century art—issues that are alive . . . . today.
> (Golding, 1975, p. 96.)

Figure 10 Kazimir Malevich, *Black Square*, 1915?, 21 × 21 ins (Russian Museum, Leningrad).

The painting itself scarcely needs description: an unmodulated black square placed against a white ground or, if you like, framed by a white edge; there is an element of ambiguity. The reductive imagery and colour clearly mark a radical break visually with Malevich's earlier work (see Figs 4 and 8 and Plates 3 and 4), but Malevich, although he saw the *Black Square* as representing a new beginning, saw no discontinuity of intention between this and the work preceding it. We have seen that the process of denying painting as a merely representational or illustrative medium was already quite far advanced in a painting like *Woman at a Poster Column* where bold rectangles of colour appear to be superimposed on, and interrupt our view of, the 'real' image. One way to see the *Black Square* is as that same process extended until the 'real' subject (or in Malevich's terms 'object') has been obscured completely.

Malevich later claimed that the *Black Square* dated from 1913, a claim which has led several historians to look for literal examples of the *Black Square*'s appearance in work firmly dated 1913, without much success.[13] It is almost certain that Malevich did not mean that he had literally painted an *image* of a black square in 1913, but that he felt that, looking back, he could identify the emergence of those processes, painterly and philosophical, which led up to the *Black Square* expressed in paintings of 1913 such as that illustrated in Plate 4.

At one level the *Black Square* is a minimalist, and you might want to suggest, a nihilist image. But Malevich interpreted it as an image which was both the most *economical* possible expression of the *means* of painting and, at the same time, as an image rich in potential content.[14] To understand why, you might pause to consider the kind of analogies you might use to describe the relationship between the black and white areas of the picture (like positive *versus* negative, for example) and the associations the 'colours' and image carry with them. In a strict geometrical sense the square is a primary form, like the triangle and the circle. It is both capable of containing, and being contained by, other primary forms (e.g. a square can be inscribed within a circle, or vice versa). It is also, like the triangle and the circle, a form from which all other geometrical configurations may be built. But besides this, throughout history, geometrical figures have also been endowed with rich philosophical and mystical associations and these associations were prominent in some of the mystic cults, such as Mazdaznan, which gained popularity in the late nineteenth and early twentieth centuries and of which Malevich may have been aware. The same kinds of considerations apply to the colours. On the one hand they are not colours, on the other they contain the potential of all colours within them. Black is the sum of all colours, white the sum of light. But, however you may interpret the painting from a *visual* point of view, it marks a radical departure by comparison with anything else we have looked at so far in the course. We have seen, in earlier units, that although Cubist paintings by Picasso and Braque from about the end of 1910 may appear as very abstract compositions, their creators continued to insist that they were still basically representational images. And Kandinsky, although he did not claim that his work was intended to be representational, was still at this date basing his compositions on representational images—abstracting from them. Malevich, on the other hand, makes a completely clean sweep with the *Black Square*.

The *Black Square* marks the beginning of what Malevich dubbed 'Suprematism', which he defined, rather eliptically, as 'the supremacy of feeling in art' by which he meant, roughly, that the primary aim, function or capacity, of the painter was to evoke emotion, sensation and reflection through the manipulation of visual means. In other words, the value of a work of art has nothing to do with the painter's capacity to depict objects from the perceived world as if they were tangibly present in the paintings; the way in which areas of colour are juxtaposed, light and shade handled, and so on, are the painter's prime means and it is only through the manipulation of these that he can communicate with the spectator.

The *Black Square* was followed by a series of Suprematist paintings of elementary forms against white grounds (see Fig. 16, p. 30), and by drawings, often on squared paper, which experiment with elementary and 'modified' elementary forms (e.g. trapezoids) in combination with one another (Fig. 11). These appear to be empirical rather than pragmatic explorations. Malevich experiments with different 'weights' through varying the density of shading on different forms. He also tries out 'incomplete' forms to suggest recession in space—shading off, for example, where you would expect an edge. What the drawings and the companion Suprematist paintings (e.g. Hamilton Fig. 187, Haftmann 359–61[15]), in which colour is reintroduced, have in common is an interest in creating tension and dynamism through geometrical forms set against (or overlapping) one another, usually against white backgrounds which evoke a 'limitless' space. Malevich tended to use a restricted palette of bright primary and complementary colours, in addition to black and white, in his Suprematist paintings; but despite his many theoretical writings of this period[16], which attempt to define a philosophy of Suprematism and to place Suprematism in relation to other recent movements such as Cubism and Futurism[17], Malevich does not seem to have felt any need to justify the persistent use of particular colours and combinations of colours (unlike Kandinsky at roughly the same period—see Chipp, pp. 152–55).

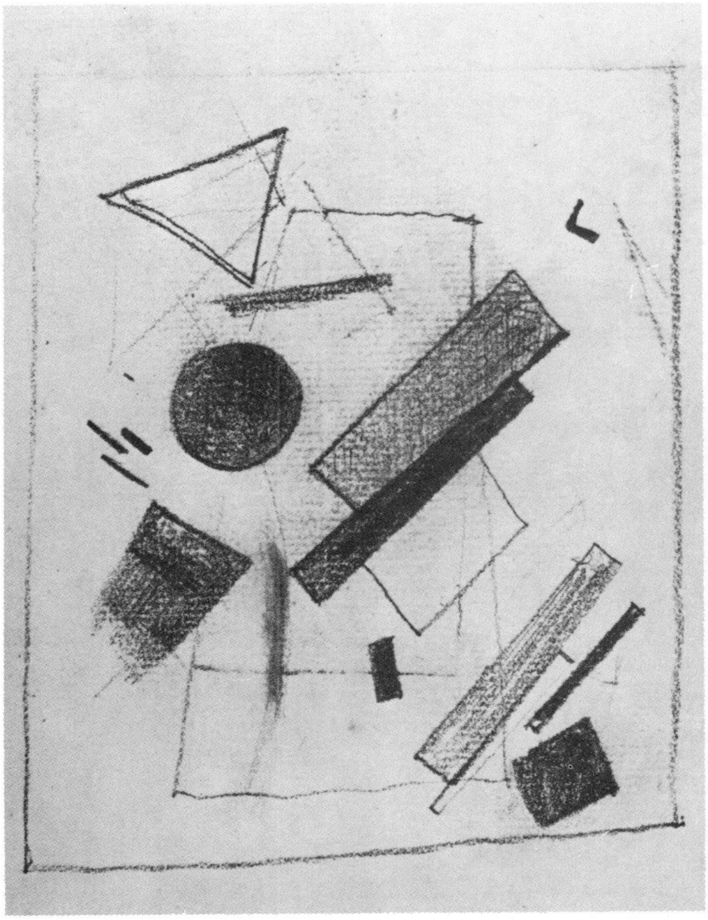

Figure 11 Kazimir Malevich, *Suprematist Drawing*, 1914/15, pencil drawing (Galerie Gmurzynska, Cologne).

Whether the evolution of Suprematism owes anything directly to Kandinsky's writings is a matter for debate, but there are certainly striking correspondences between Malevich's insistence on non-objectivity, and his preferred forms, and certain ideas in Kandinsky's writings. In his chapter 'The Language of Form and Colour' in *Concerning the Spiritual in Art* Kandinsky states that:

> 1 Either a form aims at delimiting a concrete object two dimensionally
>
> 2 Or a form remains abstract, a purely abstract entity. Such abstract entities, which have life in themselves, are a square, a circle, a triangle, a rhombus, a trapezoid, etc., many of them so complicated as to have no mathematical formula. All these forms are of equal rank in the abstract realm.

and then

> . . . there are artists who, even today, experience abstract form as something quite precise and use it to the exclusion of any other means. This seeming stripping bare becomes an inner enrichment.
> (Kandinsky, 1959, p. 84.)

In *Concerning the Spiritual in Art* Kandinsky speaks of these as 'residual organic forms' which 'possess, nevertheless, an internal sound of their own, which may be similar to that of their abstract parallel'. This 'residual organic' imagery is recognizably present in Kandinsky's work up to 1914. A single image, or fragment of an image, can be found reworked in progressively more abstract compositions (Fig. 12 and Plate 5).

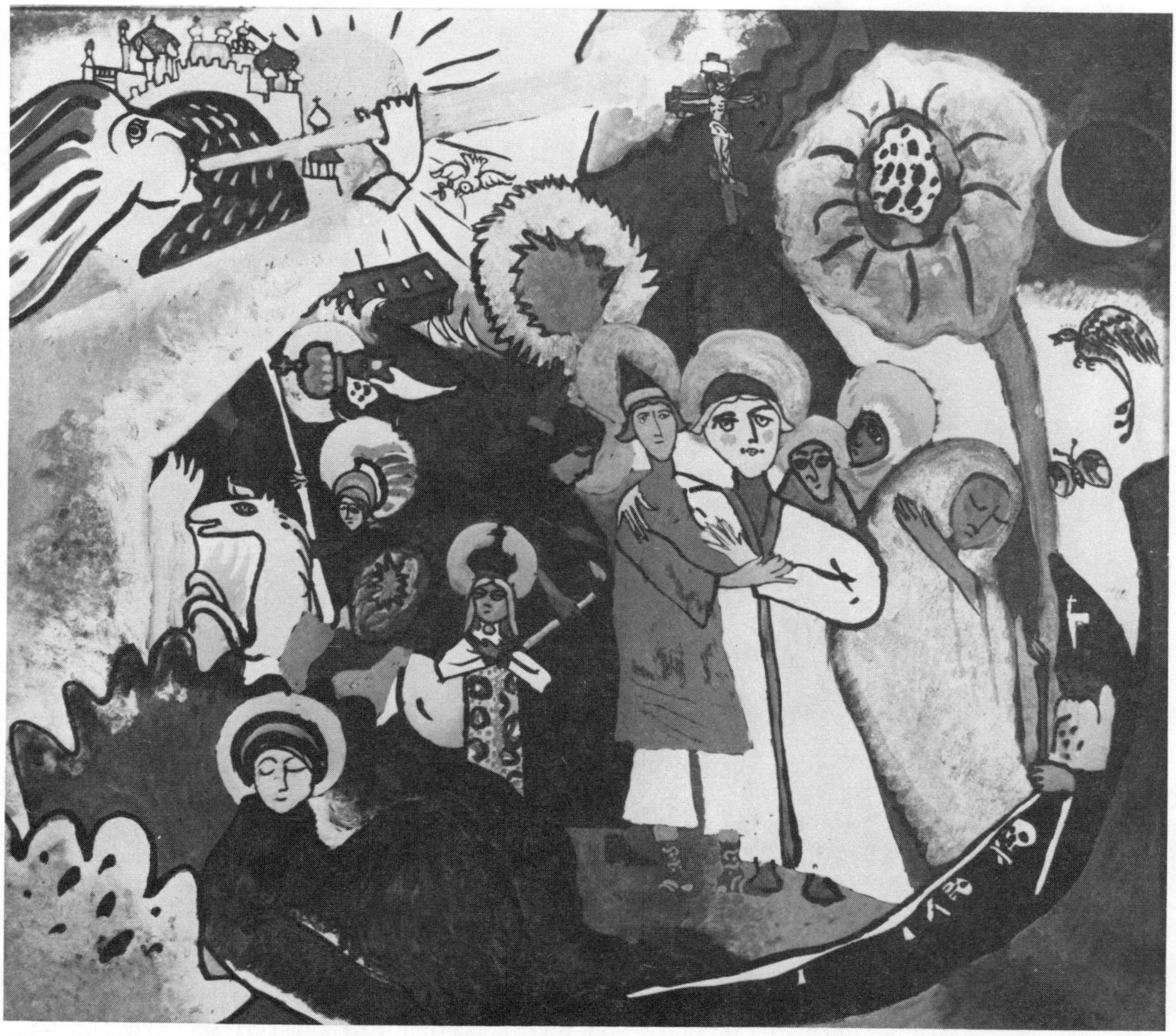

Figure 12 Wassily Kandinsky, *Allerheiligen I (All Saints' Day I)*, 1911, oil on glass, $13\frac{3}{8} \times 16$ ins (Städtische Galerie im Lensbachhaus, Munich).

Unlike Kandinsky, Malevich always denied that any residual representational imagery should be read into particular forms or configurations of forms in his Suprematist paintings.[18] He did occasionally give titles to his Suprematist compositions which suggest the presence of residual images: *Painterly Realism of a Football Player* (Plate 6) is an example, but the stress is on *painterly realism*. In other words if the painting reminded one of images in the perceived world it was because it provoked *sensations analogous* to those the spectator might experience from other stimuli.

The Beginnings of Constructivism

TATLIN'S RELIEFS AND CORNER-CONSTRUCTIONS
(See Hamilton, pp. 315–16.)

The title 'counter-relief' was not confined to those reliefs which were suspended in space, as Hamilton suggests. Tatlin seems to have used the term to convey the idea of materials 'countering' or set against one another, as well. Hamilton points to the influence of Cézanne, and of Larionov's primitivism, and rightly stresses the importance of Tatlin's visit to Paris in 1913 where he saw, in Picasso's studio, examples of the small, sometimes brightly coloured constructions on which Picasso was currently working.

Picasso's construction, *Bottle and Guitar* (Fig. 13), may look like an abstract assemblage but the references to the familiar subject matter of Cubist painting (still life with musical instrument) are still there even though transposed and inverted. A section of wooden moulding —perhaps part of a chair leg—signifies the neck and top of the bottle; the circular opening of the guitar is marked, not as we might expect by a void, but by a projecting solid. For some Russian artists the experience of seeing later Cubist work of this kind may have served to confirm their interests in the semantics of imagery, but Tatlin saw Picasso's constructions as suggesting ways in which the work of art might become the object itself, freed of any representational functions.

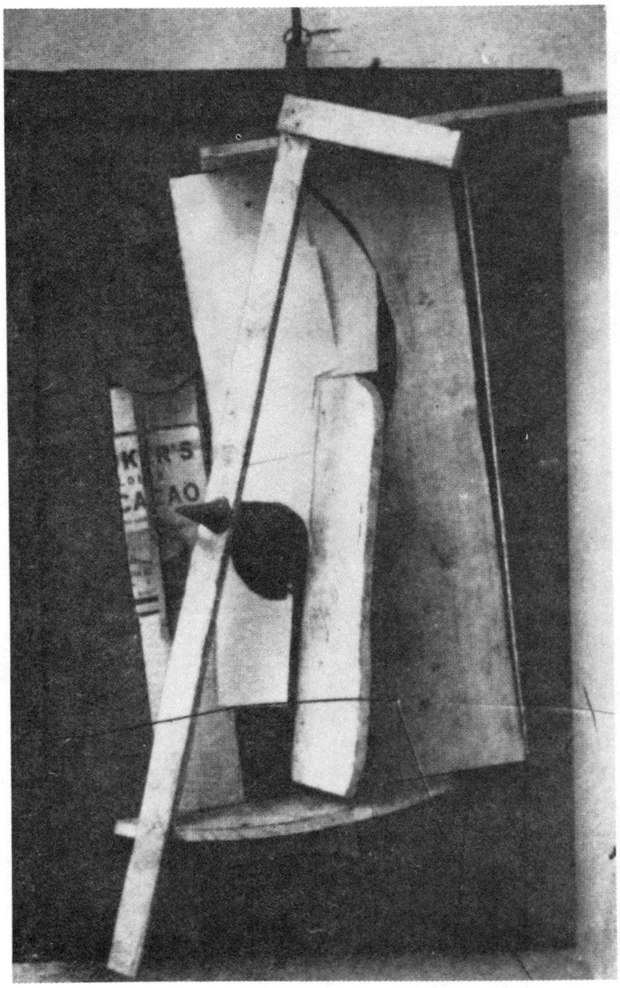

Figure 13 Pablo Picasso, *Bottle and Guitar*, 1913, construction (Original lost; photo: Galerie Louise Leiris © SPADEM, Paris 1976).

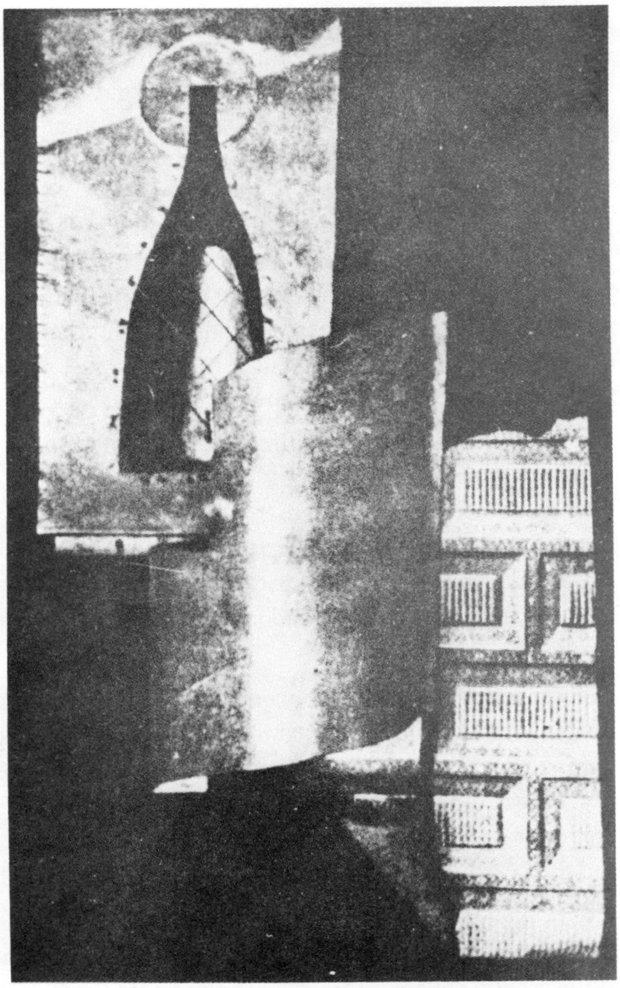

Figure 14 Vladimir Tatlin, *Bottle*, 1914 (Original lost; photo: Troels Andersen).

Tatlin's early reliefs (of the kind illustrated in Fig. 14) fall somewhere in between painting, collage and sculpture, and owe as much visually, perhaps, to some of the contemporary 'sculpto-paintings' of Tatlin's fellow countryman Alexander Archipenko (1887–1964)[19] as to Picasso's sophisticatedly allusive constructions of this period. Although Tatlin at first incorporated fragments of recognizable objects into his constructions, he soon abandoned this practice, seeming to feel that such images ran the risk of being interpreted as ingredients in a still life. He was concerned to suppress any literal and associative references, and to use fragments of 'found' material only for the character of the material itself, material which could be manipulated as an element in a composition. Tatlin described this approach in pseudo-scientific terms, as the 'culture of materials'. Hamilton illustrates an example of a later construction on p. 316.[20] This shows Tatlin using wood, scraps of metal (e.g. part of a tin with its label still attached) and painted glass nailed and clipped together and battened on to a painted board. Tatlin uses paint to 'shade' an area of the glass crosspiece and paints a shadow along the left hand side of the plank, on the 'ground'. Real projections and marks suggesting flatness are played off against one another, and the hardness of the materials against the relative 'softness' of the painted marks.

Tatlin exploits the ambiguity of these reliefs between painting and sculpture, in some cases making relief constructions which employ real volumes which can be seen to mirror painted descriptions of volume in contemporary Russian painting (compare, for example, Haftmann, 354 and 357[21]), in his corner-constructions the sculptural references are more overt (Fig. 15).

Exercise

1 Compare Tatlin's corner-construction (Fig. 15) with his reliefs (Fig. 14 and Hamilton Fig. 188).

2 How would you compare Figure 15 with those of Boccioni's sculptures which are assembled from heterogeneous materials (e.g. Unit 9, Figs 108–9)?

Discussion

1 The corner-construction is no longer a relief which hangs against the wall like a painting; it is suspended in space (although it uses the wall for support) and thus has the three-dimensional characteristics of a sculpture. There is neither a literal frame nor any vestige of a framing element (such as the painted board on which the construction in Hamilton, p. 316, is mounted). But there are still references to painting, e.g. shaded edges and shading used to suggest cast shadows; and the construction has an optimum viewpoint from directly in front, like a painting.[22]

2 Apart from the obvious differences that Boccioni's sculptures are still basically representational whereas Tatlin's are not, you might have noted that the materials Tatlin uses are inherently constructional in themselves whereas Boccioni's are not. Boccioni uses a variety of materials but they seem to be used for descriptive and anecdotal purposes. In both cases the viewpoint is frontal, the assemblages cannot easily be imagined in the round, although in both cases their extension in the round is implied.

The corner-constructions are sometimes seen as marking a radical departure in Tatlin's work yet he continued to make reliefs to hang against the wall and which impinge in various ways on the surrounding space, either through projecting volumes (e.g. Haftmann 354) or through the use of elements which extend beyond the edge of the frame and thus suggest the extension of the construction into surrounding space and the possibility of 'architectural' applications which he would later exploit (see Fig. 28, p. 53).

During the second half of the decade Tatlin, like Malevich, began to attract a group of followers and collaborators, who experimented with assemblage techniques and pursued Tatlin's 'culture of materials'.

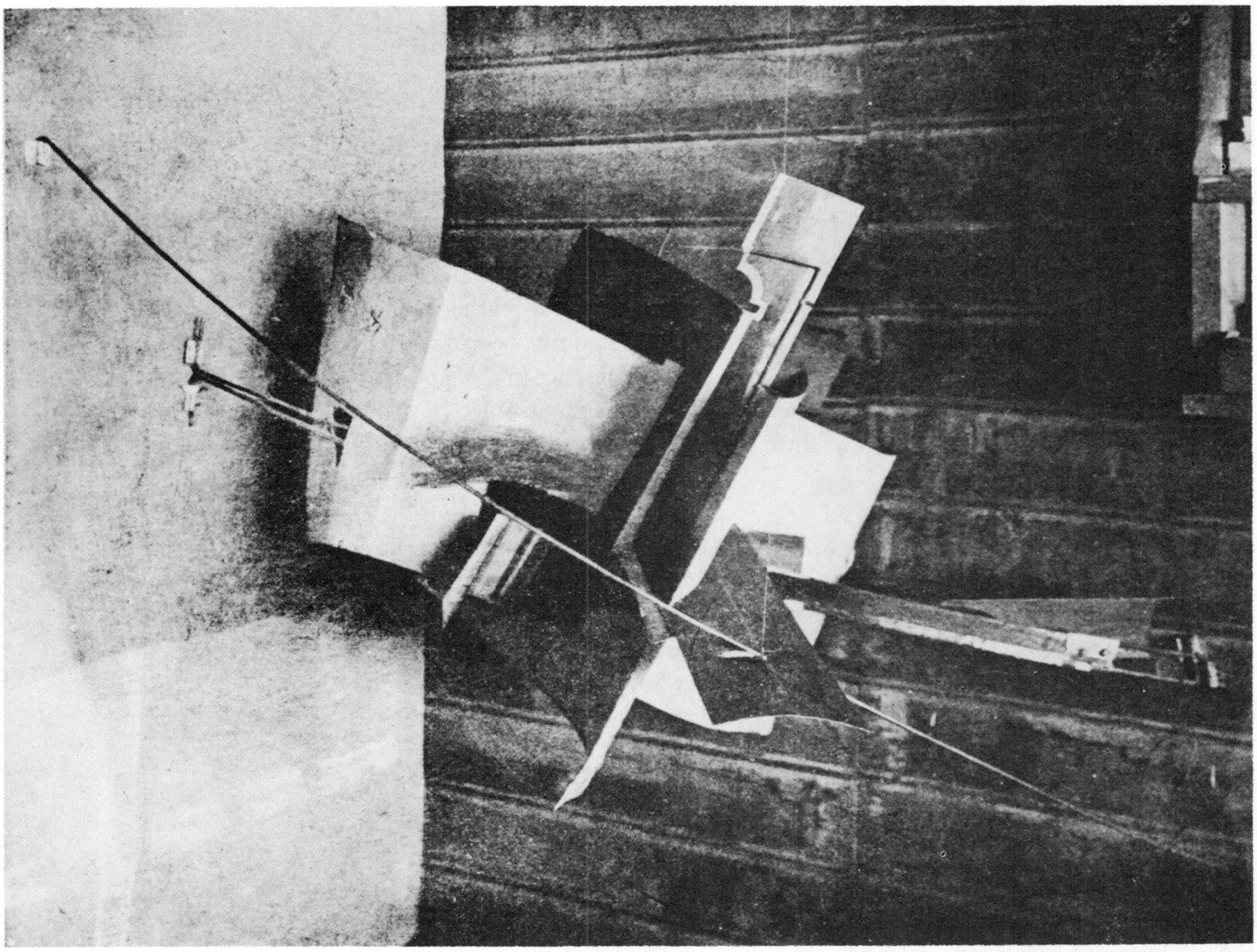

Figure 15 Vladimir Tatlin, *Corner-construction*, *c.*1915, collection of materials, iron, aluminium, primer (Original lost; photo: Troels Andersen).

Despite its common origin in Picasso's Cubism, by 1915 Malevich's and Tatlin's work looks very different, yet we can list certain characteristics that they have in common. For one thing they have both, to some extent, rejected traditional fine-art values and associations (in imagery and, in Tatlin's case, materials), but, whereas Tatlin literally assembles pieces of random material into objects which are nailed, welded and bolted together, Malevich still uses traditional fine-art techniques for his new imagery. And clearly Tatlin's work has a much more forceful physical presence than Malevich's. Malevich's renunciation of certain painterly means, such as modelling, tends to give his paintings the suggestion of an elusive physical character. Beginning with the most minimal or *economic* of means both artists use a technique of *assemblage* to *construct* their compositions. These qualities of assemblage and construction were to be characteristic of the art of the years following the Revolution, but developed and infused with new meanings.

‘0.10: The Last Futurist Exhibition’

(See Hamilton, p. 313.)

As Hamilton notes, Malevich and Tatlin regarded themselves as rivals. Both, by about 1915, had begun to accumulate their particular supporters.

The exhibition was held in St Petersburg in December 1915 as the second exhibition of the Futurist group (the first exhibition having been ‘Tramway V’ earlier in the same year). Before the exhibition opened Malevich announced that he had renounced Futurism for Suprematism and that he wished to be allowed space in the catalogue to outline the principles of Suprematism; other members of the group objected to his proposal. In October 1915 Malevich wrote to his friend, the writer and composer Mikhail Matiushin:

> The whole of our exhibition group has protested against my leaving Futurism and against my wish to write a few words in the catalogue and to name my contribution Suprematism. They’ve put the harness on me, but I’m not so sure that they’ll really manage to harness me. The reason for it [the others’ objection] is: ‘neither are we Futurists any more, but we still don’t know how to define ourselves and we’ve had too little time to think about it. . . .’ I gave in to them for the sake of keeping the exhibition intact.
> (Quoted in E. Kovtun, ‘The Beginning of Suprematism’, in Galerie Gmurzynska, 1974, p. 45.)

Malevich did not give in completely to pressure; copies of his essay ‘From Cubism to Suprematism’, which contained a statement of Suprematist principles, were on sale at the exhibition and Malevich gathered some of the other exhibitors to support Suprematism. Although Malevich had agreed not to list his paintings merely as ‘Suprematist compositions’ in the catalogue and that he would give them individual

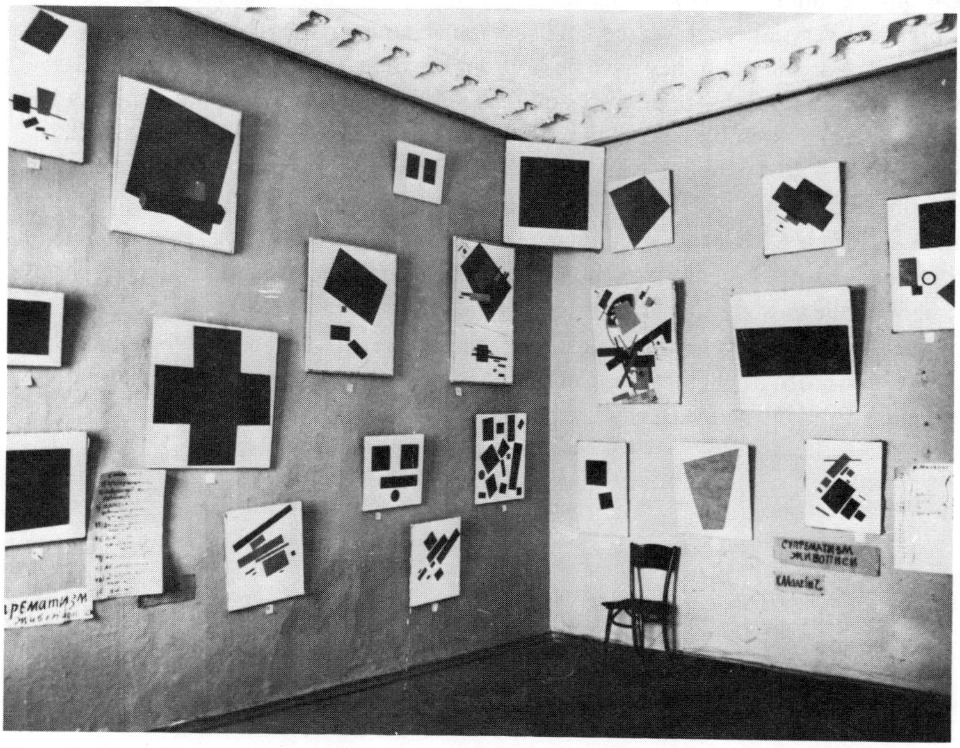

Figure 16 View of the Malevich exhibit of Suprematist work at ‘0.10: The Last Futurist Exhibition’, Moscow, 1915 (Photo: Galerie Gmurzynska, Cologne).

titles he managed to slip in a catalogue note to warn against reading the titles as clues to the subjects of the paintings:

> In naming some of these paintings, I do not wish to point out what form to seek in them, but I wish to indicate that real forms were approached in many cases as the ground for formless painterly masses from which a painterly form was created, quite unrelated to nature.
> (Extract from '0.10' catalogue; quoted in Gray, 1962.)

The paintings were clearly labelled as Suprematist compositions when hung (Fig. 16). (Note particularly the position given to the *Black Square*, hung high up at the corner of the room.) Malevich's Suprematist work provoked considerable hostility amongst some of his fellow exhibitors, because it was seen to subvert the Futurists' position. (In sheer quantity Malevich's work dominated the exhibition.) The *Black Square* might be seen as the 'reduction to zero' of painting, a supreme gesture of iconoclasm but, on the other hand, Malevich asserted that it was also a positive statement, and the quantity of Suprematist paintings (with the seemingly infinitely variable configurations they suggested) was there to prove it.

The five years between 1918 and 1921/22 saw an apparently remarkable coalition of interests between avant-garde artists and the new government. Many avant-garde artists were appointed to positions in the central ministry for cultural affairs (*Narkompros*: the Ministry of Enlightenment), to regional Commissariats of Fine Art, and to posts in the reorganized teaching institutions. By 1922 many of those who were most active had been dismissed, resigned, or changed jobs several times; and between 1921 and 1922 a large number of prominent avant-garde artists, including almost all of those who had been working in Europe until the outbreak of war (Kandinsky, Chagall, Gabo, Pevsner, etc.), emigrated to Europe.

Histories covering the art of the Revolutionary years are notably reticent on these issues, tending to suggest, by omission, that the exodus of avant-garde artists should be seen rather in the light of the fate of German International Style artists a decade later: that is, as a persecuted radical minority driven out by a totalitarian government intent on imposing a monolithic policy of 'socialist realism'. This was a view in which many exiled artists colluded, sometimes because they believed it to be true, but also sometimes for reasons of personal advantage, and occasionally because the experience of going into personal exile was too traumatic for them to wish to discuss the issues involved. The history of the period is still very far from being clear; but it is likely to be a good deal more complicated than the scheme outlined above.

Hamilton, pp. 313–14

'The new society . . . . within a few months': Very over-simplified, even as a summary. The Civil War continued until 1921.

'In Berlin . . . . artistic events': Paris and Berlin in the 1920s both had large colonies of White Russian émigrés. If artistic émigrés were 'powerless to affect the course of artistic events' in the 1920s in Russia, they were not powerless in the later making and transmission of the history of Russian art up to *c.*1922. A number of Russian intellectuals who were basically sympathetic to the new government were based in Berlin and acted as cultural emissaries between East and West, continuing to do so throughout the decade. (Berlin was even known for some time as 'extra-territorial Russia'.)

A number of avant-garde artists welcomed the Revolution, not always for reasons of specific political sympathies as much as for the reason given by the poet Vladimir Mayakovsky: 'October to our eyes represented a way out of an impasse'; in other words the Revolution was seen to offer the possibility of an end to artists' sense of alienation from society, and a vindication of their former position. However, the relationship between pre-Revolutionary 'radical' artists and post-Revolutionary society must be a complex one. In the remainder of the unit I have had three general questions in mind:

Did their art change (to reflect new circumstances)? If so, how? and to what extent?

How were artists involved, and to what extent did avant-garde artists' involvement reflect official policy? (And thus suggest sanction or approval.)

What circumstances may have contributed to the emigration, or apparent lack of prominence, of avant-garde artists after *c.*1922?

To discover whether the work of the pre-Revolutionary avant garde was seen as the most appropriate art after the Revolution we have to consider what policies for art may have existed and how these artists were viewed by their patrons. The first point to stress is that in a country with a largely peasant population and a high rate of illiteracy art did not come very high on a list of priorities. Insofar as Lenin appears to have conceived of a specific kind of art it was didactic and commemorative, thus almost by definition *illustrative*. Lenin's view seems to be loosely based on the *Civitas Solis* (*City of the Sun*), written by the seventeenth-century Italian ex-Dominican revolutionary monk F. T. Campanella. The *City of the Sun* was a utopian tract which conceived of an ideal city ruled by Hermetic priests. The 'city' of the title refers to a model form of social organization rather than a physical city but Campanella did use an architectural analogue for his description of the social and intellectual relationships within this system. At the centre of the city was a circular sun temple; radiating out from this were concentric rings painted on either side with representations of all the phenomena of the natural world on one side, all those of the spiritual world on the other. In other words it was an encyclopaedic system in which art played an entirely didactic role. Lenin's view of art as a didactic tool expressive of social and cultural relationships, above all a public art, is in the same mould as that outlined by Campanella, whose ideas were well known in socialist (and in mystical) circles at the turn of the century. It was to be reflected in the programme for public monuments and in the public festivals and agit-prop activities that mark the years after the Revolution.

LUNACHARSKY, NARKOMPROS AND AVANT-GARDE ART

At the end of 1917 A. V. Lunacharsky (1875–1933) was appointed Commissar of the newly formed Commissariat of Enlightenment (*Narkompros*). As its name suggests, this was very much more than a ministry of education. It brought together the former ministries of Public Education and the 'Palace Ministry' which had controlled the Imperial theatres, museums and academies of art. *Narkompros* included departments responsible for all levels of general and specialist education, public health, housing, the arts (theatre, music, literature, the visual arts—including film and photography), museums, libraries, archives, publishing and telecommunications.

Lunacharsky was a philosopher by training. From the turn of the century until 1917 he spent most of his life in exile, both in Russia and abroad. During these years he devoted much of his time to the history of art and questions of aesthetics, and religion and its relationship with Marxism, as well as taking an active part in émigré politics. Between the end of 1911 and 1915 Lunacharsky lived in Paris, contributing articles to the Russian press on current literature and art as well as on questions of theory. He was a regular visitor to exhibitions and also visited artists' studios. The articles he wrote during this period included discussions of Italian Futurism as well as articles on contemporary art in France. Lunacharsky was also in touch with Russian artists working in Paris.[23]

Lunacharsky's first hand knowledge of and interests in avant-garde art and literature gave him certain sympathies with avant-garde artists and writers and it was partly for this reason that these came to the fore in official positions during the years immediately after the Revolution.

THE CHANGE IN STATUS OF THE AVANT-GARDE ARTIST

The Bolshevik government effectively removed the kinds of private patronage on which avant-garde artists had been dependent and substituted another more public and directly challenging form of patronage.[24] In broad terms, those who were prepared to work with the new government were eligible for its patronage. Although avant-garde artists were amongst the first to offer to collaborate with *Narkompros*, they were by no means the only ones: numerous academic artists and teachers as well as artists who had held posts in the civil service (as museum curators, and so on) also joined *Narkompros*, and one of the major artistic programmes of 1918/19 (see below) was largely carried out by academic artists.

Between 1918 and 1920 many of the existing institutes and academies of art were liquidated or radically reorganized and new ones created by *Narkompros*. In the process, a number of avant-garde artists were appointed to key positions within teaching and research establishments.[25] Kandinsky, for example, was made head of *Inkhuk* (a contraction of the Russian for 'Institute of Artistic Culture') which was set up to investigate theories of art on an experimental basis.

Teachers and students were entitled to certain privileges including special rations and 'study conscription'—exemption from active military service during the Civil War. Even if they were not teaching, artists were entitled to apply for subsidies of various categories to allow them to continue with their own work. And avant-garde artists were appointed to the Commissariats of Fine Arts which were set up throughout the regions.

In spite of their relative success, avant-garde artists were not regarded unequivocally. Lunacharsky was personally sympathetic to them partly because they were among the first to cooperate and because he felt that he understood their position clearly:

> In Russian bourgeois society [the Futurists] were to some extent persecuted and considered themselves revolutionaries in artistic technique. It was natural that they felt some sympathy for the revolution and were attracted to it when it extended a hand to them . . .
> (Quoted in Fitzpatrick, 1970, p. 127.)

But this did not mean that he saw 'Futurist'[26] art as capable of transformation into the art of Revolution. Lunacharsky, like Lenin, saw 'Futurism' as a natural byproduct of the decay of capitalism, which contained within it characteristics which might be used to stimulate the growth of a proletarian art:

> The dynamism and methods of collective, creative work which are so characteristic of Futurist art certainly stand in some sort of relationship to what the proletariat may create in the artistic field. If we cannot speak of futurism as a whole as proletarian art, we can talk of individual artists of futurist persuasion as artists close to the proletariat. . . .
> (Lunacharsky, 1919; quoted in Fitzpatrick, 1970, p. 127.)

Above all, in Lunacharsky's view, the 'Futurists' were adaptable to circumstance. Not long after this, however, Lunacharsky would be sharply critical of the 'Futurists' for using their position to try to impose their own ideas to the exclusion of all others.

Many of the civil servants belonging to the institutions absorbed into *Narkompros* had either disappeared or refused to recognize or work for the Bolshevik government. Lunacharsky's first appointments were of colleagues from the political-intellectual circles with which he had been associated. As head of the department of fine art (*IZO*) established early in 1919 he appointed David Sterenberg (1881–1948), a painter who had been living as an émigré in Paris and returned to Russia only after the Revolution. Sterenberg had been on the fringes of the Cubist circle and his work was known and admired by Lunacharsky. Sterenberg, perhaps as much as Lunacharsky, was responsible for supporting the 'Futurists' and, besides, brought back to Russia up to date information about activities in Paris over the last few years. Nikolay Punin, the art critic, recorded that:

> I went to see him [Sterenberg], cautiously began to talk about young Russian art and so-called futurism, and was taken aback when Sterenberg pulled out photographs of his work and began to talk about Picasso and Picabia and the new French masters. . .
> (Quoted in Fitzpatrick, 1970, p. 122.)

IZO's general function was to stimulate the development of 'artistic culture' throughout the country, and several avant-garde artists were given positions in the various sections and branches of *IZO*.

Narkompros published a periodical, *Iskusstvo kommuny* (*Art of the Commune*) from 1918; begun as the journal of the theatre and music departments of *Narkompros*, issues 4–10 of the first year were edited by Wassily Kandinsky. In 1919 the journal became the official journal of *Narkompros-IZO*, but it was replaced later in the year by *Khudozhestvennaya Zhizn* (*Artistic Life*), a bulletin on art which discussed the programme for the reorganization of art teaching, museums, etc., reviewed progress and raised issues of the theory and practice of art.

THE PROLETKULT

The initial impetus for the foundation of the *Proletkult* (an association of proletarian cultural organizations) came from the theory developed by A. A. Bogdanov (1873–1928) a scientist and Marxist philosopher and politician who joined the Bolsheviks in 1904, later resigning from the party. Bogdanov spent many years before the Revolution in exile. His associates in exile included Lunacharsky (who later became his brother-in-law) with whom Bogdanov studied and debated questions of philosophy, politics and aesthetics.

Bogdanov came to believe, in opposition to Lenin, that the spheres of economics, politics and culture were autonomous (rather than interdependent) and that it was possible for a spontaneous proletarian culture to express itself independently of a developed proletarian political and economic base.

By the end of 1917 the *Proletkult* was firmly established as an independent body with branches in Petrograd and Moscow. It began to oppose *Narkompros*'s policy of inviting the cooperation of bourgeois specialists and to demand that the responsibility for all cultural questions should belong to the *Proletkult*. The *Proletkult* also began to declare that the proletariat had no need to assimilate the culture of the past and even that it should reject the culture of the past wholesale and seek immediate expression of its own culture. There were two seemingly opposed views of how this might be achieved: on the one hand the *Proletkult* itself would be a vanguard force, 'a laboratory . . . in a well equipped factory (*Narkompros*) conducting energetic and intensive work to improve the organization' and on the other 'proletarian culture must be worked out in the process of independent activity at the grass roots, among the working masses' (quoted in Fitzpatrick, 1970, p. 95).

Lunacharsky supported the main principles of the *Proletkult* but disapproved of its rejection of the 'bourgeois' art of the past. Lenin opposed both the premises on which the *Proletkult* was founded and its activities and influence. In Lenin's view proletarian culture would emerge only with the raising of the general level of cultural and political consciousness among the masses and must grow organically from an understanding and assimilation of the culture of the past.[27] He was highly critical of those within the *Proletkult* who believed that 'proletarian culture is a sort of chemical reaction which can be produced in the *Proletkult* retort with the aid of a group of selected people' and he suspected the *Proletkult* of promoting bourgeois and reactionary attitudes because it had, in fact, a large number of bourgeois amongst its members and leaders. The *Proletkult* was absorbed into *Narkompros* in 1918 on Lenin's insistence; but although it was sponsored and subsidized by *Narkompros* it retained its autonomy until the reorganization of *Narkompros* in 1920–21.

ART IN THE STREETS

Insofar as direct patronage of particular kinds of artistic activities was exercised it was mainly through the programme for public sculptures and monuments to the ancestors of the Revolution and in commissions for street decorations and mass festivals.

Most of the sculptures were very far removed from the kind of art we have come to associate with the 'revolutionary' art of the period. The programme's didactic intention required an illustrative art, in the form of recognizable portraits; it also required, in a time of extreme shortage of materials, permanent or semi-permanent results. For avant-garde artists the illustrative requirements of this programme were anathema and much of the work executed under the programme was in the tradition of academic naturalism, although a number of sculptures attempted to ally Futurist or Cubist forms with naturalism, with rather crude results (Fig. 17). With one significant exception (Tatlin's *Monument to the Third International*, Fig. 27, p. 51), avant-garde artists were scarcely involved in one of the major programmes for public art of this period. The general direction in which their sculpture was tending is partly illustrated in the work of an artist such as Naum Gabo (see Hamilton, pp. 353–54), that is, towards constructions which embody engineering/architectural analogies or symbolism in their form, materials, method of construction, and projected scale.

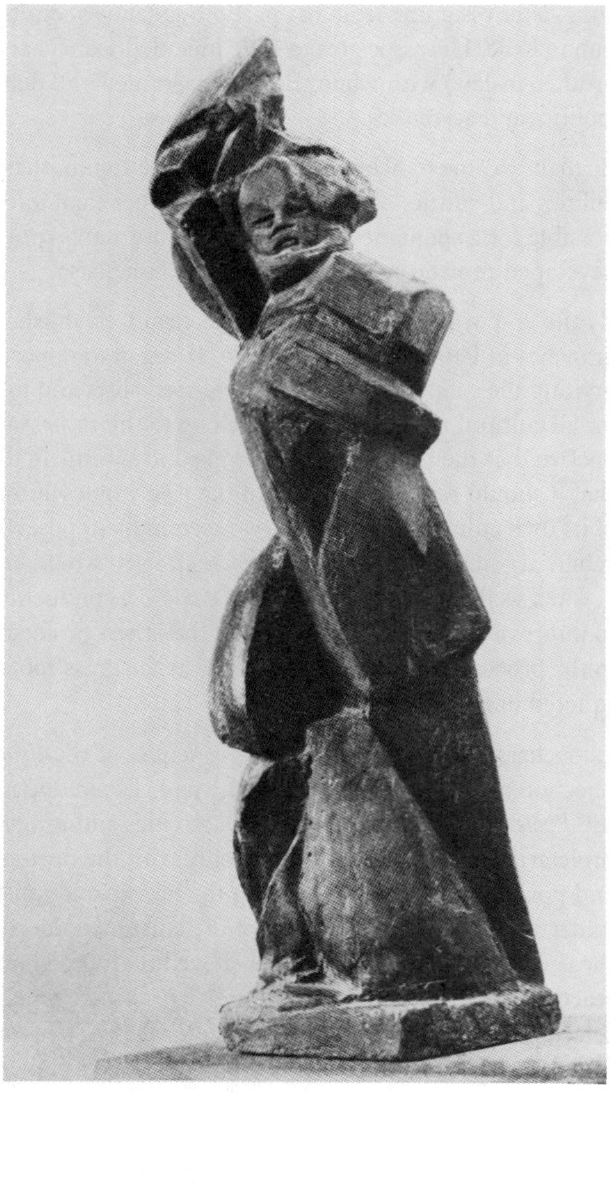

Figure 17 B. Korolev, model for *Bakunin Monument*, 1918 (*Soyuz Sovetskii Khudozhnikov, Agitatsionno-Musovogo Iskusstvo*, 1967).

It was in the programmes for mass-spectacles, temporary street decorations and agit-prop materials (i.e. all those kinds of activities which demanded improvisatory, spontaneous skills) that avant-garde artists came into their own.

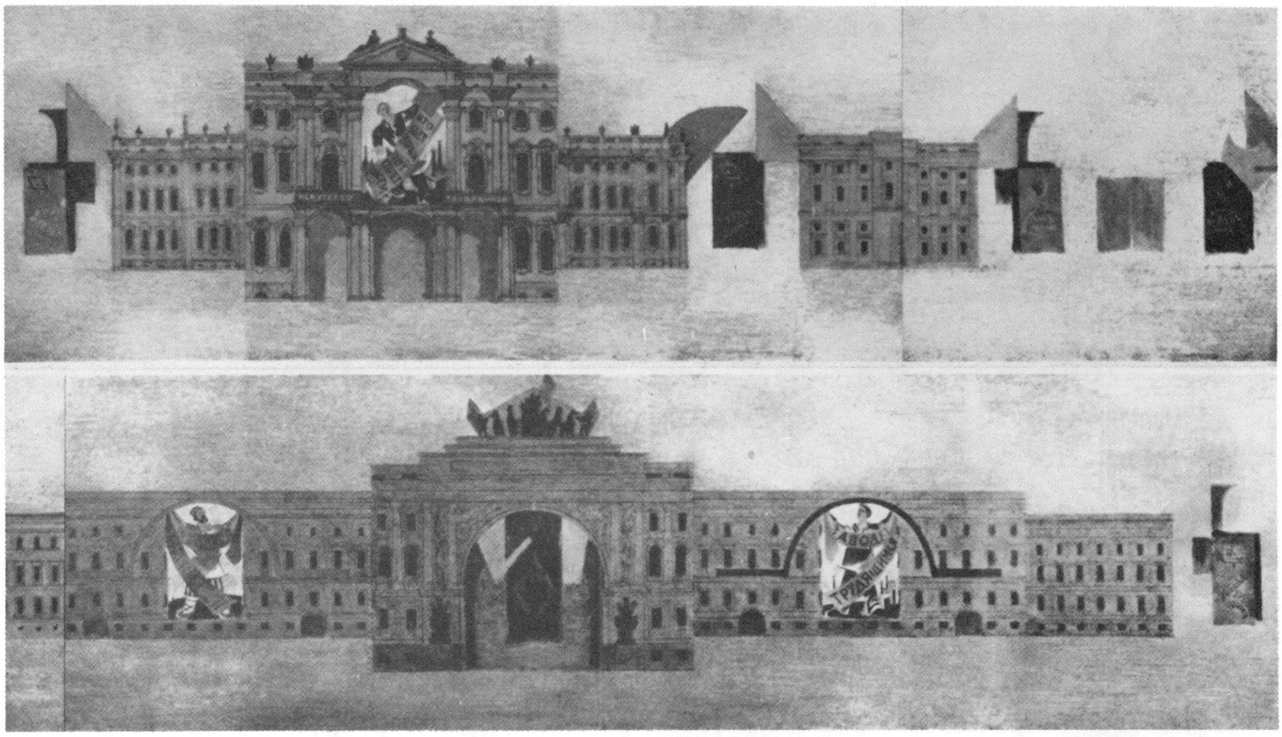

Figure 18 Nathan Altman, design for decorations to celebrate the first anniversary of the Revolution, October 1918 (Taken from Camilla Gray, *The Great Experiment: Russian Art 1863–1922*, 1962, Thames and Hudson).

Figure 18 and Plate 7 show examples of decorations designed for the celebration of the first anniversary of the October Revolution in Petrograd, by Nathan Altman. The entire square in front of the Winter Palace was requisitioned and the buildings decorated with vast paintings on canvas of figures bearing banners with slogans and huge abstract constructions placed at the entrances and in the centre of the square. The scale of other revolutionary celebrations was often similarly massive; in 1920 Altman, Ivan Puni and Xenia Boguslavskaya designed the 'sets' for the open-air re-enactment of the Storming of the Winter Palace which involved a 'cast' of several thousand (Fig. 19). One of these mass events, *The Symphony for*

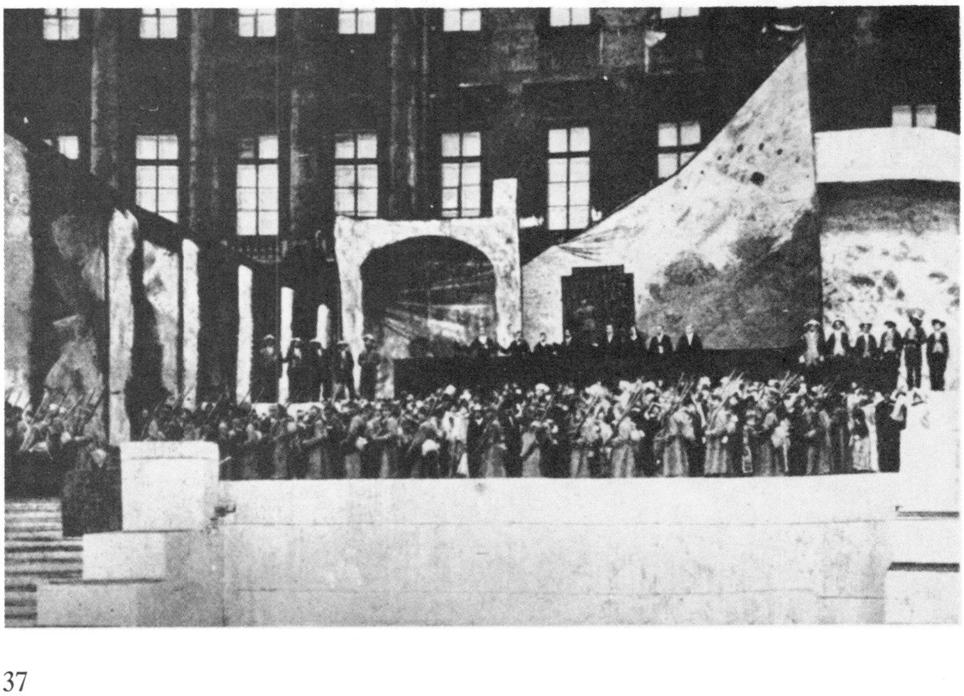

Figure 19 Nathan Altman, Ivan Puni *et al.*, the re-enactment of the Storming of the Winter Palace (Taken from Camilla Gray, *The Great Experiment: Russian Art 1863–1922*, 1962, Thames and Hudson).

Factory Sirens, involved factories all over Moscow and required coordination from the rooftops by worker 'conductors'.

Rosta (the Russian Telegraph Agency which came under the wing of *Narkompros*) commissioned a number of window displays: typically these were like enlarged *lubki* or comic strips in form—sheets with stencilled illustrations and captions—presenting educational, instructional and propaganda material (Fig. 20). In a sense these are reminiscent of the Futurist books we considered earlier not only because they draw on popular sources in format, but also because they often brought together artists and writers in collaboration, a pattern of working which continued into other forms of graphic art in the 1920s. Vladimir Mayakovsky and Alexander Rodchenko, for example, collaborated on poster design (Fig. 33, p. 57).

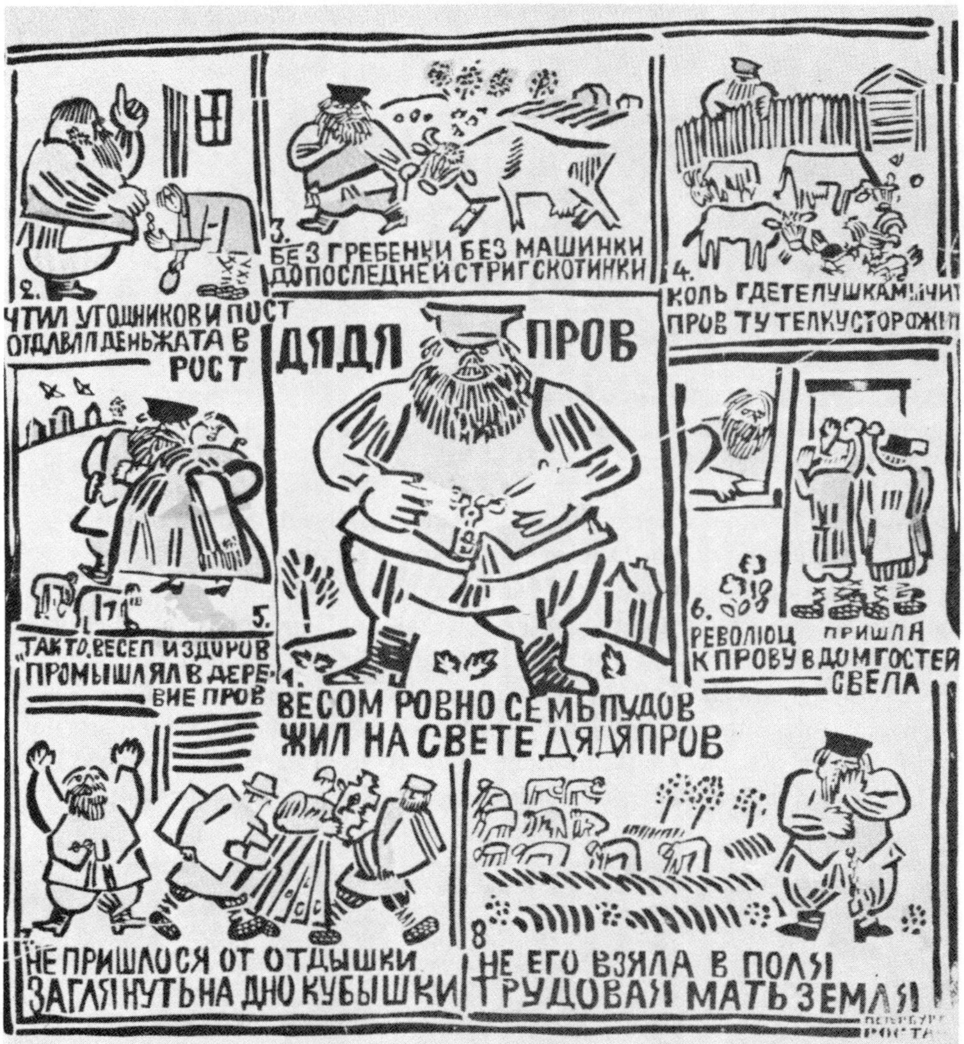

Figure 20 Vladimir Lebedev, *Old Man Prov*, *Rosta* poster, 1920, Petrograd (Taken from Syzmon Bojko, *New Graphic Design in Revolutionary Russia*, 1972, Lund Humphries).

Russo-German Links

By the end of 1918 *Narkompros-IZO* had established an International Bureau, run by a committee which included Kandinsky, Lunacharsky, Punin, Sterenberg, Tatlin, whose first major task was to establish contact with German artists. The reasons for this priority are not difficult to understand. Germany in the autumn of 1918 was in a state of social ferment which many people believed would develop into a fully revolutionary situation; soldiers' and workers' councils were established in many towns and regions (in imitation of Russian 'soviets'). Many German intellectuals were directly active in these councils, or in arts councils set up on an analogous model. In Berlin artists, writers and architects formed themselves into two groups of this kind, the *Arbeitsrat für Kunst* (*AfK*: 'Works' Council for Art') and the *Novembergruppe* ('November Group') both of which were established in November 1918.[28]

German artists evidently watched developments in Russia with considerable interest, perhaps seeing in the operations of *Narkompros-IZO* and the programme for the reorganization of the art schools a blueprint for what they were aiming for themselves.[29] Walter Gropius, a key figure in German avant-garde architectural circles and chairman of the *AfK*, wrote to Ludwig Bähr, a German intermediary with the Russians:

> Today I have once more with great interest studied the Russian artists' programme[30] and given it much thought. Brilliant ideas are expressed in it. From the material that Taut has handed to you[31], you will be able to see for yourself that they essentially correspond with our efforts, except for one point that has not been fully developed in the Russian programme and which we consider especially important, i.e. 'the association of all forms of art under the cloak of the "great" architecture.' This idea, which is an important and characteristic feature of our movement, we should like you to pass on to the Russian artists. Art should liberate itself from the salons and again come out of the isolation in which it has so far existed. . . .
> (Letter from Gropius to Bähr, part of extract quoted in *Khudozhestvennaya Zhizn*, 1920, numbers 4–5; quoted in this translation in Andersen, 1966.)

And Russian artists knew, at least in outline, the programme upon which the Bauhaus was founded. Kandinsky commented of the principles of the Berlin groups that they were beginning to be put into practice at Weimar, and noted the differences in emphasis of the Germans.

Extracts from a letter from Gropius to Bähr published in *Iskusstvo kommuny* contained references to aspects of the educational theory formulated in the *AfK* which were embodied in the initial Bauhaus structure and teaching programme.

The extent of direct contacts between groups such as the *AfK* and Russian artists working in *Narkompros* and their significance is not established in any detail; but it is clear that besides being linked by a similar atmosphere of revolutionary enthusiasm (in a general, as well as a specifically political sense), they shared ideas of collectivity, of a union or interdependency between the arts, and of the role of art in society. Not surprisingly, Kandinsky, with his recent German background, seems to have played a part in these exchanges, as well as attempting to develop further the ideas of correspondences between different art forms and of artistic synthesis with which he had experimented in Germany before the war.

In 1919 Kandinsky wrote an article for *Khudozhestvennaya Zhizn* entitled 'The Great Utopia', suggesting that an international congress of artists should be convened with representatives drawn from as wide a spectrum of the arts as possible (and here he included popular entertainment—e.g. circus and music hall—as well as literature, dance, music, painting, sculpture, architecture, etc.). For this purpose, he suggested, a 'universal' building of art should be constructed to house all existing forms of art and making allowance for any new forms which might be discovered in the future (if that sounds strange, you should remember that film was still a relatively new medium then and that artists saw the 'synthesis' of different art forms as potentially leading to new forms). Clearly although this utopian project was conceived for a particular kind of 'function' it is really a symbolic concept of unity and collectivity and, as such, has something in common with Bruno Taut's more or less contemporary conception of the '*Stadtkrone*' ('City Crown')[32], a 'universal' building with no practical function, to be constructed entirely of glass and intended to represent symbolically the summit of human aspirations, spiritual needs, etc.

KANDINSKY IN RUSSIA 1915–22

Kandinsky had returned to Russia in 1915; at the end of 1915 and beginning of 1916 he spent several months in Stockholm where both he and Gabriele Münter held exhibitions. During the years he spent in Russia Kandinsky's output was very small compared with that of the last years in Munich, not surprisingly. From the end of 1917 to the middle of 1919 Kandinsky did not produce a single work. (The same was probably true of other artists actively involved in the organization of artistic activities during this period, but there is also no doubt that Kandinsky was disorientated by his return to Russia.)

During his years in Germany Kandinsky had maintained a keen interest in artistic activities in Russia, as well as acting as a kind of intermediary between East and West during the years before the war; but despite feeling like a Russian in exile in Munich, Kandinsky did not fit easily into the avant-garde art world in Moscow when he returned. He had lived for nearly twenty years in Germany, and although he was respected in Russia as both a painter and theorist, as well as for his organizing skills, he was also distrusted by many Russian artists for what they saw as his 'Germanic' ideas.

During these years Kandinsky supervised the publication of the Russian edition of his memoirs (first published as *Rückblicke*, Munich, 1913) which was published under the imprint of *Narkompros* in 1918 (with many of the Christian references deleted). He also attempted to arrange publication of a complete Russian version of *Über das geistige in der Kunst*, accepted for publication in 1921 (extracts had been translated and published at the Pan-Russian congress of artists in 1911); however the full text was never published in Russian. After the Revolution Kandinsky was active as an organizer, teacher, writer and theoretician in the years up to 1921. He was nominated in 1919 as a teacher at the Moscow Free Studios (which became the *Vkhutemas* in 1920). As a member of *Narkompros* he edited several issues of *Iskusstvo kommuny* and contributed articles to its successor *Khudozhestvennaya Zhizn*. He was also appointed to a committee established within *Narkompros* to edit and contribute to an encyclopaedia of fine arts which was to include biographical entries and to discuss questions of artistic theory.

KANDINSKY'S PAINTINGS OF THE RUSSIAN PERIOD 1915–21

Many of the larger oil paintings Kandinsky did in Russia are fairly clearly related to the kind of work he had been doing in Munich from *c.*1911–14; the smaller works (watercolours, drawings, etc.) on the other hand, show a variety of style and subject matter. In several of the paintings a loosely painted border or framing motif is employed (Fig. 21)—a device which Kandinsky had used already in some of the paintings in the Munich period. (The formal point of departure for this device can be seen in Fig. 12, p. 26, and Plate 5.)

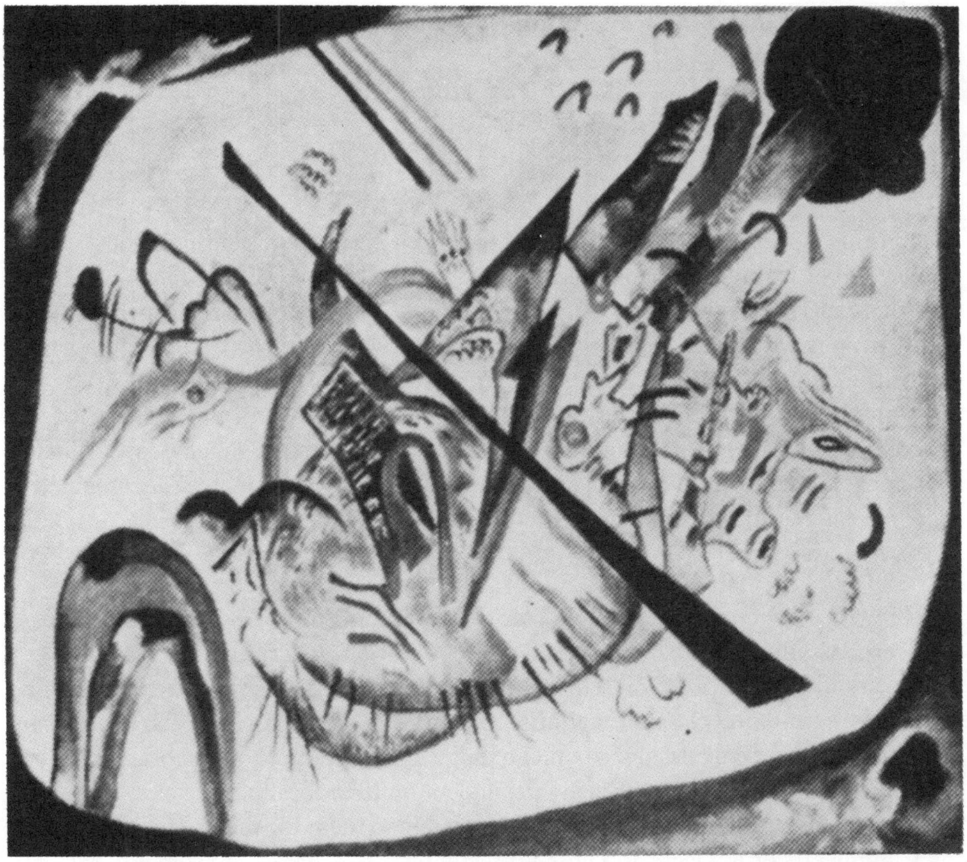

Figure 21 Wassily Kandinsky, *White Oval (Black Border)*, 1919, oil, $31\frac{1}{2} \times 36\frac{5}{8}$ ins (Formerly Tretiakov Gallery, Moscow; photo from Willi Grohmann, *Kandinsky*, 1956, Thames and Hudson, copyright DuMont Schauberg, Cologne).

The paintings done after the break between 1917 and 1919 mark a change in direction which must be related both to Kandinsky's other activities of these years and to the general 'constructivist' climate. Hamilton illustrates (Fig. 201, p. 338) a painting of 1921 which indicates the change. Geometric, hard-edged shapes (circles, triangles, etc.) are combined with more fluid shapes derived from the 'residual organic' motifs of the earlier paintings. But the general compositional schema is still recognizably related to the earlier paintings. What Hamilton's rather dark illustration unfortunately does not bring out very well is the variety of technical, painterly demonstrations in this picture: modelled forms played off against hard-edged ones, forms whose colour changes to suggest their location 'behind' or 'in front of' other coloured forms, and so on. It is almost as if Kandinsky had at last come to terms with the second of the two ways to abstraction which he had spelt out ten years earlier (see p. 25).

Art Education after the Revolution

(See Hamilton, pp. 314–15, 318–19.)

Hamilton, p. 314

'In addition, special pleading . . . general outline.': Nearly a decade after the publication of Hamilton's book this is still one of the key problems. 'The most vigorous experiments were carried out in Moscow' (p. 315), but it is clear that experiments of considerable interest were carried on outside these centres. Attention has concentrated on the Moscow *Vkhutemas* largely because it numbered some of the most prominent members of the avant garde among its members and because its programme appears to correspond rather closely to that of the Bauhaus, especially in its emphasis on industrial design; however, there is still no adequately documented account available of the teaching programme and work of the school during the decade or so of its existence.[33]

Narkompros-IZO established Commissariats of Fine Art in various regional centres with responsibility for the organization of art education programmes to include organization of exhibitions, museums, schools of art, crafts, architecture, art teaching in schools, extramural classes for adults, conservation of local collections, supervision of decorations for festivals, and so on. To judge by the example of Vitebsk, the regional Commissariats were directly dependent on their local party committees for accommodation and funding as well as responsible to them for the programme. But the Commissars of Art were appointed directly by *Narkompros*, and sometimes had to invoke Lunacharsky's personal authority in order to obtain the necessary funds from their local authorities. Chagall spent a good deal of his time as Commissar of Art for Vitebsk travelling to and from Moscow to seek support for his schemes. For obvious reasons, local authorities were not always willing to make funds available; Chagall quotes a typical encounter with a member of the local soviet:

> 'Which do you think is more important Comrade Chagall, to have an emergency repair done to the bridge or to allocate money to your Academy of Fine Arts?' (Chagall, 1961, p. 141.)

The Commissariats of Art were also required to set up 'Museums of Artistic Culture' with the art and crafts of different periods displayed in comparative formal groupings rather than in chronological sequences. The museums were intended to serve both a general educative role and to stimulate new creative work. Examples of recent avant-garde painting were allocated through a central fund established by *Narkompros* which acquired work by avant-garde artists especially for distribution for regional museums; these were intended to demonstrate the possibilities of new experimental techniques. The fund included examples of all those tendencies of the last fifteen years or so which could be labelled 'progressive' from *Mir Iskusstva* through Suprematism to Constructivism. Through this scheme some of the most advanced abstract work could be seen in provincial museums—a situation unparalleled in most of Europe at this time, with the exception of the Weimar Republic.

ART EDUCATION AND THE ROLE OF PROGRESSIVE ARTISTS: VITEBSK AND UNOVIS

I have concentrated on Vitebsk mainly because a fairly detailed account is available of Chagall's activities there (in Meyer, 1964) and it is possible to piece together a wider picture of some of the practical, ideological and artistic problems of the period.

In September 1918 Marc Chagall was appointed Commissar of Fine Art for the town of Vitebsk and its region. By the spring of 1919 he had established an art school of which he was director; by the end of 1919 he had resigned after confrontation with Malevich and his suppporters.

To understand Chagall's position it is necessary to know something of his background and his ambitions for the development of the artistic life of the town after his appointment as Commissar. Chagall was born and brought up in Vitebsk, a modest provincial town half way between St Petersburg and Kiev which had developed as a trading centre in the late nineteenth and early twentieth century by virtue of its situation on a rail junction and its river port. It was almost entirely built of wood; few of its streets were paved and in character it retained a village-like atmosphere: there was little industry and many of its inhabitants were small traders. Vitebsk was within the 'Pale of Settlement'.[34]

When Chagall returned to Vitebsk after the Revolution it was with a strong sense of the personal liberation which the Revolution had brought him. As a former victim of repression and discrimination himself, he wanted to share this sense of liberation; he described his aim as:

> to implant Art there . . . making ordinary houses into museums and the average citizen into a creator. . . .
> (Chagall, 1961, p. 145.)

The first major task on which he worked was the supervision of decorations to celebrate the first anniversary of the October Revolution. The project was to cause one of the first in a series of conflicts between Chagall and the local party administrators. Chagall mobilized all the town's artistic skills, gathering together house painters and sign painters and craftsmen to execute the designs.

The scheme of decoration included temporary triumphal arches which were set up at points around the town, banners and flags and the repainting of shop fronts and public transport. Many of the designs appear to have been Chagall's own, of which one is illustrated (Fig. 22). Its message seems unexceptionable but the decorations evidently included some of Chagall's more idiosyncratic subjects. He was immediately attacked for wasting scarce materials and on artistic grounds:

> 'Why is the cow green and why is the horse flying in the sky? Why? What has this to do with Marx and Lenin?'
> (Chagall, 1961, p. 139.)

Chagall planned to create a complex of related art and craft workshops to include a people's art school, community workshops (through which all commissions would be channelled and shared out) and a school of arts and crafts. All kinds and levels of creative activity were to be catered for. In the first few months Chagall organized lectures, public discussions and issued directives aimed to encourage the participation of the 'artistic' community as well as to publicize the school's aims. Painters, decorators, architects and craftsmen were invited to contribute to the planning and to give practical support by joining the proposed community workshops, so that students would be able to learn by example; there would be no hierarchical distinction between fine and applied arts or crafts..

Scarcely any of this plan was to materialize. The first stage was the creation of the art school and subsequently the museum. Chagall had a building at his disposal but no funds, and he applied for a grant with which to establish the art school in November 1918. In the next two months he spent a considerable amount of time in Petrograd trying to enlist avant-garde artists to teach in Vitebsk and succeeded in persuading Ivan Puni and his wife Xenia Boguslavskaya (Puni had been a signatory of the Suprematist manifesto on the occasion of '0.10'), and a former teacher of Chagall's from Petrograd to join him in Vitebsk. He appointed all of them to membership of the

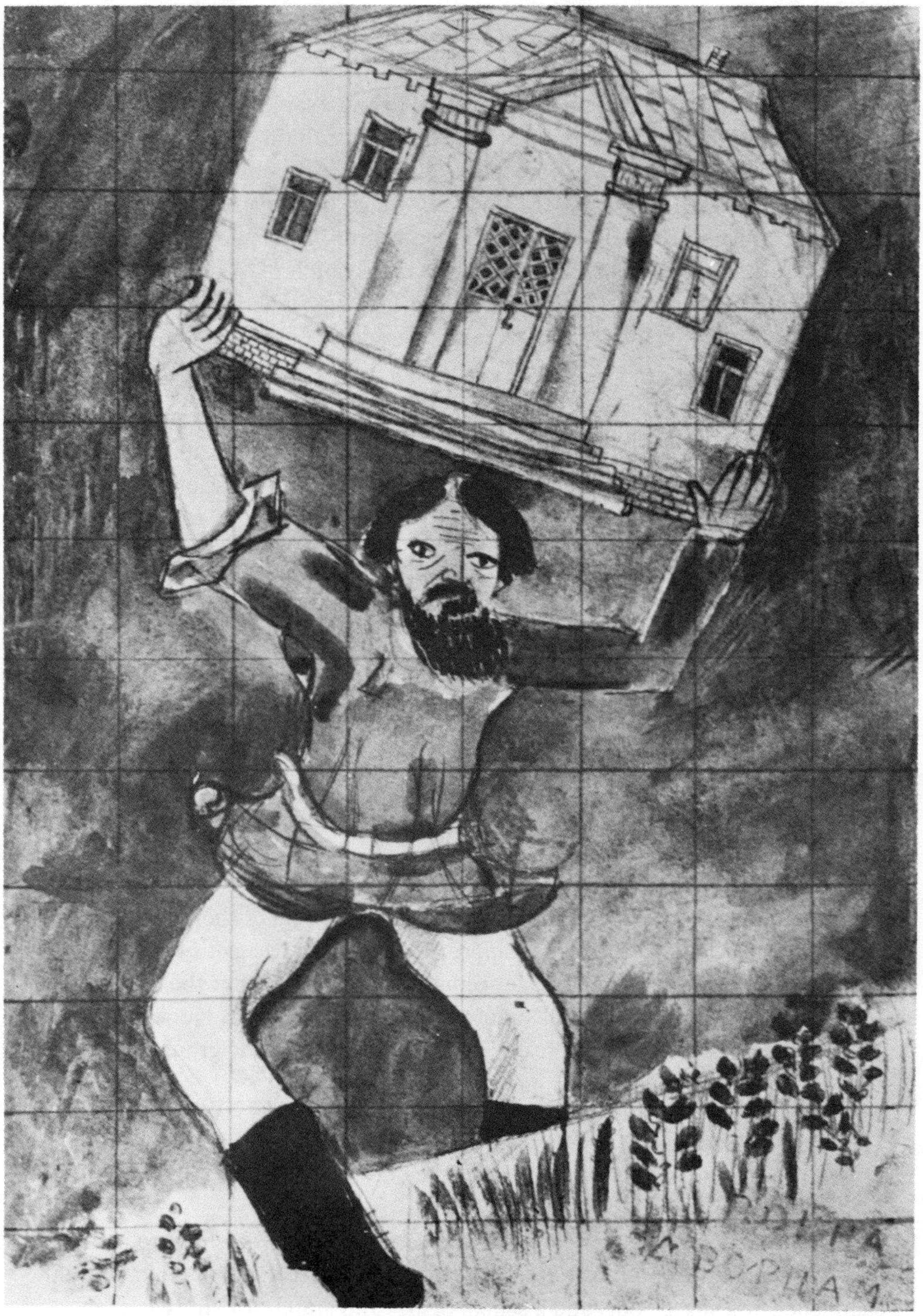

Figure 22 Marc Chagall, '*Down with Palaces*', 1918/19, Vitebsk (From *Soyuz Sovetskii Khudozhnikov, Agitatsionno-Musovogo Iskusstvo*, 1967).

Commissariat as well, probably to strengthen his hand in dealings with local functionaries. The Commissariat soon provoked protests against its 'futuristic' dictatorship through—among other things—making the decoration of all buildings subject to permit.

During the spring of 1919 funds were allotted for the expansion of the museum's collection by the acquisition of work of local interest. The core of the existing collection was formed from a private collection expropriated under decree in 1918; to this were added from the *Narkompros* fund examples of work by avant-garde artists such as Robert Falk, Malevich and Olga Rozanova. Chagall tried to expand the modern collection by petitioning *Narkompros* for examples of work by artists such as Bakst, Benois, Goncharova, Kandinsky, Larionov, Rodchenko and Tatlin, but with no success, as Vitebsk had already had a major share from the fund. A plan to make a representative selection of Chagall's own work (as a native born artist) never materialized.

The activities of the school were attacked by the local party, which demanded illustrative realism. Chagall's reply is worth quoting:

> The art of today like that of tomorrow wants no 'content'. The real proletarian art will succeed with simple wisdom in breaking inwardly and outwardly with all that can only be branded as 'literature'. . . . Proletarian art is neither an art for proletarians nor an art by proletarians. . . . It is the art *of the proletarian painter*. In him 'creative talent' is combined with proletarian conscience, and he knows full well that both he and his gifts belong to the collectivity. . . . In contrast to the bourgeois painter, who endeavours to meet the taste of the crowd, the proletarian painter never stops fighting against routine. He draws the crowd along in his wake. (From *Revolutzionnoie iskusstvo*, Vitebsk, 1919; quoted in Meyer, 1964.)

(Although Chagall's own painting remained essentially representational it did not escape the kind of criticism quoted previously. See Haftmann 495–96 for examples of his work from this period.)

Besides attacks from outside the school there was soon dissatisfaction within it. The reasons why are probably substantially those outlined by Chagall in *My Life*[35]; his personal enthusiasm for the success of the school within the community (he gave up painting almost entirely and resigned his post as Commissar in order to devote all his energies to the school) was not shared by his staff. (Chagall claimed that they invited criticism from the community by abusing their privileged position as teachers in various ways.) Then there was also the question of a conflict of artistic ideologies within the school and its effect on personal loyalties, which led eventually to his resignation.

By June 1919 when the school held its first public exhibition it offered a preparatory course as well as classes in painting, drawing, sculpture, typography, crafts and architecture. An art club and library had been started. Some of the original staff had left, but there were also new teachers, including El Lissitsky. Lissitsky had gone to Germany to train as an architect before the war (having failed to obtain high enough secondary-school grades to enter a Russian school of art under the quota system for Jews), returning to Russia after the outbreak of war. Lissitsky and Chagall knew each other in Petrograd during the war years, through their common activities in the Jewish Artists' Circle, and they had collaborated together on illustrations for Hebrew texts. Lissitsky's illustrations of the period are closely modelled in style on Chagall's. Chagall later invited Lissitsky to take charge of the graphic department and of architectural design at Vitebsk. It was Lissitsky who insisted that Malevich should be invited to join the staff, and in September 1919 Malevich arrived in Vitebsk.

Before the end of the year Chagall had resigned as a result of disagreements with Malevich, and despite the support of a number of students. At the end of the year he returned, at the request of his supporters, but soon after resigned again and returned to Moscow. Chagall's account of this period, in his autobiography, is very sketchy and the synoptic method he employs in the narrative makes it difficult to follow the sequence of events. And surprisingly, despite much recent literature on Malevich, there is no real account of the episode from Malevich's point of view. Certainly Malevich would have been intolerant of Chagall's paintings. Malevich had disparaged realism and was highly critical of artists' attempts to express mood in painting by using non-naturalistic colours on naturalistic forms. Chagall, on the other hand, thought Malevich's vocabulary of forms too reductive and imprecise to achieve the kind of psychic realism Malevich claimed for them. He was also critical of Suprematism's pretensions to non-objectivity; in Chagall's view a square or a cross was no less an object (and no less associational in its way) than a chair, or a figure.

Besides particular disagreements about painting it is likely that Chagall and Malevich would also have disagreed over the organization and function of the school. Chagall wanted the school to be as open and democratic as possible, with different tendencies represented, Malevich would have been likely to try to impose Suprematism at all costs. However, Malevich evidently soon gained considerable support within the schools for his views.

UNOVIS

Malevich's followers at Vitebsk formed themselves into a group first named *Pronovis* and subsequently titled *Unovis* (contractions respectively of the Russian for 'Followers of the New Art' and 'Affirmers of the New Art'), a change which perhaps can be seen to represent the difference between giving support for the principles expressed in Malevich's essay 'On New Systems in Art' and developing these principles in practice. During the years of its existence first in Vitebsk (1919–21) and afterwards in Petrograd, *Unovis* artists produced scores of Suprematist works; not only paintings, drawings and sculptural constructions, but also designs for pottery, kiosks, and so on. They were not concerned with utilitarian aims, however:

> *Unovis* distinguished between the concept of functionality meaning the necessity for the creation of new forms, and the question of direct serviceableness. They represented the view that the new form is the lever which sets life in motion, if it is based on suitability of the material and on economy. This new form gives birth to other forms which are totally functional, and through them is itself enriched, modified and further developed.
> (El Lissitsky, 'On New Russian Art', 1922; quoted in Lissitsky-Küppers, 1968, p. 336.)

The stress on economy and suitability of material sounds very much like the language of the Constructivists (see p. 55), but Lissitsky's statement maintains the primacy of artistic considerations over material expediency. Neither Lissitsky nor Malevich ever accepted the Constructivists' view that artistic activities should be directed towards purely utilitarian ends. Malevich viewed Constructivism as a tendency which posed the same kind of threat to Art (by which he meant the capacity to induce feeling, reflection, sensations which transcend the material world of everyday experience) as he had identified in naturalistic art.

The implications of Malevich's title 'Suprematism' are not entirely fortuitous; Lissitsky and Malevich both began to understand Suprematism as a 'system' which would 'transcend communism'; in other words, assert its *supremacy* not just as an artistic philosophy but as a manner of interpreting the world. Malevich does not seem to have discouraged the cult aspects which grew up around Suprematism; members of *Unovis* stitched emblematic black squares on their clothing and photographs of *Unovis* activities show versions of the *Black Square* employed in a talismanic way.

In line with the activities of *Unovis* and perhaps particularly because of his association with Lissitsky (who, you will remember, had trained as a architect) in Vitebsk, Malevich's own works become more referential or metaphorical, both in their construction and in the way Malevich described them. He began to make three-dimensional models (Fig. 23) made at first in cut paper, later in plaster, and drawings (Fig. 24) which are recognizably 'architectural' in character and in title (Malevich called them 'Architektons' and 'Planits' respectively) but which are not intended as models or projects for actual buildings,[36] although at least one design for an 'Architekton' was published together with a plan and sectional drawing added by someone else—perhaps one of Malevich's pupils. Although they were not intended as architectural models, Malevich's 'Architektons' were much admired in avant-garde architectural circles in Germany and Holland at this time.

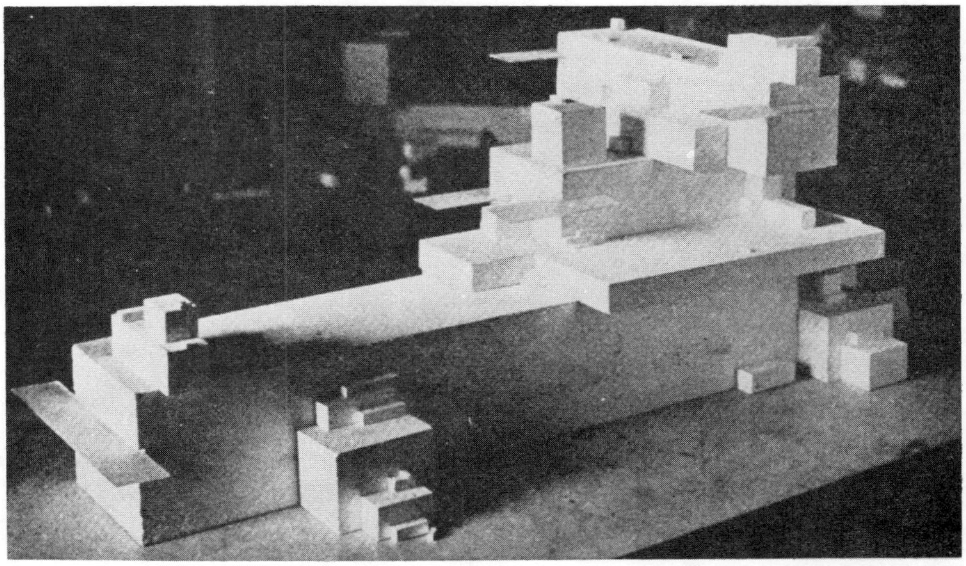

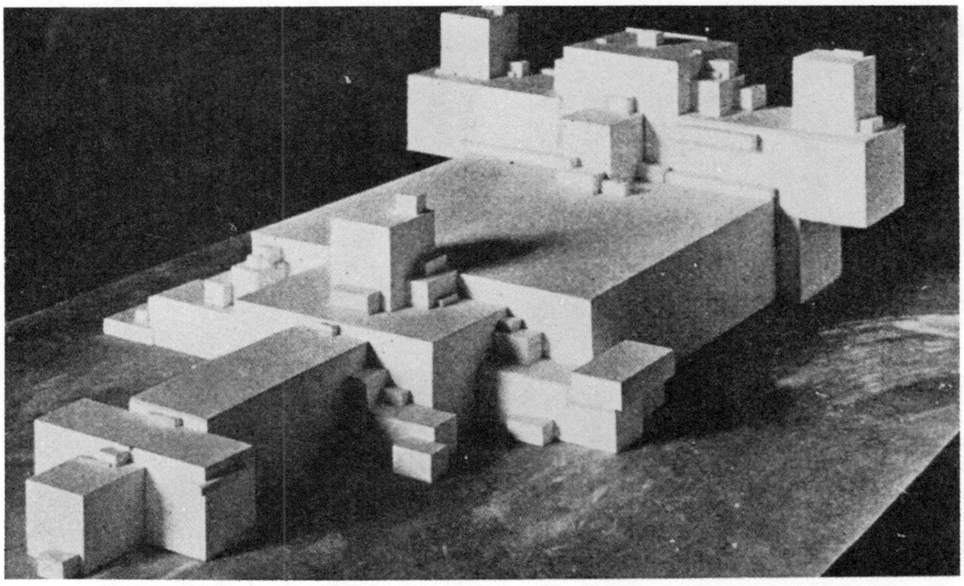

Figure 23 Kazimir Malevich, *Architektons*: upper: *Alpha*, 1923; lower: *Beta*, before 1926 (Originals lost; photo: Troels Andersen).

Suprematist forms were also modified in Malevich's two-dimensional work, in drawings which suggest architectural constructions seen in perspective (Fig. 24). It was around this time that Malevich began to speak of Suprematism as an 'aerial' system—a view which distinguishes the definitions of Suprematism given in *Die gegenstandslose Welt* (*The Non-Objective World*), published as *Bauhausbuch* No. 11, from earlier definitions Malevich gave in the years before the Revolution. Just as the emphasis in his work changed to suggest—even if only by allusion—a social dimension (in the form of the 'Architektons'), so he also adapted his philosophy of Suprematism to relate to the outside world. Malevich's teaching charts, made in the 1920s, which analyse the development of art in diagrammatic form, show Suprematist compositions set side by side with aerial photographs showing similar visual characteristics (compare the illustrations from his *Bauhausbuch*, Unit 12, Fig. 83).

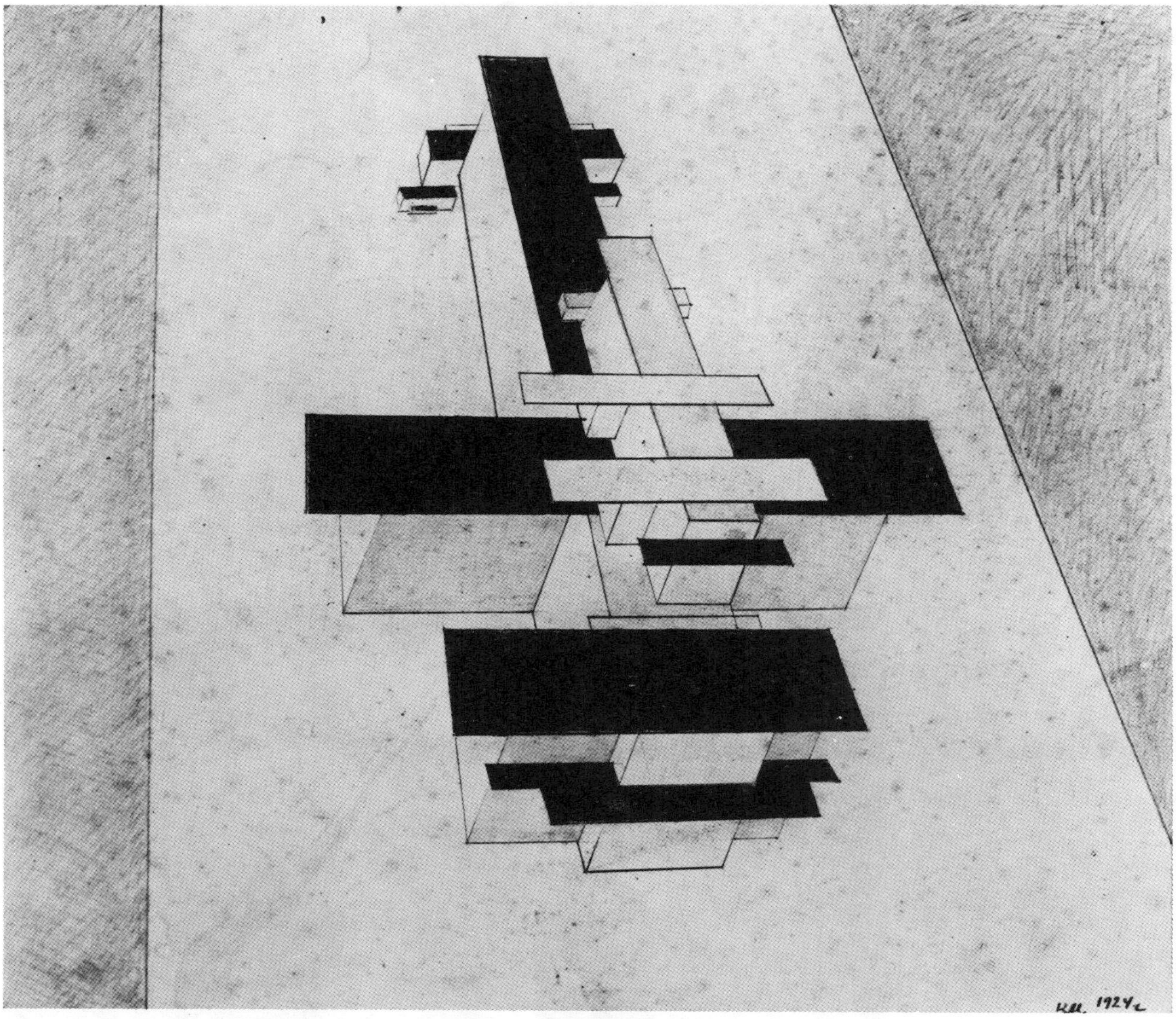

Figure 24 Kazimir Malevich, *Future Planits for Leningrad: The Pilot's House*, 1924, 12 × 17½ ins, pencil on paper (Stedelijk Museum, Amsterdam).

LISSITSKY

(See Hamilton, pp. 317–19.)

If you compare the illustration of Lissitsky's work in Hamilton (Fig. 189) with illustrations of Malevich's Suprematist work in Haftmann, you will see that there are quite striking resemblances between the two. But there are striking differences as well: Lissitsky's paintings employ stereometric images in a way that Malevich's do not; he also seems to locate his forms more precisely in relation to one another and in pictorial space by using a greater variety of treatment (more contrast, through suggestions of opacity and transparency, than in Malevich's work); and the images are less ambiguous in their architectural references than Malevich's. But a major difference as well is that Lissitsky attempts to harness the supposedly non-referential imagery of Suprematism to a fairly precisely legible meaning, particularly in his graphic work.

It is worth comparing examples of designs intended for similar purposes by Malevich and Lissitsky.

Figure 25 Kazimir Malevich, '*What have you done for the Front?*', *Rosta* poster, 1919, Smolensk (Taken from Syzmon Bojko, *New Graphic Design in Revolutionary Russia*, 1972, Lund Humphries).

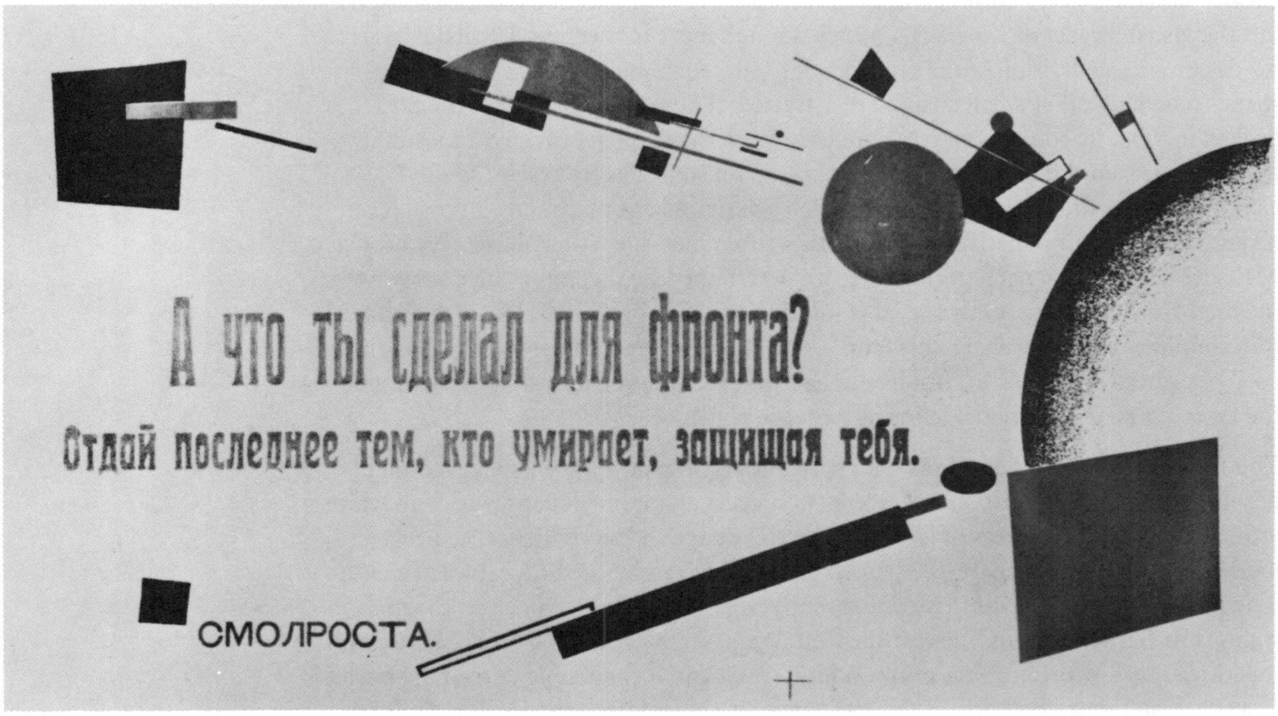

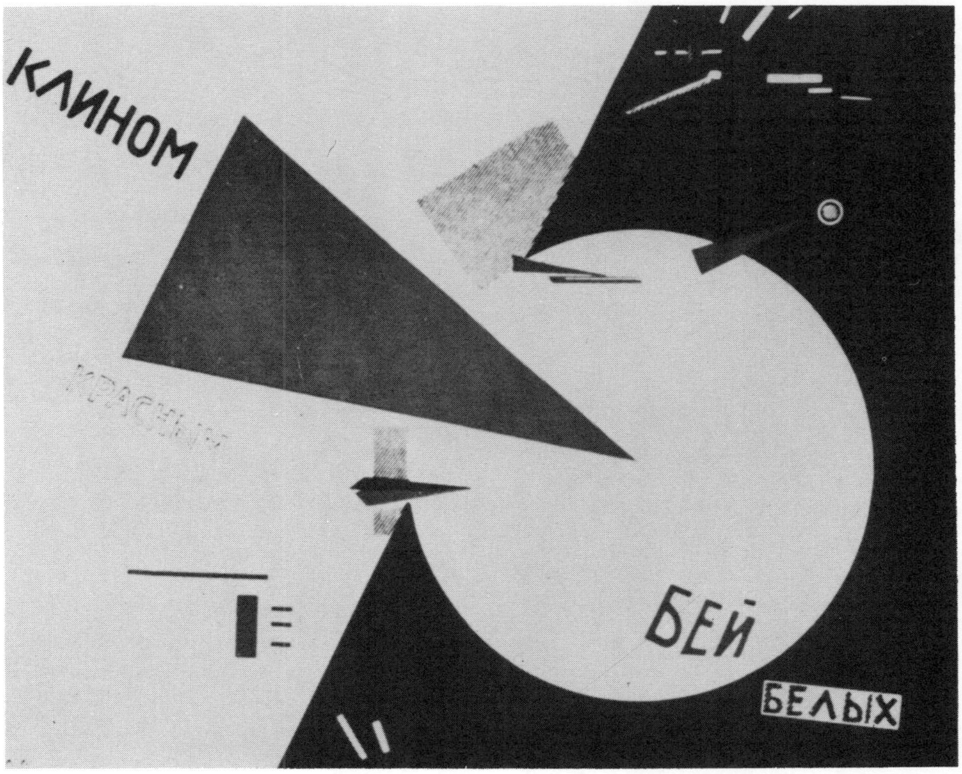

Figure 26 El Lissitsky, '*Beat the Whites with the Red Wedge*', poster, 1919, Vitebsk (Taken from Syzmon Bojko, *New Graphic Design in Revolutionary Russia*, 1972, Lund Humphries).

Exercise

Compare Figures 25 and 26. Both are propaganda posters soliciting support for the Red Army (this was still the period of the Civil War). Malevich's design was for the Smolensk branch of *Rosta*; Lissitsky's appears to have been a recruiting poster. What comments would you make on the differences and similarities between the two?

Discussion

Clearly both artists are employing similar shapes and configurations in their designs, but the visual impact of Lissitsky's poster is much more immediate. Lissitsky bases his design on the division of the rectangle into two equal but reversed geometrical shapes on which other small shapes are activated. The verbal message of the poster is broken up, and its constituent parts are used as visual elements in the composition; the lettering is in different 'weights' and sizes (and some characters are solidly coloured, others drawn in outline). Malevich's design seems more conventional (even given the use of Suprematist forms): it is a written message with a decorative border. Malevich uses traditional lettering, the size determined by the importance as part of the total verbal message. Only the label for the Smolensk branch of *Rosta* (bottom left) is in simplified, modern characters (and if the latter seem more legible to us than those used elsewhere in the poster, it is likely that Malevich's audience would have found the more familiar, traditional lettering easier to read).

You may have noted other points which distinguish the posters. Lissitsky's design, despite its use of geometric shapes, seems to suggest a simplified map: black and white areas might be read as areas of land and sea, the wedge shapes as tactical or progress markers on a campaign chart, the striped circle (upper right) as the location of a city. The poster was published in 1919, apparently as part of a Bolshevik effort to enlist support in Jewish communities for the Red Army. In the autumn of 1919, Petrograd was threatened by the advance of the White Army, and it is possible to read the poster as a schematic representation of the area around Petrograd and the Gulf of Finland.

One striking characteristic which can be seen to link the work of a number of artists is the use not only of a method which is constructive in character but also of imagery which suggests the idea of reconstruction or conjures up associations with industrial/engineering/architectural constructions. These metaphors of construction can be found in the work of both those artists who moved increasingly towards the view that art should serve utilitarian needs (e.g. the Productivists, see below) and those who were opposed to this view (e.g. Malevich). Tatlin's *Monument to the Third International*, 1919–20 (Fig. 27), is a prime example of this type of metaphor, as well as one of the most compelling images of the period.

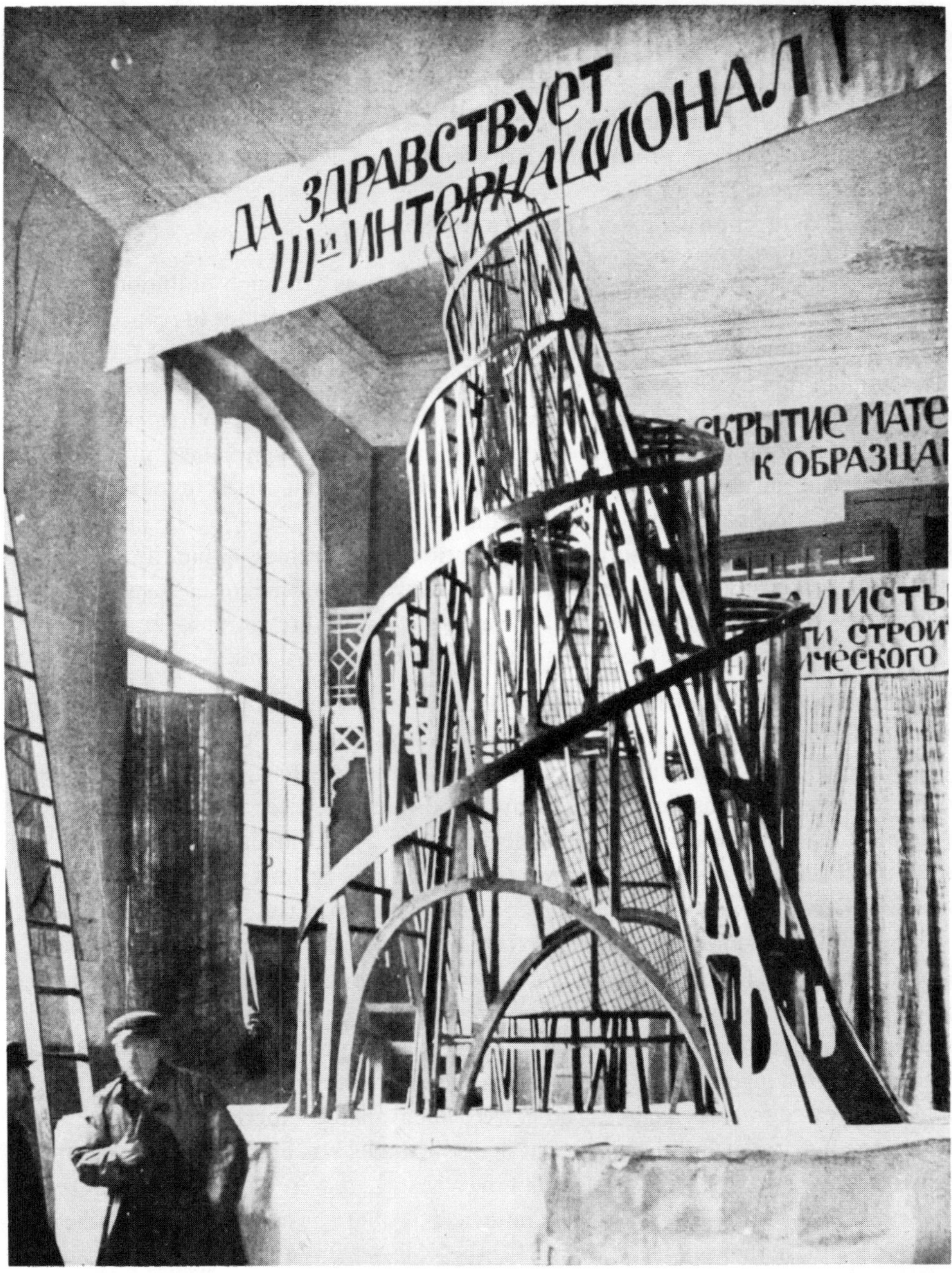

Figure 27 Vladimir Tatlin, *Monument to the Third International*, 1919–20 (Photo: Troels Andersen). Tatlin with pipe in hand is speaking to a seaman friend.

The *Monument* was commissioned by *Narkompros* to celebrate the founding of the Third International[37] in 1919. It was an exception in the programme for public

monuments and sculpture in being a monument to an institution and an idea which was fully contemporary, rather than to commemorate a historical figure.
A contemporary critic described the project:

> The main idea of the *Monument* is based on an organic synthesis of the principles of architecture, sculpture and painting. It was to comprise a new type of monumental construction, combining a purely creative form with a utilitarian form . . . the monument consists of three great rooms in glass, erected with the help of a complicated system of pillars and glass. These rooms are placed on top of one another and have harmonically corresponding forms. They are able to move at different speeds by means of a special mechanism. The lower storey, which is cubic in form, rotates around its axis at the rate of one revolution per year. This is intended for legislative assemblies. The next storey, which is pyramidal, rotates around its axis at the rate of one revolution per week. Here the executive bodies are to meet. . . . Finally the uppermost cylinder, which rotates one revolution per day, is reserved for centres of an informative character: an information office, a newspaper, the issuing of proclamations, pamphlets and manifestos—in short, all means for informing the international proletariat; it will also have a telegraphic office and an apparatus that can project onto large screens. . . . Radio masts will rise up over the monument. . . .
> (Quoted in this translation in Andersen, 1968b, p. 57.)

From this description it seems clear that the project was extremely ambitious in its intended scale and technological sophistication. But it is important to realize how these same characteristics are used to underline the symbolic intention of the project. The utopian rhetoric is given a gloss of functionalism and an image of constructional daring which made it seem ambiguous to some contemporaries who treated it primarily as a prototype for a real 'building' rather than as a symbolic expression given some of the characteristics of a building. The symbolic character of the *Monument* is expressed in a variety of ways: in the spiral of the frame—for the idea of the continuing dynamic of Revolution; the operation of hierarchies within the International—in the location, shape, and speed of movement of the forms suspended within the spiral; the transmission of the message of world revolution—in the provision of the most up to date communications technology and so on.

The *Monument* was made in various versions as a model several metres high with a wooden frame and, in the example illustrated, with the suspended forms made out of paper stretched on paper and painted with criss-cross lines to suggest glass and metal construction (the forms were attached to a hand-operated mechanism and could be rotated at differential speeds). The model in Figure 27 was made without either a scale model or detailed working drawings, according to Tatlin's assistant (whose account is given in Andersen, 1968b), and both the form of the *Monument* and its method of construction are designed to take account of the constructional possibilities of wood. (Some of the laths are over 13 feet long and only about 2 × 1 ins thick, and yet have not warped.) But, as far as possible, both the materials and the means of construction were disguised, to suggest an engineering construction made of steel and bolted together: the laths were painted and the nails which hold them together treated to look like bolts (bolts were not available—there were extreme shortages of material and the construction of the model was held up for three months when no nails or string were available). Given that there were some 2000 separate pieces in the model, the fact that such immense trouble was taken to suggest other materials and methods of construction for the *Monument* is a key to the importance Tatlin placed in the engineering symbolism of the image.

In its fusion of concepts drawn from sculptural, engineering and architectural sources, the *Monument* is clearly related to those of Tatlin's earlier works—such as the corner-constructions—which combined characteristics derived from different media. The corner-constructions had environmental implications and employed industrial materials, yet they were still intended to be seen within the limited context of the fine art object, whereas the *Monument*, in its projected scale, supposed function and its form, assumed a fully social dimension. A stage towards this social dimension can be seen in the architectonic decorations which Tatlin made, together with the Armenian painter and stage designer Georgii Yakulov, for the 'Café Pittoresque' in Moscow in 1917 (Fig. 28).

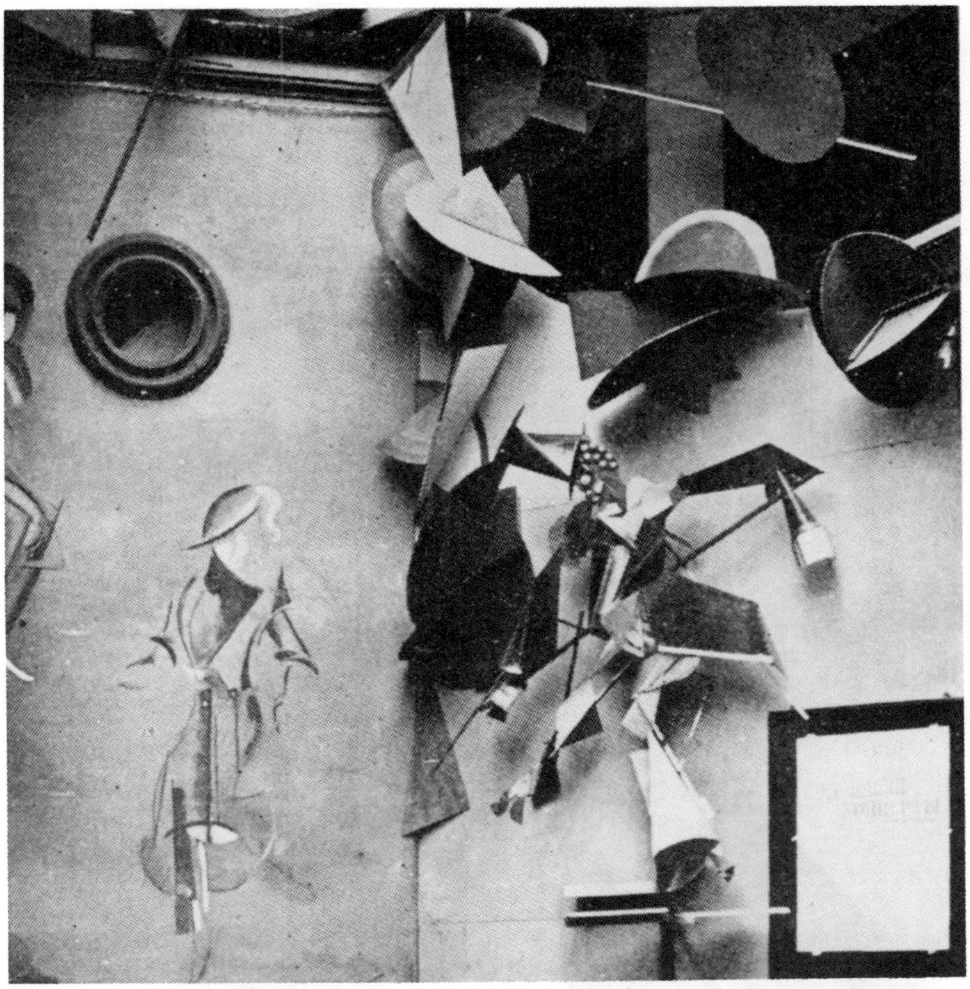

Figure 28 Vladimir Tatlin and Georgii Yakulov, decorations for the Café Pittoresque, Moscow, 1917 (Now destroyed; taken from André Salmon, *Art Russe Moderne*, 1928 Editions Laville).

The spiral motif which Tatlin adopts for the *Monument* recurs, like a *leitmotif*, in numerous designs of this period, as a symbol of the *dynamic* of Revolution. But both the spiral and the tower form can be related also to national antecedents[38] and, in a wider historical spectrum the *Monument* can be related to the idealistic projects of an earlier Revolutionary tradition.[39] In its proposed height and in its technological sophistication the *Monument* also made a claim for an impact of world scale: at 1300 feet high it would have been the largest structure in the world (the Eiffel tower, still in 1919–20 the tallest structure in the world, was a mere 984 feet high), and its communications apparatus was to be capable of transmitting the message of revolution across the world.

Suprematist imagery, as we have seen in the example of Malevich's 'Architektons', began to employ metaphors of construction in three dimensional forms. But it was also turned to similar ends in graphic work. Lissitsky's *Tale of Two Squares* (Fig. 29), a children's book written and illustrated in 1920, is a good example.[40] This is a kind of do-it-yourself manual in the 'language' of Suprematism: the story is a parable of Revolution and of the 'active' role which Lissitsky sees Suprematist ideology playing in the reconstruction of society. Two squares (one red and one black) fly towards the earth (Fig. 29a); they witness a storm in which everything 'flies apart' (Fig. 29b); they intervene as stabilizing elements (Fig. 29c). In the final figure captioned 'this is the end; let's go on' the red square presides over the reconstructed world; the black square floats into the distance, its role completed (Fig. 29d). Lissitsky injects a topical content into the language of Suprematism and at the same time appears to vanquish the mystical attributes of Malevich's black square.

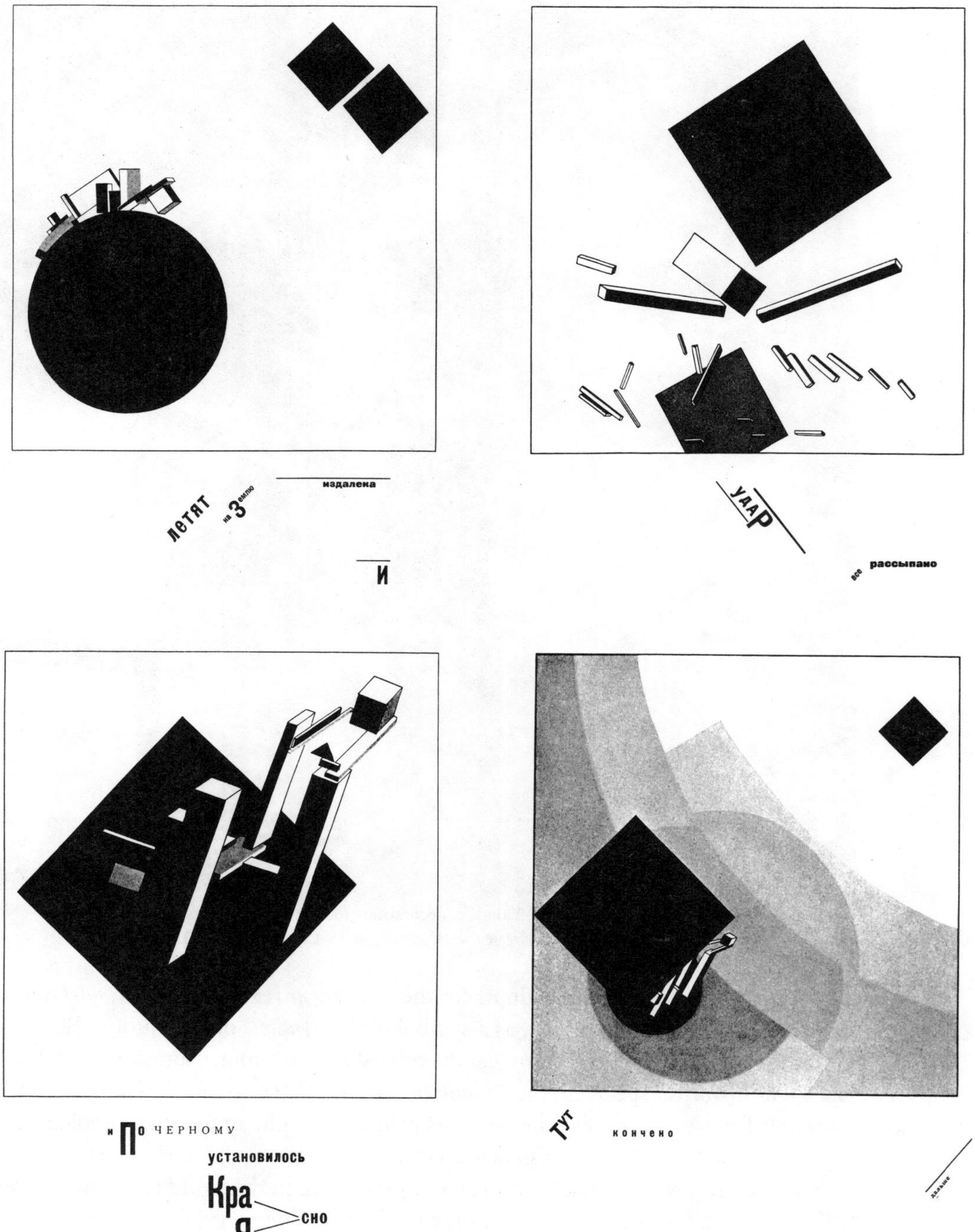

Figure 29 El Lissitsky, four pages from the *Tale of Two Squares*, 1920 (Novosti APN, courtesy S. Lissitsky-Küppers).

CONSTRUCTIVISM

In terms of what came to be known as Constructivism in Europe in the 1920s and since, the work of artists like Gabo, Lissitsky and Malevich[41] could be described as 'constructivist' in tendency, using elementary forms, assemblage methods and, in the cases of work by El Lissitsky or Gabo, often using architectural or engineering analogies in imagery. But by *c.*1920 the phenomenon known as Constructivism in Russia was distinct from all of these and had particular associations.

Constructivism was identified specifically with a group within *Inkhuk*[42] which included the artists Alexander Rodchenko (1891–1956), Varvara Stepanova (1894–1958), Liubov Popova (1889–1924), Olga Rozanova (1886–1918), Alexander Vesnin (best remembered now for his architectural designs of the 1920s), the Stenberg brothers (Georgii, 1900–1933, and Vladimir, born 1899) and Alexei Gan (1889–1942). This group identified the essential character of the culture of all industrial societies as 'Constructivist'; they believed that the full development of Constructivism, however, was only possible under the circumstances of the proletarian revolution:

> Constructivism is advancing—the slender child of an industrial culture.
>
> For a long time Capitalism has let it rot underground. It has been liberated by—the Proletarian Revolution.
>
> A new chronology begins with October 25, 1917.
> (Gan, *Constructivism*, 1922; translated in Bann, 1974, p. 36.)

Essentially Constructivism was the application of Marxist dialectic to artistic labour. Gan stated that:

> The socio-political system conditioned by the new economic structure gives rise to new forms and means of expression.
>
> The emergent culture of labour and intellect will be expressed by intellectual-material production.
>
> The first slogan of Constructivism is 'down with speculative activity in artistic labour.'
>
> We—proclaimed the Constructivists in their programme—declare uncompromising war on art!
> (Extract from *Constructivism*, 1922; translated in Bann, 1974, p. 37.)

The Constructivists saw art in capitalist society as divorced from its proper role and thus inaccessible to its proper audience; art had become the property and prerogative of the privileged few. In declaring 'uncompromising war on art' they were rejecting this condition; the first condition for cultural development was the creative labour that would result from the transformation of the economic base of society. Constructivist artists, on the basis of their investigations into the processes of art, might play a role in stimulating the development of this creative labour by themselves participating in the processes of industrial production. In Rodchenko's view:

> It is now no longer enough to be an inventor or, at worst, a theorist. One must also be a doer, a builder and a master. . . .
> (A. Rodchenko, 'Remarks on Composition', 1920; translated in Galerie Gmurzynska, 1975, p. 33.)

Much Constructivist work is fully abstract, exploiting only the character of the material, whether wood, metal or paint, and the ways in which it can be manipulated, for visual effect. But compared with either Rodchenko's construction (Fig. 30) or Popova's *Architectonic Construction* (Plate 8), Vladimir Stenberg's construction (Fig. 31) seems markedly referential: although it exploits the materials from which it is made to describe constructional tensions, it also clearly has representational associations.

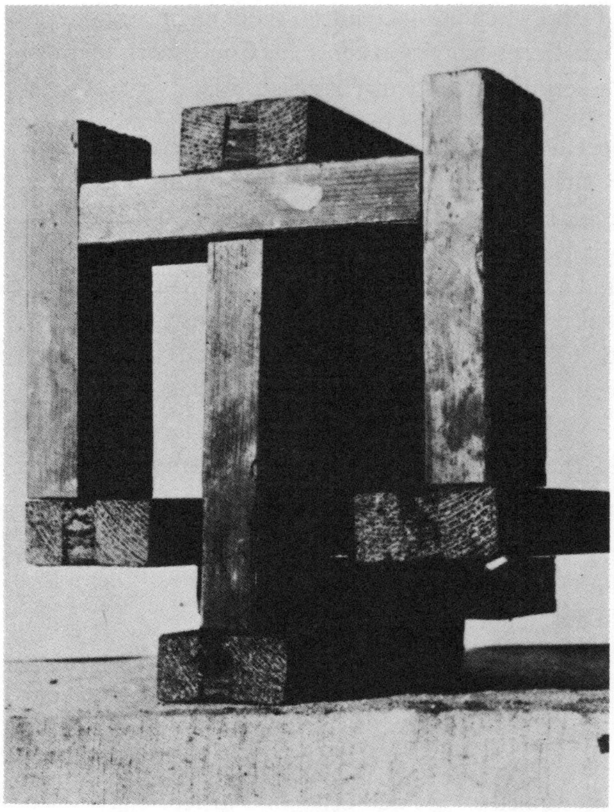

Figure 30 Alexander Rodchenko, *Construction*, 1920/21, wood, (Galerie Gmurzynska, Cologne).

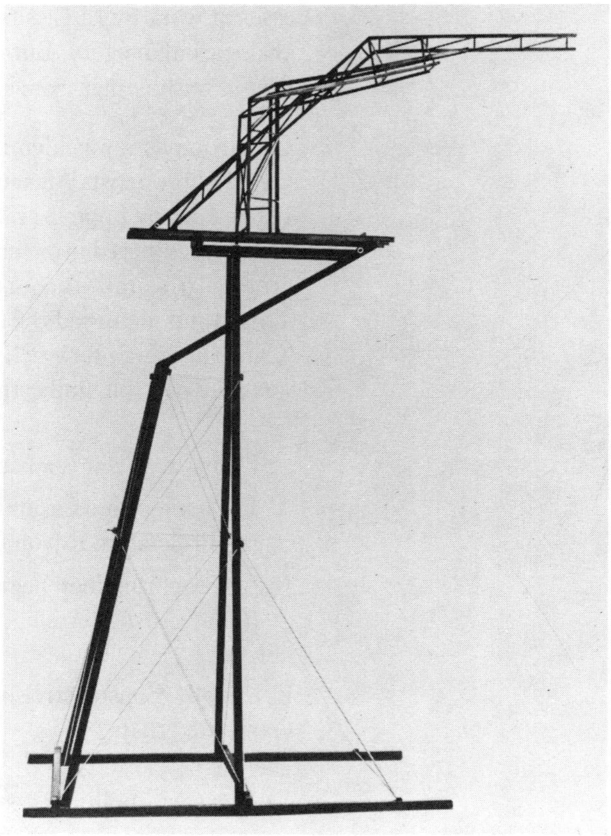

Figure 31 Vladimir Stenberg, *Construction KPS6*, *c.* 1921, angle iron assembled with bolts and welded, $30 \times 11 \times 61\frac{3}{4}$ ins, base: plastered wood lacquered black, steel stays $70\frac{7}{8} \times 27\frac{1}{2} \times 52\frac{3}{4}$ ins (Reconstruction 1972, Annely Juda Gallery).

THE 'LABORATORY' PERIOD

What has come to be known as the 'laboratory' period is primarily identified with work of the Constructivists *c.*1918–20 (although the term has also been used, more or less indiscriminately, to include the activities of those—some of them later Constructivists—who took up Tatlin's 'culture of materials' from *c.*1915). Between *c.*1918 and 1920 the Constructivists were concerned with the mastery of materials and techniques which still fall within the category of 'fine' (as opposed to applied) art.

Exercise

Compare Liubov Popova's *Architectonic Construction* (Plate 8) with Malevich's *Suprematist Painting* (Plate 9)—one of a series of all-white paintings. What are the most striking differences (e.g. from the point of view of handling)?

Discussion

Apart from the reduced colour of the Malevich, compared with the bright primary colours of the Popova painting, the most obvious differences are to do with the treatment of surface. In the Malevich painting any sense of the painting as a physical presence is elusive; the brushwork is scarcely visible and the use of what we normally think of as a non-colour incapable of tonal gradation for both 'figure' and 'ground', to suggest mass against space, also tends to emphasize elusiveness. Where we would expect to be able to read the left-hand edge of the 'form', figure and ground merge with one another, and we cannot easily define ground since it appears to be both in front of and behind the figure. Painted surface and illusionistic space are thus held in continual tension. Note also that the surface shows very little sign of its handling.

The Popova in contrast shows every sign of its processes: it is a flat surface treated with paint which can be handled in a variety of ways from the point of view of colour and texture. The surface is given a definite, almost measurable presence by the thickly built up paint. The character of colour and its ability to be varied in tone are demonstrated, but colour is scarcely used for modelling at all. Such definition as there is of planes as entities in a pictorial space, overlapping or intersecting one another, is created by the use of white to suggest light. The painting is an exploration of the physical properties of the elements of painting, which are clearly seen to have distinct roles (quite unlike their role in the Malevich).

It is easy to ignore or deny the possibility that such semantic differences exist between two paintings which are *visually* very similar. Yet such differences were observed by both artists and critics of the period; the manner of *handling* of a painting could be interpreted as charged with implications of a wider kind, and these differences were emphasized by the artists' own theoretical writings.

THE TRANSFERENCE FROM CONSTRUCTIVISM TO PRODUCTIVISM

What came to be known as 'Productivism' (from *c.*1920) was essentially the extension of Constructivist principles to the problems of design for industrial production. Some artists abandoned 'fine' art altogether to devote themselves to the problems of design for mass production, adopting the slogan 'art into production' (Figs 32–34).

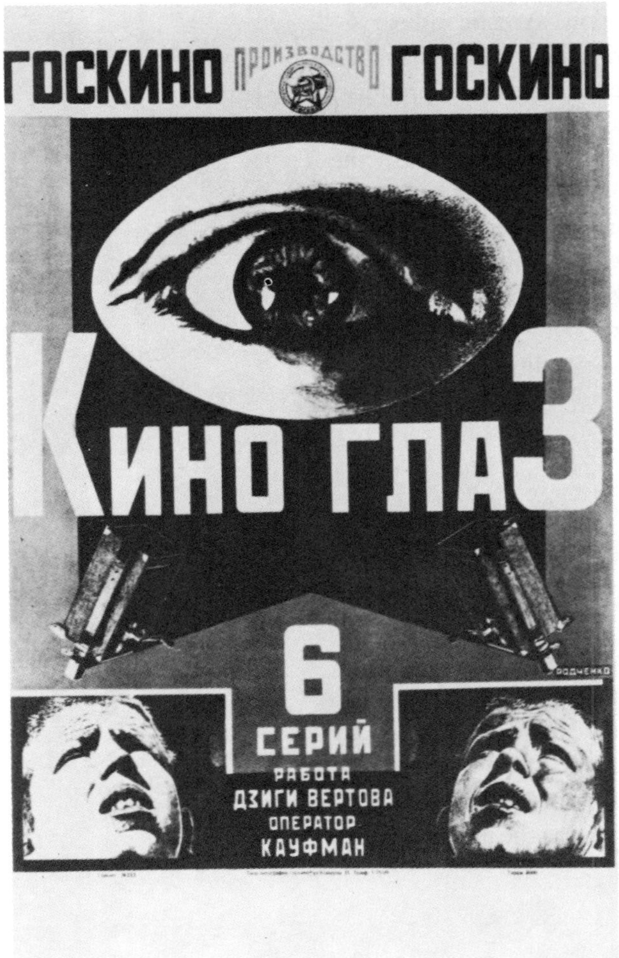

Figure 32 Alexander Rodchenko, film title for *Kino-Pravda*, 1924 (Taken from *Sovetskiy Reklamnii Plakat*, Izdatelstvo 'Sovetskiy Khudoznik').

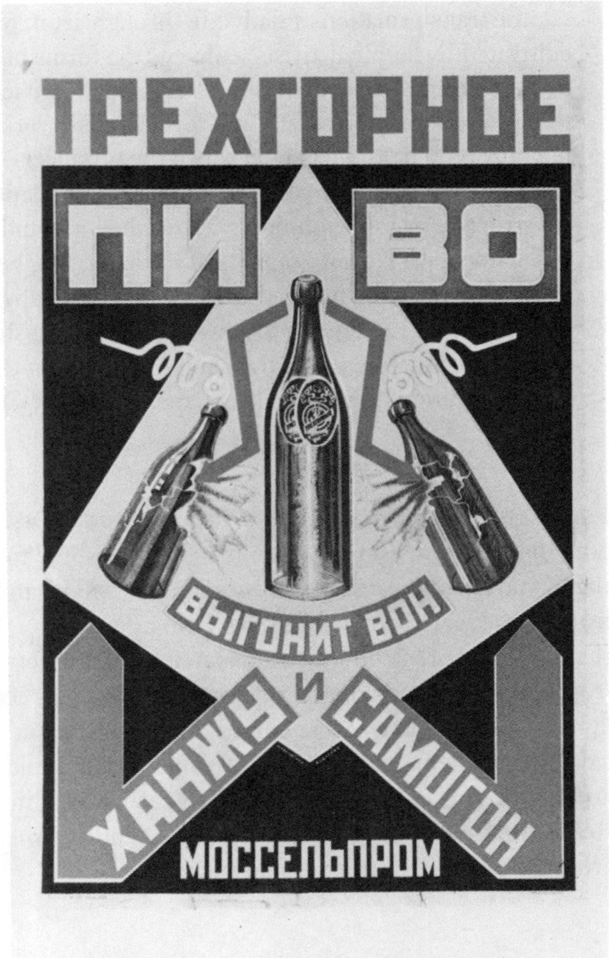

Figure 33 Alexander Rodchenko and Vladimir Mayakovsky, poster design for beer advertisement, 1923 (Taken from *Sovetskiy Reklamnii Plakat*, Izdatelstvo 'Sovetskiy Khudoznik').

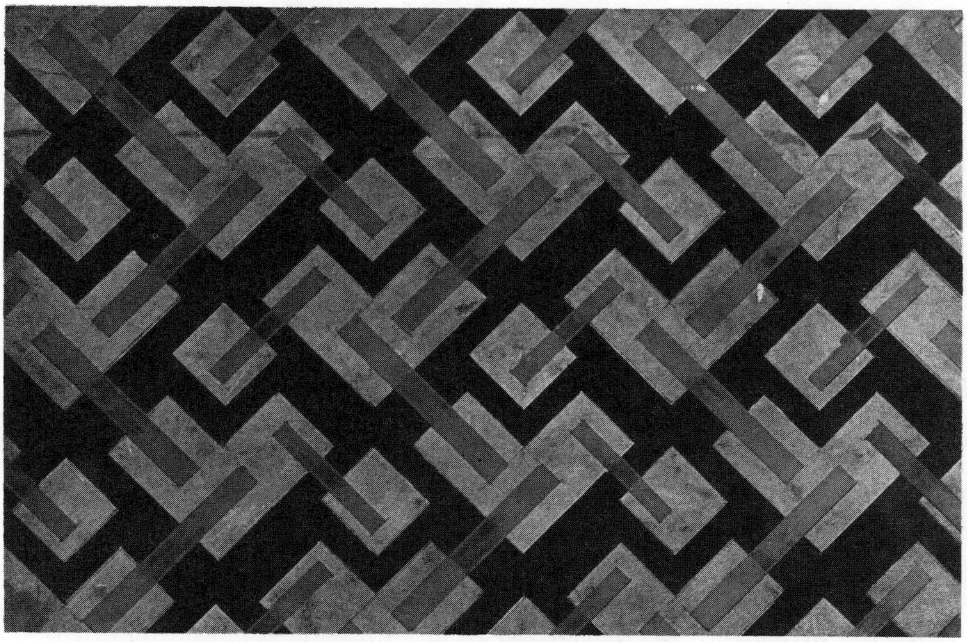

Figure 34 Varvara Stepanova, fabric design (Taken from *Izistoriy Sovetskogo Kostyuma*, Izdatelstvo 'Sovetskiy Khudoznik').

The Productivist slogan 'art into production' implied very much more than that the proper role of the artist was to be in the applied arts or industrial design. Tarabukin defined the role of art in production as

> . . . the transformation of daily life through art in production. 'Artistic industry' cultivated by 'applied artists' enlivens the forms of exterior life without changing them, whereas Constructivist mastery applying itself to each stage of the production process transforms first and foremost the work itself in exercising its effects not only on the products but also on the producer—the workman. That is why the results of this work are not only 'pleasing' but adapted to their function and constructive from the point of view of the form and the use of material. Thus understood, art is really capable of changing life, because it transforms work, the basis of life, making it into a skilful, creative, happy activity. The art of the future will not be the indulgence of a few, but work transformed.
> (N. Tarabukin, 1923; this translation made from the French edition *Le dernier tableau*, Editions Champ Libre, Paris, 1972, p. 53.)

A NOTE ON SOCIALIST REALISM

For reasons of space it is not possible to get into the issue of Socialist Realism here (and there is a television programme, TV 7, devoted to the subject). I have assumed that if you are interested in the question you will try to follow up some of the material listed in the recommended reading. I would warn you, however, against assuming that the issues are to do with clear-cut oppositions between *styles* or modes of painting (realism *versus* abstraction, for example), or of rigid recommendations as to particular kinds of subject matter. The phrase 'Socialist Realism' has come to be associated with a dogmatism in matters of style and subject matter initiated in the Stalinist period, and it is thus usually used in a pejorative sense. But, insofar as a theory of Socialist Realism existed in the 1920s, it was not as crudely programmatic as the mainstream art of the period after 1932 would suggest.

1922 and After

The standard English-language history (Gray) stops at 1922, for no very clearly defined reason. (I have also taken 1922 as a terminal date for this unit, for the reasons stated in the introduction.) It is sometimes assumed (though not always acknowledged overtly) that from *c.*1922 avant-garde art in Russia was 'suppressed' by a régime bent on imposing a monolithic dogma and style of 'socialist realism'. Like all simplifications, including style labels, a generalization of this kind has its uses as mental shorthand, as long as checks and balances are used against it to sustain its usefulness. But, as both recent exhibitions and articles have shown, a good deal of the earlier vitality survived in Russian art of the 1920s. It is probably true, however, that by 1922 a good deal of the impetus that sustained avant-garde art in Russia up to this date had begun to be dissipated, for a variety of reasons, of which one, certainly, was the beginning of a shift in attitude towards avant-garde art and the role of the 'Futurists'. To some extent the climate was changing in Russia towards avant-garde art, but the ways in which this affected particular artists is not at all clear. And the reasons for this change are complex.

The effects of the introduction of the New Economic Policy (NEP) in 1921, which restored a measure of free enterprise, should not be ignored. It brought back to favour (because it reintroduced a limited possibility of private patronage) a number of academic artists. And it is no accident that in 1922 the *Mir Iskusstva* group held its first exhibition since the Revolution, in Leningrad.

THE EMIGRATION OF ARTISTS

Throughout the years after the Revolution, but particularly around 1921/2 a number of artists emigrated from Russia (mainly to France and Germany; some of them later to the USA). Many of those who left (Chagall, Gabo, Pevsner, Exter, Kandinsky) had already established bases for themselves in European artistic circles before the war, but had returned to Russia on the outbreak of war and had been waiting for a suitable opportunity to return to Europe. Although artists like Chagall and Kandinsky had been willingly and energetically involved in artistic activities in the first few years after the Revolution they had gradually become disillusioned (as much by what they felt was the intolerance of their fellow artists as by personal attacks on their work). The part played in their decision to leave by the sheer physical difficulties of everyday life should not be underestimated either. Chagall lived a penurious existence after leaving Vitebsk.

Both Chagall and Kandinsky had had to leave behind in Europe a considerable body of work, when the war began, and both believed that they would have sufficient funds from the sale of this work on which to subsist while they established themselves. The reality was rather different. Chagall discovered that although a number of the works he had left with Walden[43] in 1914 had indeed been sold during the intervening years and the proceeds lodged with a lawyer on his behalf, the post-war inflation in Germany had reduced the money to a derisory amount.

Artists like Chagall and Kandinsky were easily reabsorbed into the current mainstreams of the European avant-garde. Kandinsky went to Berlin at the end of 1921; by 1922 he had taken up an appointment at the Weimar Bauhaus. Chagall emigrated in the summer of 1922, first to Berlin to collect his hoped-for funds from Walden[44], and later to Paris where he was taken up by the Surrealists, like the Spanish painter Joan Miró, as a natural 'naif' painter—a view which Chagall was not anxious to refute.

Besides the emigration of a number of prominent artists to Europe, there was also the 'emigration' of fine artists (e.g. Rozanova, Stepanova) to production (the move from the easel to the machine implied by the title of the unit) and into the 'mass'-media of film, poster design and so on.

> . . . We had a vision of a new world, industry, technology and science. We were inventors and transformers of the world. . . . We created new concepts of beauty and broadened the concept of art itself. . . . We were opposed because of our slogans of 'Death to art, long live production'. We were taken to task for not recognising 'pure art', for being printers, photographers, designers of fabrics and shop displays—because we made graphic layouts for newspapers.
> (A. Rodchenko; quoted in Bojko, 1972, p. 19.)

RUSSIAN ART IN EUROPE

There had been many exchanges of information between Russian artists and avant-garde groups in Berlin and elsewhere before 1922; and much Russian work was known through reproduction in periodicals and books such as Konstantin Umansky's *Neue Kunst in Russland 1914–1919* (*New Art in Russia 1914–1919*), published in 1921.

But the major impact of Russian art in Europe was felt through the *Erste russische Kunstausstellung* ('First Russian Art Exhibition') organized at the Van Diemen gallery in Berlin, in the autumn of 1922. The exhibition contained several hundred paintings, sculptures, constructions, drawings of which only part could be labelled abstract or specifically Constructivist[45] but it was these works which were important. It was the sheer collective strength and variety of work in an identifiably constructivist vein, and the brilliant colour of much of this work, allied with catalogue introductions identifying the revolutionary content of the exhibition, which made an impact on European artists.[46] The exhibition coincided with the hardening of the division between Constructivist and Expressionist tendencies at the Bauhaus and, not surprisingly, it tended to reinforce the constructivist tendencies in the work of Bauhaus students. The exhibition was also shown, appropriately enough in view of the constructivist tendencies of the *De Stijl* artists, in Amsterdam later in the same year. (Other countries rejected the exhibition on the grounds that it was bound to be subversive and propagandist.)

Conclusion

As a way of summing up this unit, I would like to make some general points about the study of Russian art of this period. By comparison with what we know about European art of the same period, our knowledge of both the general outline and specific artists is relatively fragmentary and crude. The reasons why are various, but fairly obvious and I shall list only some of them. There has always been, both for Western and Soviet art historians, a problem of access: much material has been lost or destroyed, and surviving documentary material—often including the paintings, sculptures, etc.—has not been always readily accessible (even to *bona fide* researchers, let alone art historians with a general interest in the period). Of course, by no means all the work has disappeared: that of those artists who emigrated to the West is, on the whole, fairly well known, although there are areas which have not been thoroughly studied (e.g. Kandinsky's work 1915–21, by comparison with his earlier and later work). But the work of those artists who remained in Russia (Tatlin, Rodchenko, even Malevich) is much less well known. With the exception of the collection of Malevich's work in the Stedelijk collection in Amsterdam (acquired by a lucky accident), there is no major collection of work of the latter part of the period in Western museums. There has also been a tendency among Western art historians, until very recently, to rely on the 'evidence' of those artists who emigrated from Russia in the 1920s and slotted into prominent roles in the European avant garde (Kandinsky, Gabo), but whose evidence was sometimes fragmentary and frequently partisan (which is why I suggested a qualification to Hamilton on p. 32).

Besides problems of access, and of the history handed down by émigrés, there is a continuing problem of ideological perspective which has inhibited discussion of both the role of the pre-Revolutionary avant garde in the years following the Revolution and of subsequent developments in the 1920s. If your view of the history of art is a self-contained one in which, to put it crudely, only paintings breed paintings, then you may say that the question of the relationship of modern art to its particular social context is not of importance. Seen in this light, Malevich's 'Architektons' to take an example, are explorations or extensions of formal 'problems' suggested by the Suprematist paintings; and the fact that they—like other constructional images—begin to appear *c.*1918/19 is fortuitous. If, on the other hand, you think that art has a social dimension, you will be likely to want to consider its relationship to its social context as well as its self-contained formal tradition. So Malevich's 'Architektons' may be seen as related to both purely formal developments within his own work, and to more widespread tendencies.

POSTSCRIPT

By any reckoning the Russian contribution to the history of modern art of the first quarter of the century was an important one; however you calculate who should belong in your pantheon of 'pioneer' abstract artists, Russian (or Russian-born) artists of the decade 1912–22 will always occupy a major and probably a dominant position. While art historians have long recognized that Russia produced some of the most consistently formally radical and seminal art anywhere during this decade, there has always been an embarrassing paradox—the absence of most of the key works. The major reputation of an artist like Vladimir Tatlin has rested largely on anecdote, reminiscences, the partisan view promoted by El Lissitsky of the artists of his generation, and a handful of photographs of the works—scarcely enough of them to constitute a picture of a year's activities, let alone a working life of great richness spanning several decades.

Can you have a 'heroic' period in the history of art if few of the canonic works necessary for the definition of a 'heroic' period survive? Evidently not. There is now a boom in the 'reconstruction' of some of the prime works of the period. In much the same way as Duchamp's canonic lost *Bottle Rack* has been reproduced in a 'limited edition', growing interest amongst Western art historians and dealers has begun to result in 'reconstructions' of Russian work of the Revolutionary period, sometimes 'sealed' with the approval of the surviving artist.[47] Whatever advantages a three-dimensional visualization of, say, a construction by Stenberg or Rodchenko may have over an old (and probably much repeated) view of the original in a photograph, or a sketch, such advantages are balanced (and possibly outweighed) by disadvantages. Reconstructions tend to be 'completed': that is, they are made with the degree of fine finish, or the materials, for which the original design was supposedly intended. As 'documents' they tell us as much, if not more, about our own period, than the period in which they were designed. But they cannot tell us what, in any view of Russian art of the first decades of the twentieth century, it is important to remember: the exigencies of the times, the circumstances of physical hardship in which the originals were designed, from Tatlin's early reliefs to Gabo's designs for kinetic constructions. Particularly in the post-Revolutionary period the very fact that there was no immediate possibility of constructing such designs as Tatlin's *Monument*, or really using beautifully finished industrial materials, such as perspex, was central to the conception of these works—they were expressions of optimism and utopianism, of a belief that revolutionary change might build a new and better world, in which the artist would have an integrated place. In removing the *ad hoc* character of the originals, reconstructions tend to suppress the necessary imaginative dimension in our perception which would remind us of one of the most compelling reasons for looking at the period at all.

Notes

1 You will usually find them referred to by the Germanic transcription of their surnames as von Werefkin and Jawlensky.

2 For example: *Ver Sacrum* (Vienna), *Pan* (Berlin); these often covered literature as well as visual arts.

3 However, the question of the relationship between patronage in its wider sense (i.e. including dealers and progressive museum directors like von Tschudi in Berlin and later in Munich) and the development of avant-garde art in this period in Europe has not been given serious attention.

4 Quoted in Gray, 1971, p. 80.

5 The collection was published in 1913 (in Ryabushinsky's magazine *Apollon*) with commentaries and numerous illustrations in black and white and colour.

6 Although initially Shchukin hesitated over Matisse's *Dance*, he later wrote to Matisse to confirm the commission: 'I find your panel *The Dance* of such nobility, that I am resolved to brave our bourgeois opinion and hang on my staircase a subject with nudes'.

7 Edward Fry (1966, p. 189) lists *Three Women* as 'formerly in Stein and Shchukin collections'.

8 Including other Matisse patrons such as K.-E. Osthaus of Hagen, whose purchase of Matisse's *Bather with a Turtle*, 1908, is said to have inspired Shchukin's purchases of the large figure compositions of 1908–9.

9 Here it is worth noting that Shchukin also patronized Russian avant-garde artists. He later bought one of Tatlin's corner-reliefs which caused a *succès de scandale* at an exhibition in 1915.

10 It is important to note, however, that until very recently semantic issues in European painting (e.g. the use of typography in Cubism) have been largely neglected. Robert Rosenblum's essay (1973) is one of the first serious studies of the subject.

11 'A so-called Old Believer, member of a dissident religious faction, is threatened by a barber who wishes to cut off his beard, an action which was a gesture of debasement for an Old Believer.' (Bowlt, 1974.)

12 I.e. the alphabet in use before Peter the Great reformed and 'westernized' the cyrillic alphabet by reducing the number of characters and simplifying the forms of some of the remainder.

13 The best clue that can be found is in the descriptions of Malevich's stage sets for a Futurist opera *Victory over the Sun* which include references to a black square.

14 As time went by Malevich built up the iconic significance of the *Black Square*. In 1920 he wrote: 'It's worth dwelling on who it is and what it contains. . . . And I, too, am peering into its mysterious black space—one which is becoming a kind of form of the new face of the Suprematist world, its external appearance and its spirit. Perhaps you consider my ideas excessively audacious. Oh, no. I see in it what people at one time used to see before the face of God.' (Letter from Malevich to Paul Ettinger, 3 April 1920; quoted in Galerie Gmurzynska, 1974, p. 54.)

15 Note that the dates given in Haftmann and Hamilton are not definitive.

16 See Andersen, 1968a.

17 Which Malevich sees as evolutionary stages in the development of Suprematism, contributing both theoretical and formal bases for Suprematism, but *superseded* by Suprematism (note here the significance of Malevich's choice of 'Suprematism' as a label).

18 But it should be noted that by the time he published *Die gegenstandlose Welt* (*The Non-Objective World*), in the *Bauhausbuch* series, in 1927, Malevich took a rather different view of the relationship of Suprematist imagery to the perceived world (see Unit 12, Fig. 83).

19 Archipenko had settled in Paris in 1908. (Hamilton illustrates two works of this period, Figs 158 and 159, neither of which is quite what I have in mind.)

20 Although Andersen (1968b) queries whether this particular relief is by Tatlin.

21 The date given to Haftmann 357 may be incorrect, but the illustration makes the point.

22 Any discussion of Tatlin's work must be of a provisional and speculative kind. Scarcely any of his work has survived intact. It is known mainly from photographs, some of which have been heavily retouched for the purposes of publication or to enhance particular qualities. Although some reconstructions have been made, they cannot be relied on as definitively correct.

23 Chagall recalled Lunacharsky visiting his studio in Paris before the war with the intention of writing an article on Chagall's work.

24 Private collections were expropriated. By the end of 1918 the Shchukin and Morozov collections had been nationalized and named the First and Second Sections of the Museum of Modern Western Art respectively. They were subsequently amalgamated. (The items originally belonging in these collections have now been dispersed among the national museums in Moscow and Leningrad.)

25 There is an interesting parallel to note here with the situation in Germany; the establishment of the Weimar Republic placed many Expressionist artists in positions of authority in artistic institutions.

26 'Futurist' was used pretty well indiscriminately for all avant-garde tendencies.

27 This is very important for any understanding of the way in which Russian art and architecture would develop in the later 1920s and 1930s.

28 For an account of these organizations' membership, structure and activities, see Franciscono, 1971, and for a short account, The Open University, 1975, dealing primarily with the architectural side.

29 Yefim Golyshchev, a Russian artist working in Berlin (and later a student at the Bauhaus), wrote to Gropius with the comment 'The Russian programme is a powerful model. Only willpower can turn good fortune to use!'

30 Sent to the *AfK* by Kandinsky.

31 Almost certainly a reference to the programme of the *AfK* and not the Bauhaus.

32 Published in German in 1919, but largely written a couple of years earlier. In 1914, Taut, a great admirer of Kandinsky, had written:

> Let us build together a magnificent building. A building which will be not architecture alone, but in which everything—painting, sculpture, everything together—will create a great architecture, and in which architecture will once again merge with the other arts. Architecture will here be the frame and content all at once.
> (Quoted in Franciscono, 1971, pp. 91–92.)

33 Notwithstanding the accounts given by V. Khazanova in Shvidkovsky, 1971, and by Bojko, 1974.

34 The pre-Revolutionary 'Pale of Settlement' included areas in the west and south of Russia within which the majority of Russian Jews were obliged to live.

35 Written in 1922, and earlier, but first published in French in 1932.

36 Malevich distinguished between the '*purely architectonic*, devoid of purpose' and the '*specifically architectural*, the material expression of a stated purpose'.

37 The First International (the International Working Men's Association) was founded in London in 1864 and became directly associated with Marx's ideas; it was dissolved in 1876. In 1889 a Second International was founded, bringing together a number of European Socialist parties. In 1919, the Soviet government issued invitations to found a Third (Communist) International, the aim of which was to further the cause of world revolution. The first congress of the Third International was held in Moscow in March 1919, the second in July 1920.

38 For example the ziggurat at Khorsabad, Ivan the Great's Kremlin tower, etc.

39 For example those by the French eighteenth-century architects J.-E. Boullée and J. N. Ledoux.

40 First published in Berlin in 1922, and published in the same year also in the *De Stijl* magazine.

41 The work of all these artists was seen as 'constructivist' by European artists of the period. Lissitsky was a founder member (together with Hans Richter and Theo van Doesburg) of the International Faction of Constructivists which was declared at the Congress of International Progressive Artists in Düsseldorf in 1922.

42 Including a number of Tatlin's former associates. It was members of this group who opposed the artistic programme drawn up by Kandinsky when he was head of *Inkhuk* and effectively caused his resignation. Elements of Kandinsky's *Inkhuk* programme were to reappear in his teaching programme at the Bauhaus a few years later.

43 In 1914 Walden held an exhibition of Chagall's work in the *Der Sturm* galleries. The outbreak of the war prevented the return of those works not sold by the end of the exhibition.

44 Chagall initiated a law suit against Walden for the return of those works which had been sold or payment of a sum to compensate for the loss on these sales caused by the inflation of the Mark.

45 In the sense given on p. 55.

46 But it is worth noting that it was on the occasion of the opening of this exhibition that Lunacharsky warned that the future of proletarian art was not necessarily contained in the works exhibited.

47 For a recent exhibition (1975) at a London gallery, working drawings for the reconstructions were made by the artist.

Recommended Reading

If you are not already familiar with the Russian art of the period covered by the unit, you should aim to read Camilla Gray's book (1962 or 1971) before proceeding to any of the more specialized articles or monographs. See also Hamilton's bibliography for further titles on individual painters and other general titles.

I have listed below a considerable number of titles, both to give you an idea of the scope of recent literature in English on the period and an opportunity to follow up particular artists or issues, and in order to include acknowledgements for those sources on which I have drawn and which are not mentioned elsewhere in the text.

I have also listed some titles on areas not covered in the unit such as film and poster art, which are germane to an understanding of the period after 1922. I have not listed the titles of many of the recently published books and articles in foreign languages, as these are not likely to be available in any but the most specialized libraries.

Andersen, T. (1966) 'Some unpublished letters by Kandinsky', *Artes* (Copenhagen) II, 1966. In English.
Documents some of Kandinsky's links with artists and groups in Russia, during the time he was in Munich, and his activities in Russia between 1917 and 1922.

Andersen, T. (1967) *Moderne Russisk Kunst 1910–1930*, Borgen, Copenhagen.
By one of the leading authorities on the period. One of the few books to pursue the subject into the 1920s. Unfortunately not available in English.

Andersen, T. (1968a) *Malevich: Essays on Art 1915–1933*, two volumes, Rapp and Whiting/André Deutsch.

Andersen, T. (1968b) *Vladimir Tatlin*, exhibition catalogue, Moderna Museet, Stockholm. With English translations.
The main source of information on Tatlin.

Andersen, T. (1970) *Malevich*, exhibition catalogue, Stedelijk Museum, Amsterdam. With English translations.
The only available monograph on Malevich. Contains numerous black and white and colour illustrations of Malevich's work (mainly from the Stedelijk Museum's collection).

Bann, S. (ed.) (1974) *The Tradition of Constructivism*, Thames and Hudson.
A critical anthology of texts. Parts 1, 2 and 3 include texts on Constructivism in Russia and Europe in the 1920s.

Barr, A. (1951) *Matisse, His Art and His Public*, Museum of Modern Art, New York, reprinted 1976, Secker and Warburg.
Useful for documentation of Matisse's work in the Morozov and Shchukin collections and photographs of the interior of the Shchukin residence.

Birnholz, A. C. (1972) 'El Lissitsky's writings on art', *Studio International*, March 1972.

Birnholz, A. C. (1972) 'El Lissitsky, the Avant-Garde, and the Russian Revolution', *Artforum* (New York), September 1972.

Birnholz, A. C. (1973) 'El Lissitsky and the Jewish Tradition', *Studio International*, October 1973.

Bojko, S. (1972) *New Graphic Design in Revolutionary Russia*, Lund Humphries.
On the design of posters, film titling, magazines, books, display and agit-prop material.

Bojko, S. (1974) 'Vkhutemas', *Art and Artists*, December 1974.

Bowlt, J. E. (1974) 'Neo-primitivism and Russian Painting', *Burlington Magazine*, March 1974.

Bowlt, J. E. (1975) 'Pavel Filonov: An Alternative Tradition', *Art Journal* (New York), Spring 1975.

Bowlt, J. E. (1975) 'The Art of Construction', *Art and Artists*, September 1975.

Chagall, M. (1961) *My Life*, first published in French, 1932, Orion Press, New York; another translation 1962, Peter Owen, London.

Chamot, M. (1973) 'Russian Avant-garde Graphics', *Apollo*, December 1973.

Compton, S. (1974) 'Malevich and the fourth dimension', *Studio International*, March–April 1974.
On the relationship between Malevich's Suprematist work and contemporary literature on geometry.

Dabrowski, M. (1975) 'The formation and development of Rayonism' *Art Journal* (New York), Spring 1975.

Douglas, C. (1975) 'The New Russian Art and Italian Futurism' *Art Journal* (New York), Spring 1975.

Elderfield, J. (1970) 'Constructivism and the objective world', *Studio International*, September 1970.

Fitzpatrick, S. (1970) *The Commissariat of Enlightenment*, Cambridge University Press.
On A. V. Lunacharsky and the organization of education and the arts, October 1917–1921.

Ginsburg, M. (1973) 'Art Collectors of Old Russia. The Morosovs and the Shchukins', *Apollo*, December 1973.

Golding, J. (1975) 'The Black Square', *Studio International*, March–April 1975.
On Malevich's work.

Grohmann, W. (1956) *Kandinsky*, Thames and Hudson.
The most complete monograph on Kandinsky in English.

Gray, C. (1962) *The Great Experiment: Russian Art, 1863–1922*, Thames and Hudson.
The basic reference work in English, and still one of the only *general* histories of the period. This edition is recommended, if available, in preference to the reprint (1971) for its large-format illustrations.

Gray, C. (1971) *The Russian Experiment in Art 1863–1922*, Thames and Hudson (available in paperback).
Small format reprint of the 1962 edition.

Higgens, A. (1971) 'The development of the theory of Socialist Realism in Russia, 1917 to 1932', *Studio International*, April 1971.

James, C. V. (1973) *Soviet Socialist Realism: Origins and Theory*, Macmillan.
Not concerned specifically with the visual arts, but a useful, documented introduction to this subject.

Kozloff, M. (1974) 'Malevich as a Counter-Revolutionary (East and West)' *Artforum* (New York), January 1974.

Leyda, J. (1960 and 1973) *Kino: A History of the Russian and Soviet Film*, George Allen and Unwin.
A study of the development of Russian and Soviet cinema from 1896 to the late 1950s.

Lissitsky-Küppers, S. (1968) *El Lissitzky*, Thames and Hudson.
The only recent monograph on El Lissitsky available in English. Contains translations of many of Lissitsky's writings.

Markov, V. (1969) *Russian Futurism*, Macgibbon and Kee.
Mainly on Russian Futurist literature, but contains a good deal of information on artists' activities as stage designers, book illustrators, etc. as well as interesting background material.

Matsa, I. (1972) 'Constructivism: an historical and artistic appraisal', *Studio International*, April 1972.

Meyer, F. (1964) *Marc Chagall*, Thames and Hudson.
The most complete monograph in English on Chagall's work; especially useful for the chapters covering his life and work in Russia, 1915–22.

Nakov, A. (1973) *Tatlin's Dream: Russian Suprematist and Constructivist Art, 1910–1923*, exhibition catalogue, Fischer Fine Art Ltd., London, November 1973–January 1974.

Nakov, A. (1974) 'The Iconoclastic Fury', *Studio International*, June 1974.
On Malevich.

Rusakov, Y. A. (1975) 'Matisse in Russia in the Autumn of 1911', *Burlington Magazine*, May 1975.

Schnitzer, J. and L., and Martin, M. (1975) *Cinema in Revolution: The Heroic Era of the Soviet Film*, Secker and Warburg.
An anthology including writings by some of the major directors of the 1920s. Introduction by David Robinson.

Schvidkovsky, O. A. (ed.) (1971) *Building in the USSR 1917–1932*, Studio Vista.
For Chapter 4, 'Vkhutemas, Vkhutein' and Chapter 5, 'El Lissitsky'.

Additional References

Franciscono, M. (1971) *Walter Gropius and the Creation of the Bauhaus in Weimar*, University of Illinois Press.

Fry, E. (1966) *Cubism*, Thames and Hudson.

Galerie Gmurzynska (1974) *Von Fläche zum Raum: Russland 1916–24* (*From Surface to Space: Russia 1916–24*), exhibition catalogue, Galerie Gmurzynska, Cologne.

Galerie Gmurzynska (1975) *Die 20er Jahre in OstEuropa* (*The Twenties in Eastern Europe*), exhibition catalogue, Galerie Gmurzynska, Cologne.

Kandinsky, W. (1959) *Concerning the Spiritual in Art*, George Wittenborn, New York.

Lankheit, K. (ed.) (1974) *Blaue Reiter Almanach*, Thames and Hudson.

The Open University (1975) A305 *History of Architecture and Design, 1890–1939*, Units 9–10, *Expressionism*, The Open University Press.

Rosenblum, R. (1973) 'Picasso and the typography of Cubism', in Penrose, R. and Golding, J. (eds.) *Picasso in Retrospect*.

Stein, G. (1938) *Picasso*, London.

Introduction to Units 11 and 12: The Idea of Universal Art

Two of the dominant cultural problems of the nineteenth century were the attitude to the machine and the vision of the past and both influenced the course of art. The awesome ability of the machine to reproduce as much art as the market might demand drove many advanced thinkers, including John Ruskin and William Morris, into an attitude of veneration for the Middle Ages. For these men, the prospects for the future were to be found in the past.

It was imagined that in the Middle Ages art and society coexisted in harmony, each one indivisible from the other and each characterized by the honest, happy craftsman in love with his work. It was this imaginative vision of the harmony of art and life in the Middle Ages which contributed to the idea of the *Gesamtkunstwerk* (Total Work of Art) which was profoundly to affect the course of art in the twentieth century. This idea of uniting all the arts found expression in the works of the architectural theorists Gottfried Semper and H. P. Berlage, as well as in those of the musicians Richard Wagner and Arnold Schoenberg.

De Stijl and the Bauhaus were reactions to these ideas about the past, the machine and the unity of the arts. But while *De Stijl* was a more or less cohesive group and the Bauhaus was an art school which attracted artists onto its staff, both groups, despite their intention, are remembered for *paintings*. Despite the brave idea of creating a novel, universal art which would transcend old boundaries, history has selected from *De Stijl* and from the Bauhaus the works of individuals. Certainly it is a paradox, but it does suggest that it is the individual work of art which continues to have primacy over however grand a cause.

Unit 11 *De Stijl:* The Reconstruction of Life through Art and Technology

Introduction: The Theoretical Background to *De Stijl* 73

Part I ***De Stijl***

Dutch Painting immediately before *De Stijl* 77

Van Doesburg's Early Work 86

The Foundation of *De Stijl* 89

Van Doesburg's alter egos and *De Stijl*'s Opponents 95

Dynamic Dialectics: Elementarism 99

Mondrian's Mature Style 102

Part II ***Synthesis—Architecture and Painting***

De Stijl and Architecture 104

Mondrian's Late Development 108

Postscript 109

Introduction: The Theoretical Background to *De Stijl*

(Read Hamilton, pp. 319–22.)

Piet Mondrian's *Composition* (Plate 10) was painted in 1921 four years after Theo van Doesburg had founded the *De Stijl*[1] group. The picture is typical of the movement of different personalities who developed a style and philosophy of art quite unique in European history. It was a coming together under the mercurial Theo van Doesburg (1883–1931) of a number of diverse painters, architects and musicians. Piet Mondrian (1872–1944) was *De Stijl*'s most famous and most prolific member, but at one time or another van Doesburg could claim as adherents to his group the musician George Antheil (1900–), the Dadaist Hugo Ball (1866–1927: see Unit 13), the Futurist Gino Severini (1883–1966) as well as the architects Rob van t'Hoff (1887–), Gerrit Rietveld (1888–1964) and Jacobus Johannes Pieter Oud (1890–1963).

From 1917 to 1931, when he died from an asthmatic complaint, van Doesburg tirelessly edited the magazine *De Stijl* which was the vehicle for the dissemination of the elaborate and often contradictory *De Stijl* philosophy. Not many people could tolerate van Doesburg's personality for long; although he attracted students while at Weimar between 1921 and 1923, Gropius would not invite him actually to join the Bauhaus faculty. Mondrian left the *De Stijl* group in a fit of pique in 1925 after van Doesburg had decided the year before to introduce dynamism into *De Stijl* compositions by the use of the diagonal in his paintings, and few other of the people whose names we associate with *De Stijl* stayed with the group throughout the full period of its existence. When van Doesburg died there was no one who could take complete control and edit the journal with the enthusiasm which he ceaselessly maintained and *De Stijl* was finished.

Yet, despite the frictions, *De Stijl* was an enormously influential phenomenon in the history of art. Although its history has often been written (see the Recommended Reading list on p. 110) its full influence has yet to be assessed, affecting as it has not only the direction of the Bauhaus but also of much design in the everyday world. In the world of painting, the art of *De Stijl* is the *ne plus ultra* of cerebral abstraction: like the Bauhaus, the prime movers of *De Stijl* sought the universal but, unlike the Bauhaus, not in a superficial way. It was Walter Gropius's idea to unite the arts in common pursuit of the perfect building, in imitation of the work which the different mediaeval guilds put into the creation of the cathedrals. But *De Stijl* represented a search for a much more fundamental form of universal art which had its roots in philosophy. Van Doesburg and Mondrian sought between them no less than a complete understanding of the laws of the visible world. Life and art were to be, for them, united by their new aesthetic.

Exercise

Look again at Mondrian's *Composition* of 1921 (Plate 10). It is sometimes suggested that one of the formative influences on *De Stijl* was the Dutch landscape. Do you think that this might be a valid argument?

Discussion

This question can be answered on two levels. In a sense it is possible that the flat landscape and hedgerows of Holland may have suggested this pictorial form to Mondrian (even though Mondrian himself denied that there was any reference to nature in his pictures). A more sophisticated answer would be that like the Dutch landscape, which is largely artificial,[2] Mondrian's picture also represents man giving form to the indeterminate. If there is any reference to the landscape in this picture it can only fairly be said to be an abstract one. Van Doesburg spoke of stripping nature bare and being left with the essence, in fact, 'the style'; Mondrian has not looked at the polders and made them into an abstract pattern, but has refined his experience of the natural world and expressed it in this formal way. However, there is another clue to the development of *De Stijl* painting which has its source in the character of the Dutch people. The paintings of *De Stijl* have what the celebrated Dutch historian, Johan Huizinga, called *Nederlands geestesmerk* ('Dutch spirituality'). The Dutch are traditionally, if unjustly, regarded as hard-headed, cold puritans; in Mondrian's picture is it not possible to detect a twentieth-century form of the cool, hard clarity which characterizes also the work of the great seventeenth-century Dutch painters, Philips Kooninck, Pieter Saenredam, Govaert Flinck and Jan Vermeer?

Because neither van Doesburg nor Mondrian were philosophers, but relied on philosophy to support their own aesthetic predilections, their writings (which are numerous) can sometimes appear to be hopelessly arid, contorted and impenetrable. Certainly, neither man had academic training in philosophy and it is likely that their philosophical interests were of a rather amateurish nature, not disciplined by a scholarly approach to the subject. Yet, the philosophical origins of *De Stijl* bear explanation, for it is only through an examination of the sources of van Doesburg's and Mondrian's ideas that a full understanding of the paintings can be achieved because, to *De Stijl*, painting and philosophy were closely linked and of similar stature in their vision of the world.

It is quite appropriate that the philosophical influence which affected van Doesburg and Mondrian was not derived from close readings of original texts, but came, instead, via the works of a philosopher called M. J. H. Schoenemaekers, the author of books on mathematical philosophy which enjoyed a certain popularity in the second decade of this century.[3]

Schoenemaekers's speculative mysticism had much to offer the developing artistic consciousness of Mondrian. Like Kandinsky, whose *Über das Geistige in der Kunst* (*Concerning the Spiritual in Art*) had influenced van Doesburg after its appearance in 1912, Schoenemaekers considered that, for the time being, art required a literary explanation in order for its full potential to be made manifest. He wrote in *Beeldende Wiskunde* that

> As long as our language has not yet clearly explained the new insight into the direct and general facts of nature, the plastic artists will have to try and speak in words, because the art itself is insufficient—as yet.
> (Quoted in Jaffé, 1956, p. 54.)

There was, besides the influence of Schoenemaekers, the spectre of Hegel standing behind van Doesburg and Mondrian. To van Doesburg, Neo-Plasticism[4] was the visual manifestation of laws first established by Hegel. In an article in *De Stijl* II, van Doesburg invoked the mighty German:

> The spirit is a thing infinitely higher than nature in it, divinity manifests itself more than in nature. It must thus be understood that all works which are wrought according to the spirit, must diverge from the external forms of nature and that they will diverge completely or rather less in proportion in which the spirit has come to its distinction.
> (Quoted in Jaffé, 1956, p. 55.)

Drawing on sources such as Hegel, *De Stijl*'s aesthetics could be nothing other than complicated. At other times, van Doesburg, with the careless freedom of an eclectic, drew also upon Neo-Platonism.[5] But the unifying factor throughout was the example of Schoenemaekers who made the occult available to the non-specialist.

The association of Mondrian with Schoenemaekers was not, however, a purely literary one: the two men were once neighbours in Laren, an artists' colony, and met often to discuss their common interests. What Schoenemaekers gave the painters was, like Hegel, a system which claimed to be able, by concentration, to penetrate the hidden structure of reality: natural appearance was a sham, a metaphor. Even before reading Schoenemaekers Mondrian had arrived at a similar conclusion. In Paris as early as 1911 he had thought that 'the appearance of natural things changes, but reality remains constant' (Jaffé, 1956, p. 56).

But to add to his mystical interpretation of the world, Schoenemaekers, who was by profession a mathematician, had also an exact interpretation of the qualitative values of geometrical features. He wrote

> The two fundamental, complete contraries which shape our earth and all that is of the earth, are: the horizontal line of power, that is the course of the earth around the sun and the vertical, profoundly spatial movements of rays that originate in the centre of the sun.
> (Quoted in Jaffé, 1956, p. 58.)

Throughout his life, Mondrian adhered with Messianic enthusiasm to the notion that this opposition of horizontal and vertical was a fundamental principle of natural construction.[6] Although Mondrian borrowed almost all his terminology from Schoenemaekers, his ideas were often quite distinct. Schoenemaekers, for instance, had a precise system of colour values (yellow, he thought, radiated, while red floats) which, while they may have influenced Mondrian to a degree, formed no permanent part of his aesthetic system. However, there were other qualities besides the purely philosophical which motivated the artists of *De Stijl*. What the philosophy suggested was the creation of a new life and a new reality made possible by the revelation of art. This revelation was, in sum, the universal values of life. By exposing the 'whole swindle of lyricism and sentiment' (Jaffé, 1956, p. 14) *De Stijl* not only set itself up in opposition to almost all preceding art,[7] but also posited a complete reconstruction of life. In art, representation could offer nothing. Mondrian expressed the Platonic spirit of *De Stijl* when he wrote that

> Neo-Plasticism arises from the notion of a universal conception of life. The universal can be expressed by pure relations between the subject and the universal; of the one extreme to the other.
> (*De Stijl*, Anniversary Number, 1927, p. 30; quoted in Jaffé, 1956, p. 113.)

Exercise

Despite the radical sentiments, *De Stijl* continued to use the traditional medium of painting on canvas to express its aims. How do you think painting could be used to express the universal?

Discussion

The artists of *De Stijl* considered painting to be the most appropriate means of expressing the universal because aesthetic contemplation was, to them, the principal means of perceiving the universal. Painting offered the opportunity for this contemplation; to *De Stijl* it was a means of understanding the structure of the universe in a convenient form. In the spirit of revolutionary artistic change which flourished around 1920, the presence of abstract painting provided art whose meaning was not hampered by subject matter, and whose purity was not impaired by emotional content which was inimical to equilibrium. To Mondrian, painting was the 'reconciliation of mind and matter'.

In common with other artistic movements of the time, the spirit of Utopianism featured large in *De Stijl.* Art was not an adjunct to life, but was indissolubly connected with it. The art of the past was connected with the individual, but, in the spirit of the contemporary social revolutions, the new art was to be universal.[8]

Mondrian said that

> Art is ahead of life; that which we are able to detect in present life is only the preludium to New Life.
> (Piet Mondrian, *Art and Life*, in Jaffé, 1956, p. 229*f.*)

Yet despite the fundamental position of art *vis-à-vis* life, *De Stijl*'s attention to the significance of art had in it the seeds of art's destruction. Aiming at an artistic utopia which when perfection has been achieved, like Marxism, the means of its creation shall wither away, *De Stijl*'s projected aesthetic utopia, had it come, would surely have been the end of art.

PART I *De Stijl*
Dutch Painting immediately before *De Stijl*
(Read Hamilton pp. 319–22.)

Four painters formed the nucleus of *De Stijl* when it was founded in 1917: Piet Mondrian, Theo van Doesburg, Bart van der Leck and Vilmos Huszar. Although *De Stijl*, because of van Doesburg's ambitions, was always internationalist in spirit, it nevertheless remained predominantly Dutch in membership. Of the painters named, only Huszar—who was Hungarian— was not born in Holland. The influence of the Dutch tradition in painting was, therefore, a common backcloth before which the *De Stijl* protagonists enacted their rebellion.

In the later nineteenth and early twentieth centuries there existed three dominant schools in Dutch painting. There was the Hague School, which appeared around 1870 and was characterized by the work of the Maris brothers, Jacob Henrikus, Matthij and Willem, together with Anton Mauve. The Hague School specialized in a heightened realism in their paintings, which constantly referred back to the seventeenth century, the great age of Dutch art. Although itself by no means avant-garde, it regarded the creation of certain 'moods' paramount in its efforts; the Hague School was, at least, responsible for the training of Van Gogh, whose teacher was, for a time, Anton Mauve.[9] Contemporary with the Hague School was the group of painters, including Isaac Israëls, known as the Amsterdam Impressionists; they drew their inspiration, naturally enough, from France as did the later Dutch Expressionists from Germany.

But, despite this dalliance with the advanced art of the rest of Europe, the force of nineteenth-century academic realism was still for a time, a dominant one. J. Israëls's *Child with Old People* (Fig. 35), is typical of the world of art which Mondrian was born into and which was soon to be transformed by the full influence of Post-Impressionism and the work of the Fauves.

Piet Mondrian[10] was born in Amersfoort in 1872 and was thus eleven years older than van Doesburg. After training at the Amsterdam Academy, where he spent the years 1892–4, he emerged as a conventional realist very much under the influence of his master, August Allebé, whose painting *The Custodian*, of 1870 (Fig. 36), is an almost unconscious satire on the somnolent creative flatulence of the academic painting and the museum world in the later nineteenth century.

From 1895 to 1907 Mondrian went through a naturalistic period painting traditional landscapes in and around Amsterdam which, while apparently conventional, do, as in the case of his *Woods near Oele* (Fig. 37), reveal on close examination a tendency to organize the picture into a static, well-balanced composition.

Of his predilection he wrote

> I often sketched by moonlight—cows resting or standing immovable in Dutch meadows, or houses with dead, blank windows. I never painted these things romantically, but from the very beginning I was always a realist.
> (Translated in Jaffé, 1956, p. 39.)

Woods near Oele displays a noticeable tendency to exaggerate the verticals, or, in other cases, the horizontal. It seems that even before the philosophical imperative of Neo-Plasticism required this organization of the visible world, Mondrian's own aesthetic sense had started to put nature in order in a personal way.

On first seeing the work of Van Gogh and the Fauves, Mondrian was impressed by their artistic quality, but felt that this sensual art had little to offer him which might help his own progress towards a new sort of painting. Much more influential on the

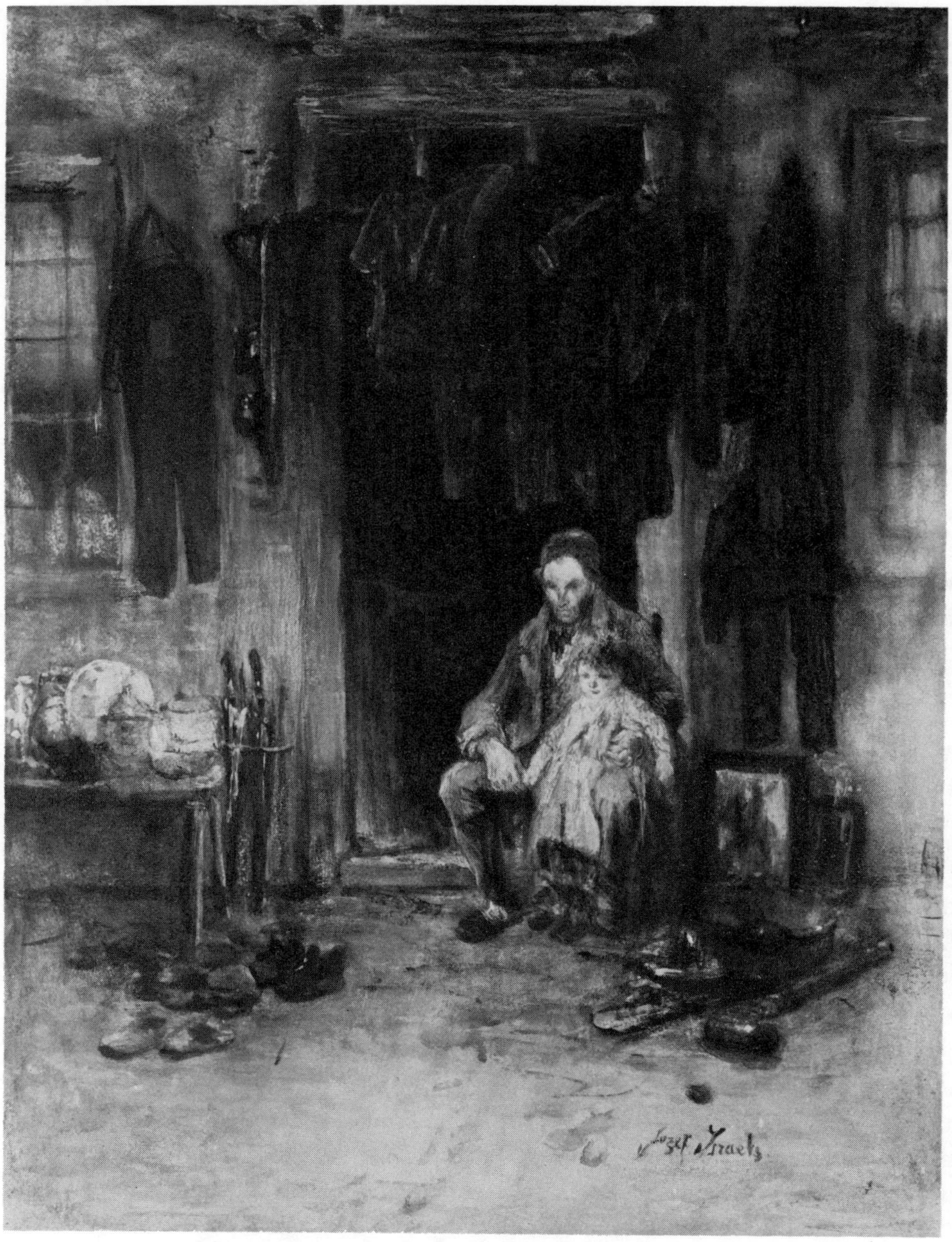

Figure 35 J. Israëls, *Zoon van het oude volk* (*Child with Old People*), 1888, watercolour, 23 × 17½ ins (Rijksmuseum, Amsterdam).

course of Mondrian's own development was the work of the Dutch graphic artist and painter, Jan Toorop.[11] Toorop began his career as a realist, with a tendency towards ostentatious sentiment: the thick impasto of his paintings is not unlike that of Lovis Corinth. But by the later 1880s he began to work in a variation of pointillist technique; parallel with this there was, as with so many other Dutch artists, an influence from Van Gogh, whose genius can be detected in, for instance, Toorop's *De Vloed* (*The Flood*) in Otterloo. But Toorop's art was to take its most significant inspiration from the Janus of Symbolism-Jugendstil, for around 1890 Toorop developed a highly original style, using flat colour and an anti-naturalistic emphasis on line to realise his own personal Catholic vision. It is easy to see what Mondrian might have seen in pictures of Toorop's mature style like *Fisherman in Katwyk* (Fig. 38): although his subject matter is more-or-less derived from observed phenomena of this world, Toorop's mature works suggest a literary unreality which is heightened by the linear quality of his designs.

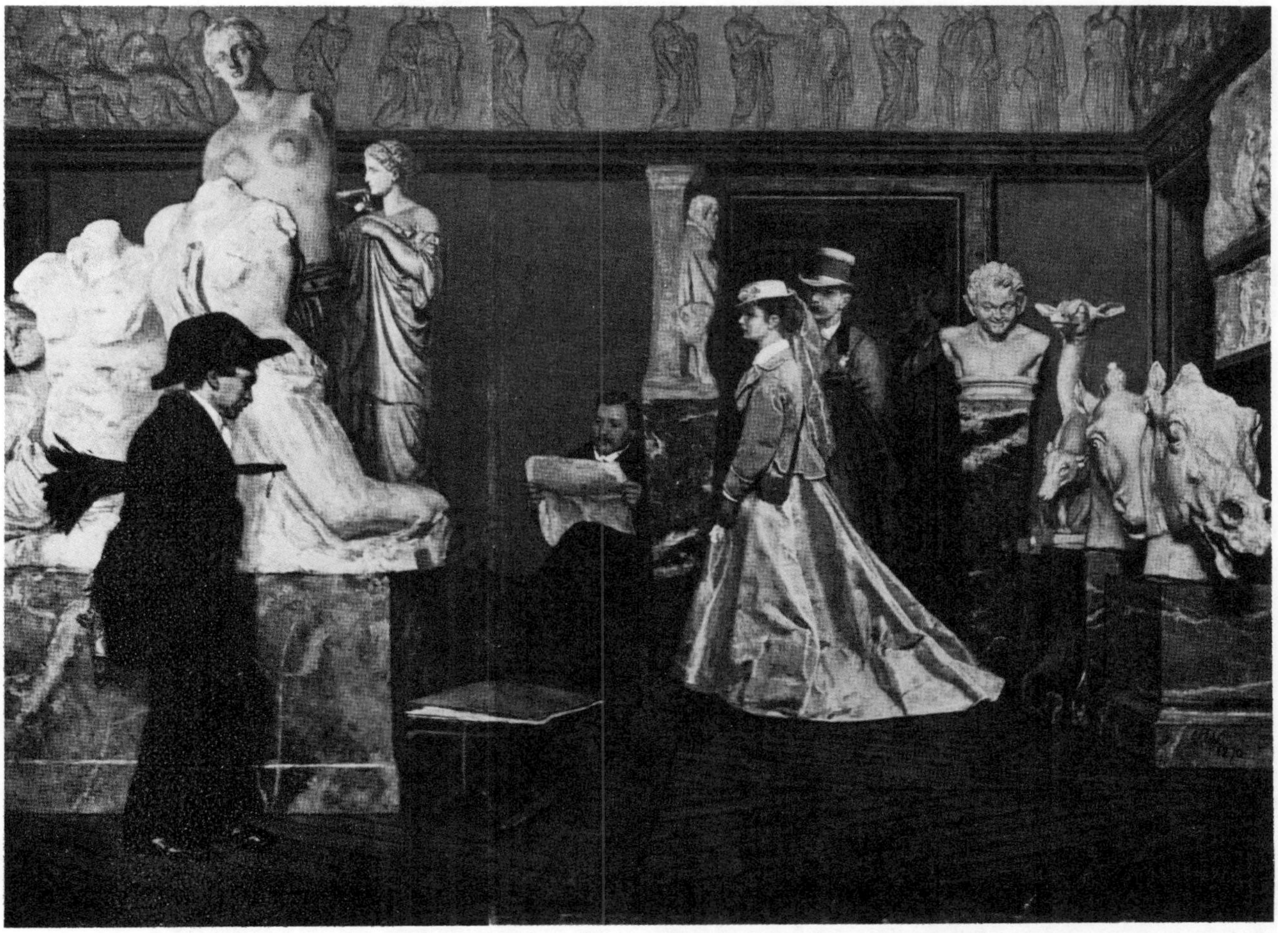

Figure 36 August Allebé, *The Custodian*, 1870, oil (Rijksmuseum H. W. Mesdag, The Hague, photo: A. Dingjan).

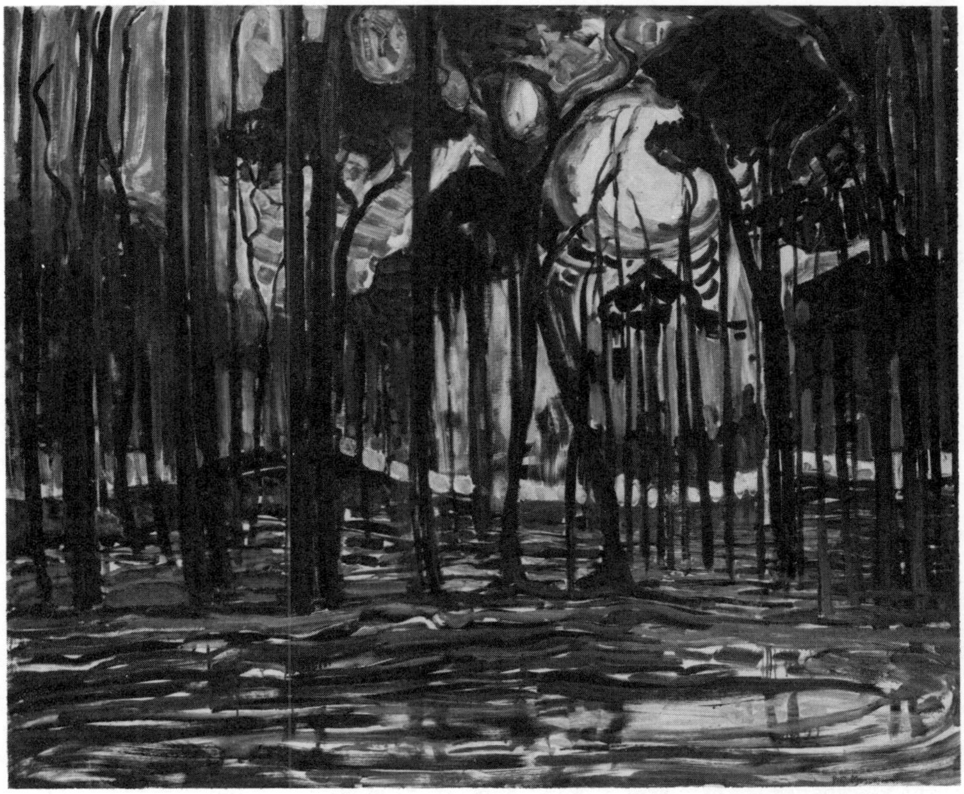

Figure 37 Piet Mondrian, *Woods near Oele*, 1908, oil, $51\frac{1}{2} \times 63\frac{1}{2}$ ins (Haags Gemeentemuseum, The Hague, courtesy Mr Holtzman).

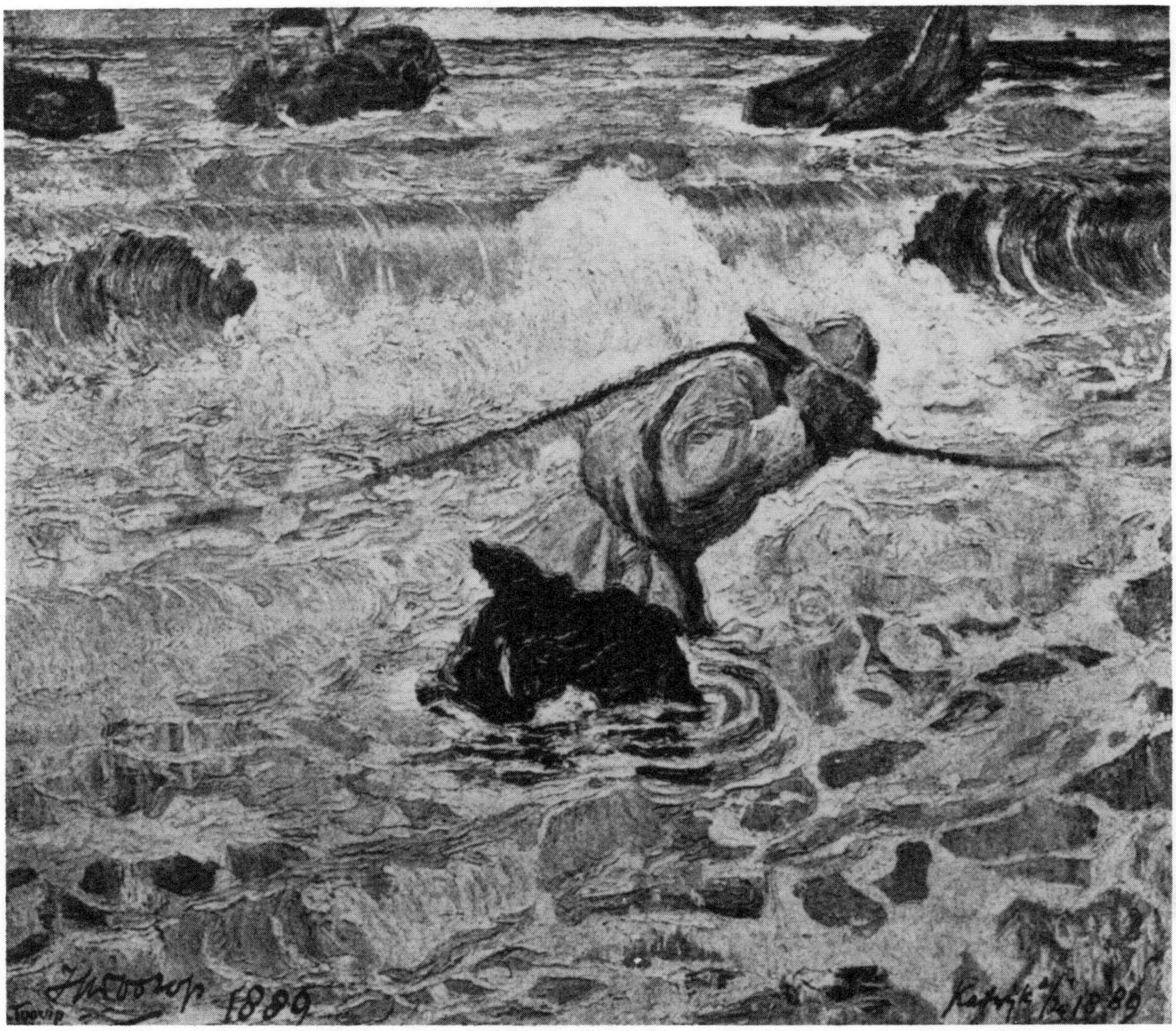

Figure 38 Jan Toorop, *Fisherman in Katwyk*, 1889 (From Miek Janssen, *Jan Toorop*, 1928, Führer-Verlag zu München-Gladbach).

But if Toorop had suggested to Mondrian a concentration on line, then it was Mondrian himself who brought about the new use of colour and the new manipulation of form apparent in his work after 1908. It was in this year that he moved to Domburg, in Zeeland, where he began a series of pictures of towers, windmills and sand dunes inspired by the local scenery. Two pictures in the Gemeentemuseum in The Hague, the *Lighthouse at Westkapelle* of 1908 (Fig. 39) and *The Red Mill* of 1911 (Fig. 40) are evidence of Mondrian's increasing simplification of colour, form and pictorial design even before his first experience of Cubism in Paris. Yet Mondrian was still under the influence of Symbolism as his triptych called *Evolution*, 1910–11 (Fig. 41) shows, but there are important changes apparent in his work. Foreshortening is beginning to disappear and the pictorial design is becoming simplified. Furthermore there is a change to the use of primary colours: 'The first thing to change', he wrote in his *Essays*

> was the colour. I forsook natural colour for pure colour. I had come to feel that the the colours of nature cannot be reproduced on canvas. Instinctively I felt that painting had to find a new way to express the beauty of nature.
> (Quoted in Jaffé, 1956, p. 40.)

In 1911 Mondrian left Holland to work in Paris and thus made the fundamental decision that was to affect his whole career. On the advice of the knowledgeable critic of the newspaper *De Telegraaf*, Conrad Kickert, Mondrian was drawn to the early work of the Cubists.

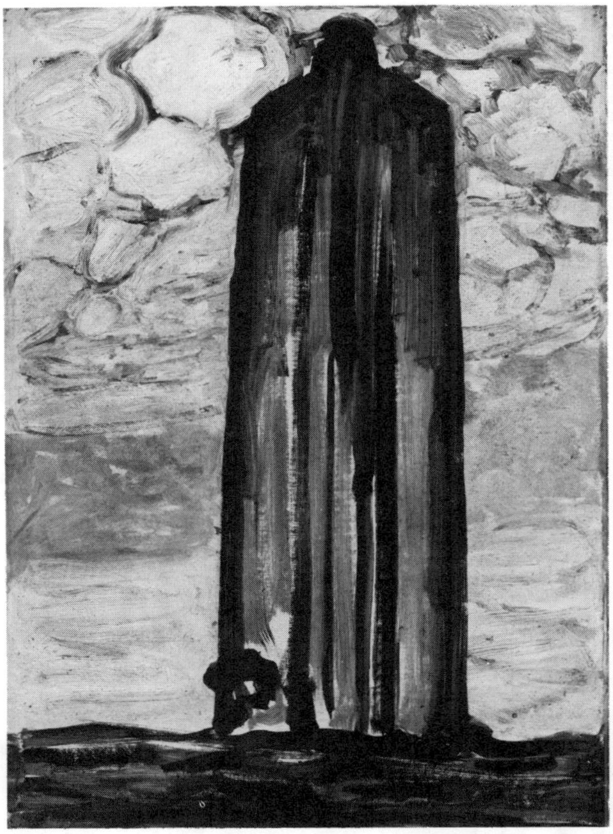

Figure 39 Piet Mondrian, *The Lighthouse at Westkapelle*, 1908, oil, 28½ × 21 ins (Haags Gemeentemuseum, The Hague, courtesy Mr Holtzman).

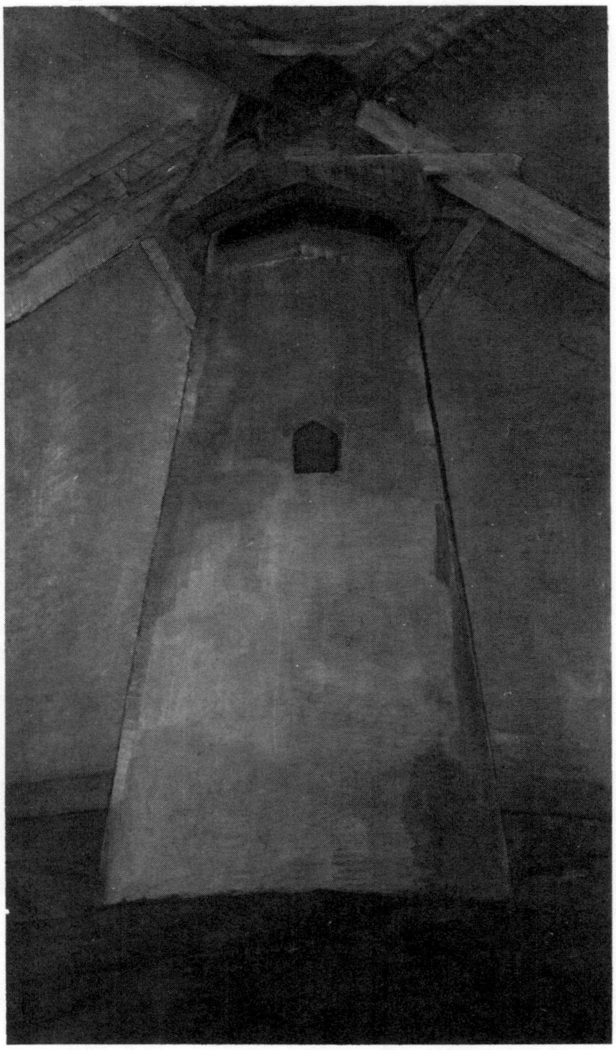

Figure 40 Piet Mondrian, *The Red Mill*, 1910–11, oil, 60 × 35 ins (Haags Gemeentemuseum, The Hague, courtesy Mr Holtzman).

In two series of pictures, one called *Still Life with Ginger Jar* and the other *Apple Tree*, painted at around this time we can see clearly the way Mondrian successively eliminates the careless arrangements of nature from his canvases and imposes on them a degree of order appropriate to his insight into the hidden order of the visible world.

Exercise

Look at Figures 42 and 43, the two pictures called *Still Life with Ginger Jar*. How would you describe the differences between the two?

Discussion

Both pictures, which were painted in 1911–12, are clearly informed by the influence of Cubism, but there are essential pictorial differences between the two treatments of the same subject matter. The first picture is a conventional enough still life in the Cubist idiom: glasses, an artist's brush, a cloth, a book and the ginger jar are clearly visible as objects set in space. But by the time Mondrian comes to paint the later picture all the individual plastic elements of the first, which exist in space, have coalesced into a two-dimensional visual pattern for which line, and not form, is the means of expression. In the second picture a balance has been achieved between the conflicting tensions of the objects in the first; the whole of the subject matter, if such shorthand notations can be considered such, is brought onto the picture plan to create a visual pattern. The artist's brush, for instance, which is clearly visible in the lower left-hand corner of the first picture is in the later canvas, reduced to a line whose literary meaning is not clear but whose pictorial responsibility is vital to the creation of

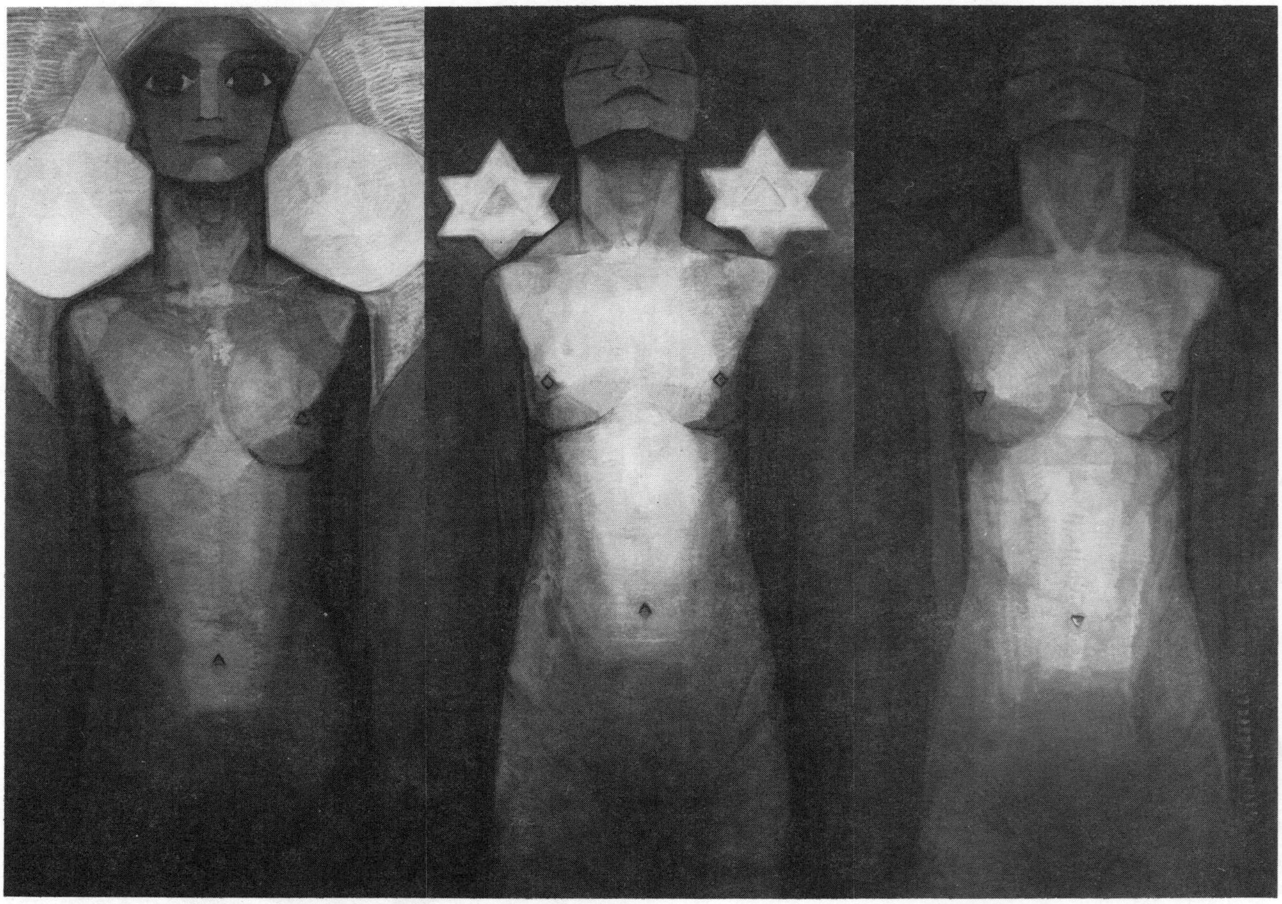

Figure 41 Piet Mondrian, *Evolution*, triptych, 1910–11, oil on panel, 71½ × 34 ins (Haags Gemeentemuseum, The Hague, courtesy Mr Holtzman).

the linear pattern. Indeed, the line of the brush which lends emphasis to the centralizing pull of the composition, is a reminder that by 1911 Mondrian was painting pictures in an oval format, rather like the Cubists whose work he then so admired.

Mondrian's escape from visual reality was no headlong fling, but, on the other hand, was a considered, measured retreat whose every step can be followed by us. His meticulous personality would have scorned any radical behaviour and he was aware of the slowness of his development:

> It took me a long time to discover that particularities of form and natural colour evoke subjective states of feeling which obscure pure reality. The appearance of natural form changes, but reality remains. To create pure reality plastically, it is necessary to reduce natural forms to constant elements of form, and natural colour to primary colour. The aim is not to create other particular forms and colours, with all their limitations, but to work toward abolishing them in the interest of a larger unity.
> (Piet Mondrian, *Essays*; quoted in Jaffé, pp. 42–43.)

Mondrian returned home in 1914 for a holiday, but was caught unawares by the outbreak of the First World War. His enforced isolation in Holland enabled him further to refine the pictorial researches which had been under way since 1907. By 1915 he was painting his famous versions of the pier at Scheveningen (Fig. 44) where the pictorial elements of sea, sky and the pier are reduced to + and — signs and where the composition is, again, an oval inspired by the centralized compositions of the Cubists.

It was at the time that Mondrian had quite independently reached this astonishing stage of development that there was the coming together with van Doesburg and the

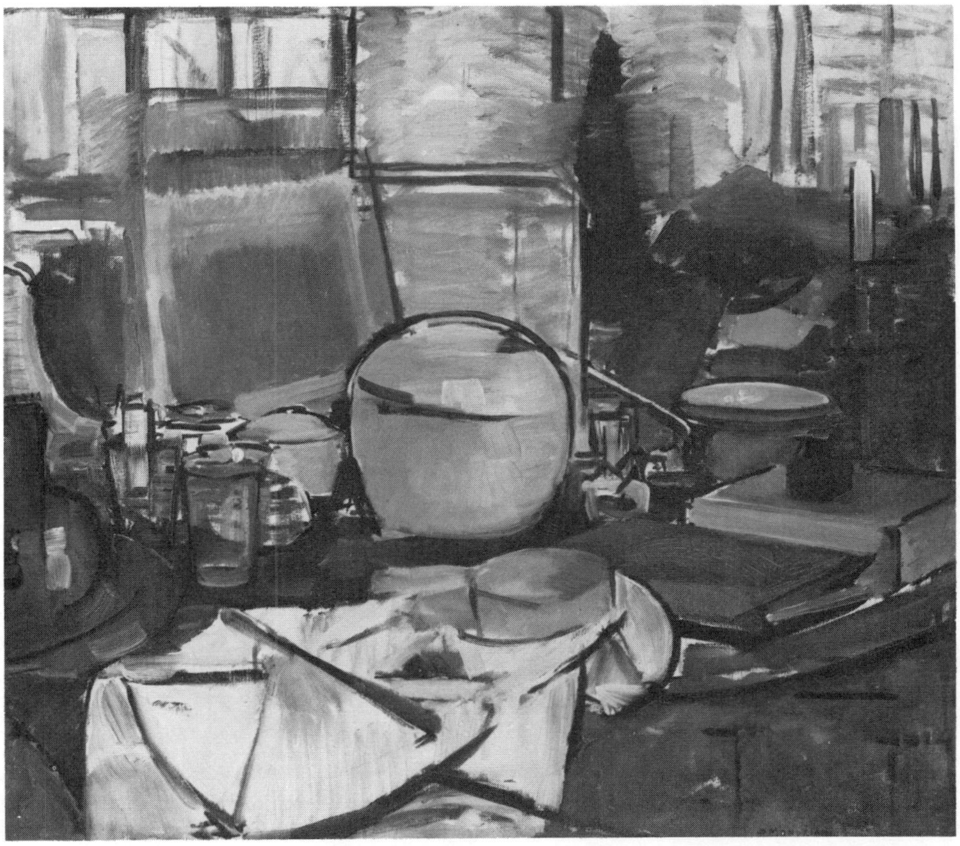

Figure 42 Piet Mondrian, *Still Life with Ginger Jar I*, 1911–12, oil, 26½ × 30 ins (Haags Gemeentemuseum, The Hague, courtesy Mr Holtzman).

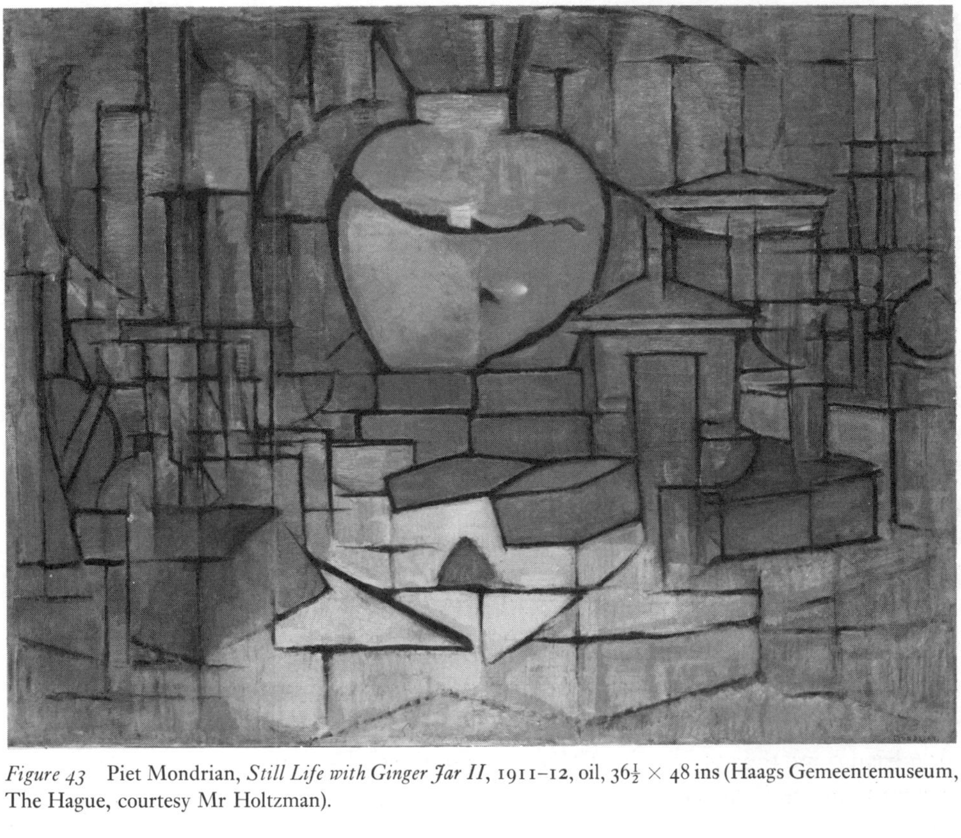

Figure 43 Piet Mondrian, *Still Life with Ginger Jar II*, 1911–12, oil, 36½ × 48 ins (Haags Gemeentemuseum, The Hague, courtesy Mr Holtzman).

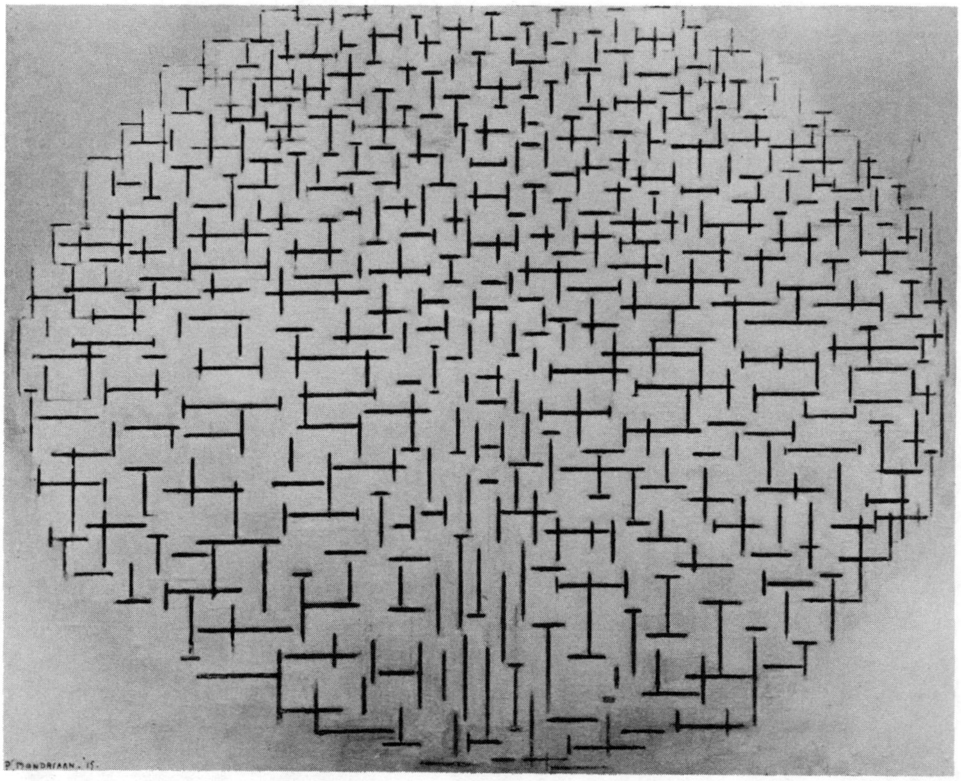

Figure 44 Piet Mondrian, *Composition no. 10: Pier and Ocean at Scheveningen*, 1915, oil, $33\frac{1}{2} \times 42\frac{5}{8}$ ins (Rijksmuseum Kröller-Müller, Otterloo, courtesy Mr Holtzman).

third great painter of the early years of *De Stijl*, Bart van der Leck. Van der Leck's pictures were relatively much more conservative than Mondrian's, but it is easy to see why Mondrian was impressed with van der Leck's work. In 1916 van der Leck was not an abstractionist, but was still painting pictures whose motifs are plainly derived from the visible world. *The Tempest* (Plate 11) is a good example of his style: it is figurative, but the figurative motifs in the picture are treated as flat planes of colour. Van der Leck was interested in simplifying form and in establishing an objective visual language but, unlike Mondrian, he had little taste for theorizing and perhaps because of that, felt unwelcome within the *De Stijl* group and did not, consequently, stay with it for long.

Van Doesburg, the genius of *De Stijl*, was considerably younger than both Mondrian and van der Leck, his cofounders. His personal style (which is treated at greater length in the next section) grew out of a combination of realism and Fauvism. In service during the war van Doesburg had expressed his interest in the theories of Kandinsky by publishing a study of one of Kandinsky's Dutch followers, Adrianus de Winter.

At the foundation of *De Stijl* the paintings of Mondrian, van der Leck and van Doesburg are virtually indistinguishable from each other. By what Hans Jaffé called a 'spiritual short cut' the three men had achieved a unity of aesthetic purpose appropriate to the beginning of a radical new modern art movement. In 1917 all three painters were producing canvases which bore no resemblance to anything which exists in the natural world. Each master used squares, rectangles and lines often of primary colours, of black and of white, to create entirely abstract compositions, sometimes suggestive of depth by overlapping and sometimes, as in the case of van der Leck's *Geometrical Composition I* in the Rijksmuseum Kröller-Müller, not.

However, despite the apparent community of intention each painter had arrived at this destination by a different route, and each had brought separate influences. From Mondrian came the experience of Cézanne and the Cubists, from van der Leck came the emphasis on the surface, and from van Doesburg came the influence of the theories of abstraction of Wassily Kandinsky. These opposing tensions were all present at the foundation of *De Stijl.* The fusion, however, was soon to fall apart. Van der Leck soon left the group to work in textiles and interior decoration while van Doesburg was to develop other interests besides those catered for exclusively by the credo of *De Stijl.* It was only Mondrian who, from 1917 on, continued a linear pattern of development which never faltered, hesitated or looked back. But that, for the time being, is another story.

Van Doesburg's Early Work

(See Hamilton pp. 322–26.)

Theo van Doesburg was such a varied and complex personality that he required four separate identities (see p. 95). Van Doesburg was not his own name—that was Christiaan Emil Marie Küpper—but when his mother married Theodorus van Doesburg after the departure of her German husband, Wilhelm Küpper, it was natural that her son should adopt the Dutch name which he felt to be legitimately his own. Indeed, whether the 'van' which he added to his name was affectation or a dark suggestion of irregular paternity will never be known.

An early painting is known from 1899, but van Doesburg's first serious phase of activity was what he was later to call his 'Brown period', a term which he adopted to describe his dependence between about 1902 and 1909 on the old Dutch masters, and in particular on Frans Hals and Rembrandt. Rembrandtesque indeed is a self portrait of 1906 where the twenty-three-year-old youth has painted a picture in strong chiaroscuro of the artist standing by an easel which clearly has as its inspiration the mature portrait style of the seventeenth-century master, but despite the opportunity which van Doesburg had at this time of exhibiting at a show in the Haagsche Kunstkring (in 1908) and thereby making a positive artistic statement, it is clear that no particular style and no particular artistic ethic appealed to him.

Afterwards, between 1909 and 1913, van Doesburg entered his so called 'Blue period', which expression he used to denote his burgeoning appreciation of the developments of modern art. By about 1912 the personality of van Doesburg with which we are familiar was beginning to emerge. Articles appeared in *Eenheid*[12] which attacked Futurism, and even Kandinsky (who was only a little later to be so influential) was criticized for indulgence. In 1913 van Doesburg's 'White period' began when he had begun to synthesize all the opposing trends of modern art and to refine from them a rigid and austere aesthetic of his own. It was at this time that he came to acknowledge the fundamental importance of Kandinsky, when acquaintance with his writings was part of a wide programme of reading which van Doesburg undertook. Of all his experience of modern art theory, van Doesburg believed that the two most influential works were Kandinsky's *Concerning the Spiritual in Art* and *Rückblicke* (*Reminiscences*). In both of them was an apology for the notion that art was more than the mere arrangement of forms in a pleasing way.

From Kandinsky came the idea of precise spiritual values in painting and a sense of a universality of artistic creation, while from the architect Berlage, whose *Studies over Boukunst Stijl en Samerleving* (*Studies on Architecture, Style and Community*) was published in 1910, came the notion that there was an art of the future which would be quite independent of any precedent.[13] In articles written at this time in *Eenheid* and elsewhere van Doesburg began to work out a philosophy of art which included as one of its essential elements the use of the straight line. The straight line will enable, he thought, 'the art of the future to create an international form' (quoted in Baljeu, 1974, p. 19). But despite the suggestions of Kandinsky's painterly semantics and the inference one can make of a desire for universalism in art there is in van Doesburg's paintings of *c.* 1914 nothing to suggest the strong and influential operation of these principles. The idea it seems, came before the means. His *Girl with Buttercups* (Fig. 45) expresses a rather maudlin theme by means of a reliance on a Futurist-Orphist mode of pictorial expression. A year later his paintings still showed no great stylistic innovations, but his philosophy was becoming clearer and there can be detected for the first time the specific elements which were later to become the aesthetic of *De Stijl*. In a lecture he gave at Utrecht which was later published in *Eenheid*, van Doesburg stated that 'nature will become idea, and idea is style (quoted in Baljeu, 1974, p. 20), a principle that is clearly, if unconsciously, derived from Hegel.

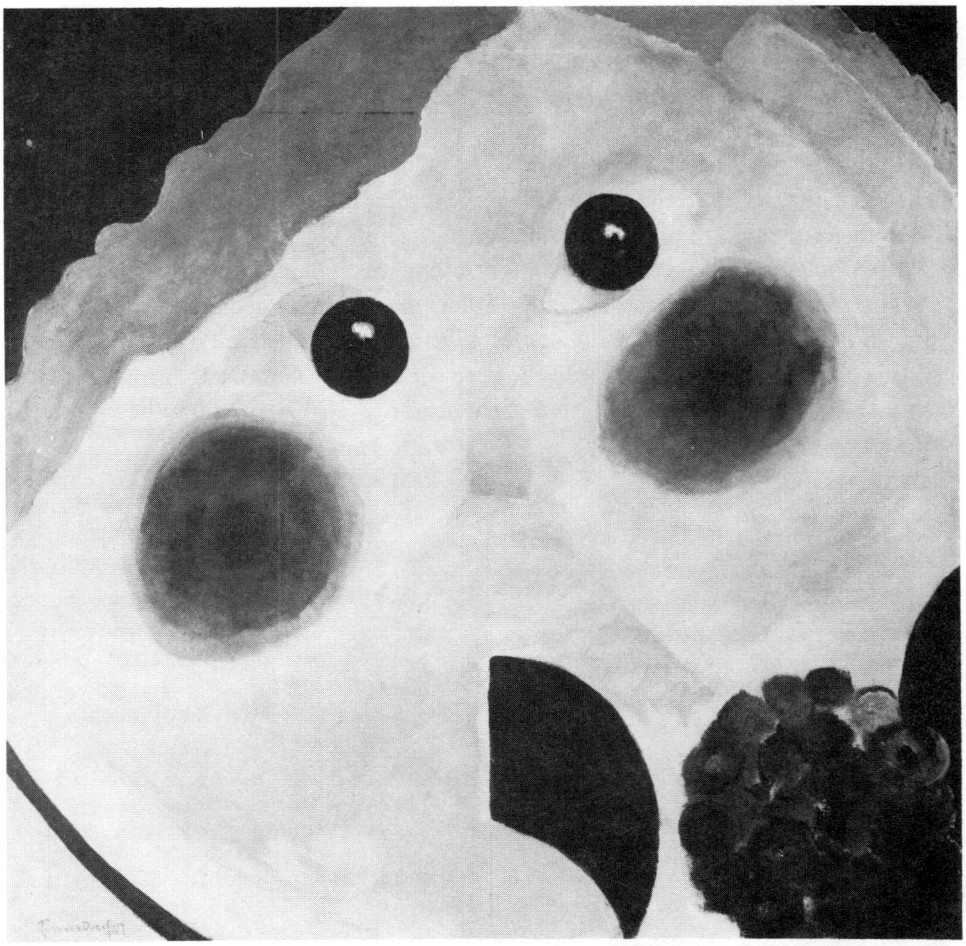

Figure 45 Theo van Doesburg, *Jeune Fille en Fleur* (*Girl with Buttercups*), 1914, oil, $31\frac{1}{2} \times 31\frac{1}{2}$ ins (Yale University Art Gallery, lent by Mr and Mrs William N. Copley).

Whether this development in van Doesburg's theory was influenced by his experience of the works of Mondrian, which he saw for the first time in 1915, in an exhibition called *Moderne Kunst* at Amsterdam's Stedelijk Museum, we do not know. Certainly though, this exhibition which, besides Mondrian, contained works by Cubist painters, must have appealed to van Doesburg as a novel experience of the possibilities of the new art. Impressed at this exhibition most of all by the works of Mondrian, in which he saw spiritual and architectural qualities which appealed to him, van Doesburg wrote to Mondrian to ask him to take part in a joint venture which would take the form of a magazine devoted to the aims of the new art which he could envisage, but not yet create. Mondrian, characteristically aloof, cold and careful, declared himself to be unready to take part in any joint enterprise. He replied

> You won't take me amiss, but good things have to grow very slowly . . . I believe that the time has not yet come for it. There is more to be achieved in that direction. I scarcely know anyone who really does produce our style of art, that is to say, art that has as yet attained some sort of perfection . . . There won't be enough material for a specialised magazine or else it will be half-hearted.
> (Mondrian to van Doesburg, 20 November, 1915; quoted in Stedelijk Museum, 1951, p. 71.)

The contrast between the two men's attitudes is a telling one. Mondrian, whose painting was by 1915 clearly in a state of rapid evolution, was unwilling to presume yet to participate in an organ of the new art, while van Doesburg who had, by 1915, painted little of moment, was anxious and excited to give presence to the nascent spirit in art by means of a new journal, even before he was ready for it himself.

But if there is one point when in van Doesburg's art theory the early speculation appears to be becoming the elemental theory of *De Stijl* it is in the second of his *Three Lectures on the New Plastic Art*. The collection was published in 1919, but the second paper 'The Aesthetic Principle of Modern Art' had appeared first in 1916. In it van Doesburg expresses the idea that the new style will be realized by a collaboration between architecture and the other arts: architecture, itself, he says, will possess characteristics related to the universal space of the new aesthetic. Yet there is still little in van Doesburg's paintings to suggest a fundamental revolution; his painting, *Tree with Houses* (Fig. 46) is still a composition whose essence is derived largely from the spirit of Cubism, but a Cubism subjected to a rigid geometrical order; nevertheless, this changing sensibility around the year 1916 marks the transition from a sense of a *nieuwe beelding* to a full realization of the aims of Neo-Plasticism in the founding of *De Stijl*.

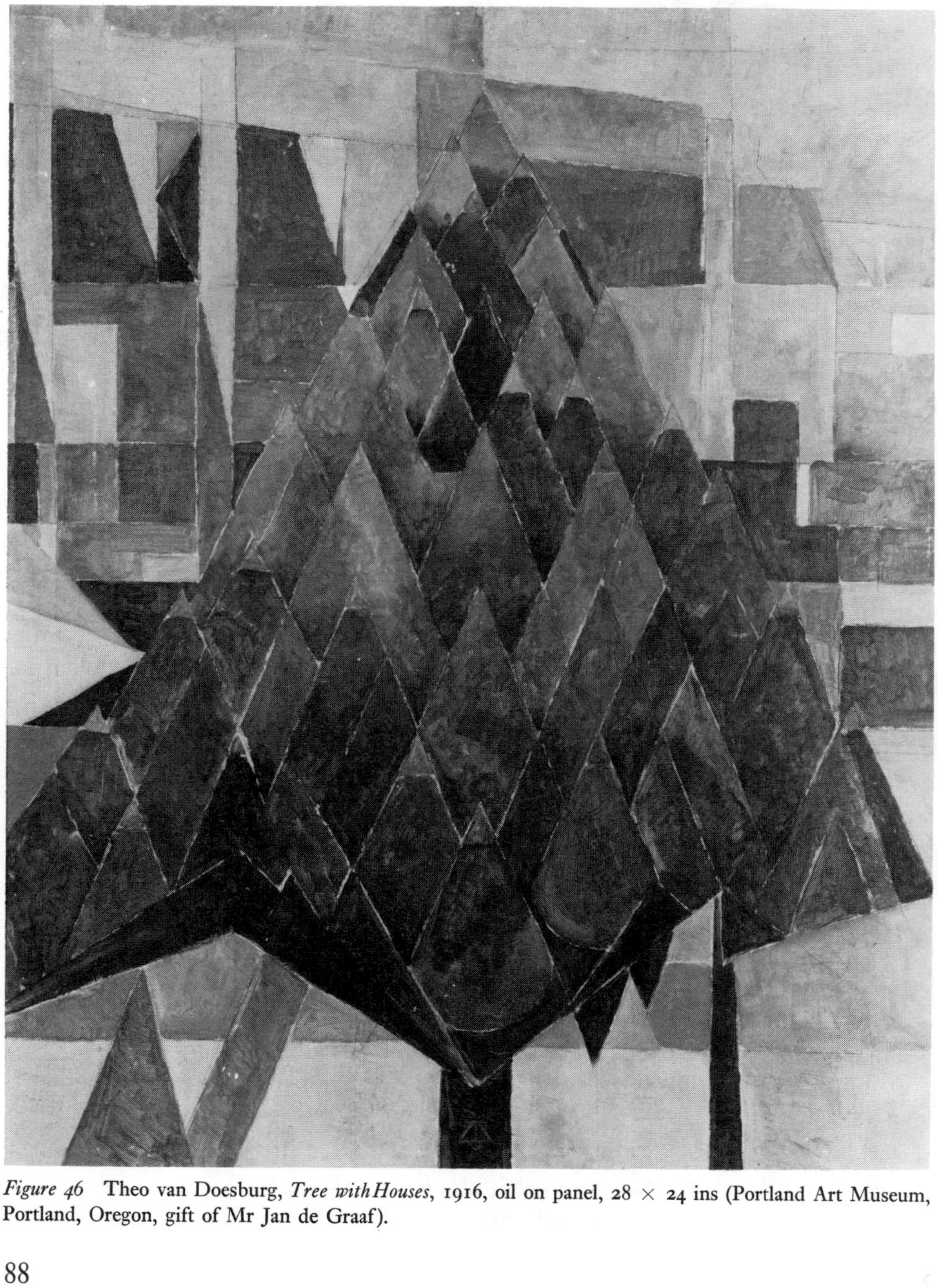

Figure 46 Theo van Doesburg, *Tree with Houses*, 1916, oil on panel, 28 × 24 ins (Portland Art Museum, Portland, Oregon, gift of Mr Jan de Graaf).

Immediately after he was demobilized in 1917 van Doesburg lost no time in discussing the foundation of his proposed magazine of the visual arts. First of all he contacted the architect, J. J. P. Oud and then the Hungarian designer, Vilmos Huszar. Although architecture was often the catalyst in all of *De Stijl*'s activities the two painters with the earliest associations with the group, Mondrian and van der Leck, were at first both unsympathetic to the idea of including architects. However, Mondrian eventually concurred in the founding of *De Stijl* on 16 May 1917, but in a passage written soon after was anxious to impress upon van Doesburg the uniqueness of his own art. He said that 'you should remember my things are still intended to be paintings' (quoted in Stedelijk Museum, 1951, p. 51). Van der Leck joined *De Stijl* the day after Mondrian and, under the editorship of van Doesburg (both Mondrian and van der Leck were unwilling to assume any editorial responsibility), the first issue of the magazine of that name appeared in October 1917. The title page was a curious amalgam of bold layout and grotesque type contrasting with traditional typography; it announced the eruption of a new influence in the world of art. The contents of the first issue were an unequivocal statement of the group's aesthetic intentions: it contained Mondrian's essay 'Neo-Plasticism in Painting', Bart van der Leck's 'Modern Painting and its Relationship to Architecture', Anthony Kok on 'The Modern Painting in the Interior', Oud on the 'Monumental Town' and comments by van Doesburg on an advanced van der Leck painting of 1917 (Fig. 47) and a short critique of a seafront scheme proposed by Oud.

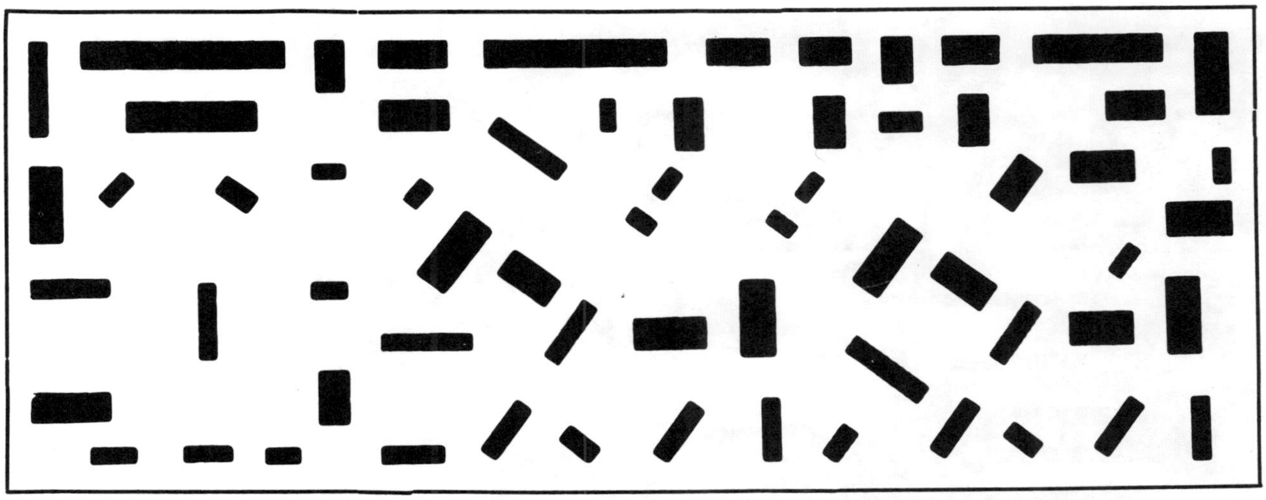

Figure 47 Bart van der Leck, *Composition*, 1917 (Present whereabouts unknown, *De Stijl*, Volume I, 1, 1917, courtesy Uitgeverij van Gennep).

Although all the contributors to the first issue of *De Stijl* were Dutch, there was always in van Doesburg's mind the question of extending the influence and scope of his group beyond the borders of Holland. In the beginning, both van Doesburg and Mondrian were attracted by Futurism: Mondrian had originally suggested that Gino Severini be invited to join the group (he even proposed Picasso as well!). Van Doesburg responded by publishing in the second issue of *De Stijl* Severini's article 'La Peinture d'avant garde'.

Exercise

Why do you think Mondrian and van Doesburg might have been interested in Futurism?

Discussion

It seems to us now that Futurism and Neo-Plasticism have very little in common and it is initially hard to see what van Doesburg thought would be gained from printing Severini's article. However, I think that two points can be made:

1 There was, around the end of the First World War, a community of feeling between the different movements of modern art which encouraged the belief that the aims, if not the means, of each movement were shared.

2 To the Futurists, and Severini stressed this throughout his article, there was the recurrent idea that the *machine* expressed certain *universal* values.

Furthermore the Futurists, as much as anyone else, had a firm conviction in the *Zeitgeist*, a feeling that there was a spirit of the time which had to be expressed. In the early years of this century the great intellectual innovations in the arts and sciences were felt to be changing for ever man's conception of the universe. This belief was common to all the movements of modern art.

Amazingly, in the same year that he was so busy getting the first issue of *De Stijl* into print, van Doesburg also managed to publish a collection of essays, which had originally appeared in *De Beweging* under the title of *De nieuwe beweging in de schilderkunst* (*The New Movement in Painting*). Also in 1917 van Doesburg painted his first pictures which express fully the aesthetic philosophy of *De Stijl*. These paintings are not yet recognizable as pure Neo-Plasticism, but they do clearly mark a significant stage on the journey from the representation of nature to the expression of the purest abstraction: *Composition IX: The Card Players* (Fig. 48) is an abstract version of a picture on the same theme which was completed almost a year before, in the figurative style of Bart van der Leck.

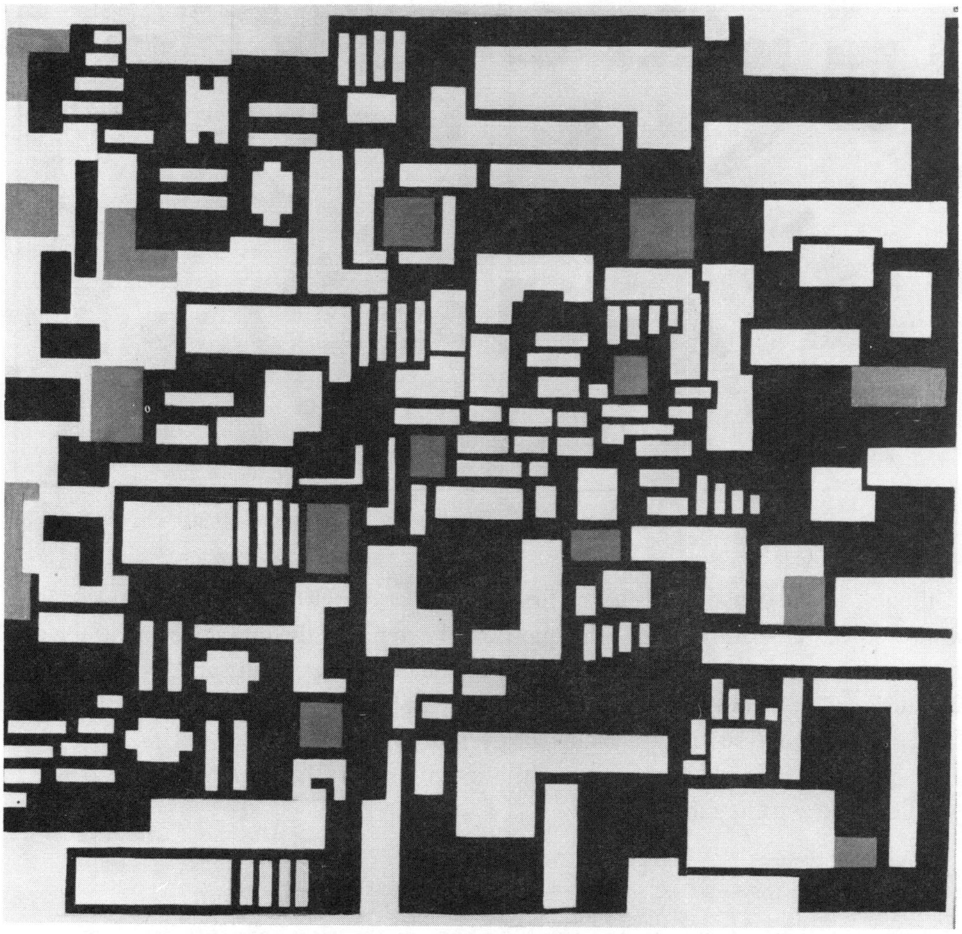

Figure 48 Theo van Doesburg, *Composition IX: The Card Players*, 1917, oil, $46\frac{1}{2} \times 42\frac{1}{2}$ ins (Haags Gemeentemuseum, The Hague).

There had been, even in the first year of publication, an attempt to achieve *De Stijl* sculpture. Georges Vantongerloo's *Construction in the Sphere* (Fig. 49) was an attempt to achieve a different goal, for the aims of *De Stijl* could not necessarily be interpreted in the medium of sculpture: architecture and painting were the movement's real media.

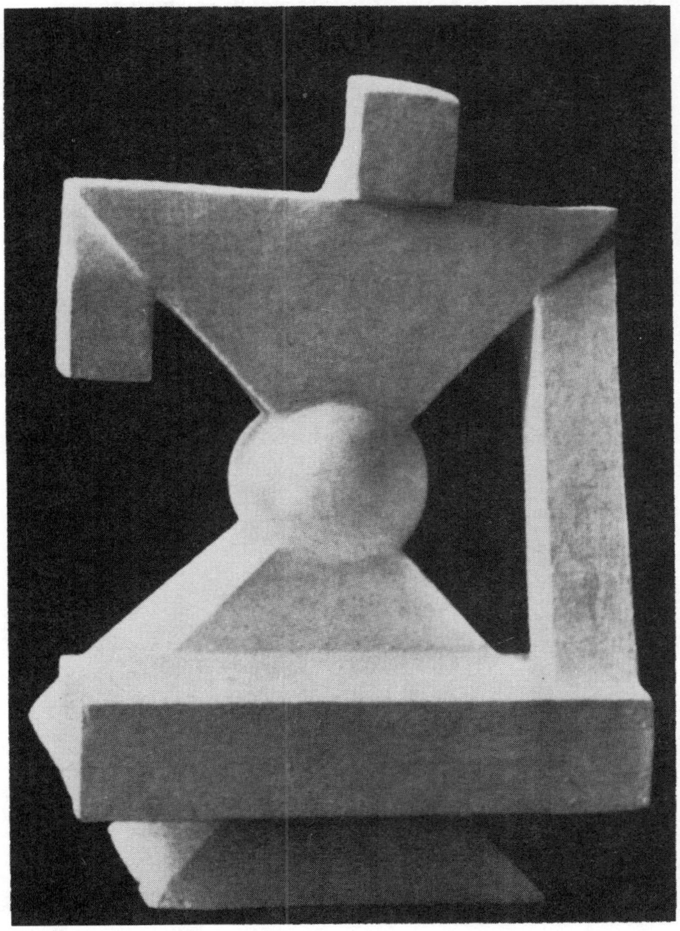

Figure 49 Georges Vantongerloo, *Construction in the Sphere*, 1917, blue painted wood, 6¾ ins high (Collection Nelly van Doesburg, Meudon-Val-Fleury; photo: Professor H. L. C. Jaffé).

It was, despite the activity of 1917, not until the next year that the real consolidation of the group took place. In Mondrian's paintings of 1918 what had been the year before floating planes of flat colour in a simple two-dimensional pattern, become regularized compositions with black lines which destroy any lingering sense of pictorial space that might have been sensed to exist in the 1917 pictures. In van Doesburg's own work the picture surface becomes fuller and more dynamic and, as with Mondrian, there is no longer any suggestion that the source of inspiration for a picture was in nature.

The most important event for *De Stijl* in 1918 was, however, a literary one. The first *De Stijl* manifesto was published in the journal in November 1918.[14] An indication of the wide ambitions and hopes which van Doesburg held for this statement of policy is the fact that the manifesto was published in Dutch, French, German and English. It reads:

Manifesto I of 'The Style', 1918

1 There is an old and a new consciousness of time.
The old is connected with the individual.
The new is connected with the universal.

The struggle of the individual against the universal is revealing itself in the world war as well as in the art of the present day.

2 The war is destroying the old world with its contents: individual domination in every state.

3 The new art has brought forward what the new consciousness of time contains: a balance between the universal and the individual.

4 The new consciousness is prepared to realise the internal life as well as the external life.

5 Traditions, dogmas and the domination of the individual are opposed to this realisation.

6 The founders of the new plastic art therefore call upon all, who believe in the reformation of art and culture, to annihilate these obstacles of development, as they have annihilated in the new plastic art (by abolishing plastic form) that, which prevents the clear expression of art, the utmost consequence of all art notion.

7 The artists of today have been driven the whole world over by the same consciousness, and therefore have taken part from an intellectual point of view in this war against the domination of individual despotism. They therefore sympathise with all, who work for the formation of an international unity in Life, Art, Culture, either intellectually or materially.

8 The monthly editions of 'The Style', founded for that purpose, try to attain the new wisdom of life in an exact manner.

9 Co-operation is possible by:
I Sending, with entire approval, name, address and profession to the editor of 'The Style'.
II Sending critical, philosophical, architectural, scientific, literary, musical articles or reproductions.
III Translating articles in different languages or distributing thoughts published in 'The Style'.
(*De Stijl* reprint, 1968, Volume I, p. 238.)

Exercise

Read Mondrian's 'Natural Reality and Abstract Reality' (Chipp, pp. 321–23). What do you think are the principal characteristics expressed in van Doesburg's manifesto and Mondrian's essay?

Discussion

Both were a call-to-arms, stirring documents which demand action. It would be possible to isolate a number of different characteristics, but you would have done well to spot:

1 The idea, perhaps derived from van Doesburg's interest in Futurism, that war is cathartic;

2 A high degree of utopianism; the new order, it seems from the manifesto, will be brought about by art;

3 A belief in the *Zeitgeist*, or the spirit of the age;

4 A practical concern to spread *De Stijl* across the Dutch borders; and

5 Neo-Plasticism is a painterly expression of the universal.

Whether or not as a direct effect of the manifesto is now known but certainly by 1919 the international membership of *De Stijl* was increasing, perhaps aided by easier communication at the end of the war. The painting, too, was progressing; van Doesburg's pictures of 1919 look very like Mondrian's of the year before, while Mondrian himself began to paint lozenge-shaped canvases with very tightly controlled patterns of squares. His *Composition: Bright Colour Planes with Grey Lines* (Fig. 50) is typical of the increasing formalism in his art. It was in 1919 that Mondrian returned to Paris (and dropped the second 'a' in his name making *that* too, cleaner and neater) while the restlessly energetic van Doesburg travelled to Belgium and Germany to enact the mandate of the manifesto. There was, however, strong criticism of *De Stijl* in Holland. This appeared to stimulate Mondrian; writing to van Doesburg he said

> I am glad that the criticism is what it is. It is all right that way. In complete opposition to our direction otherwise we would have nothing to do . . . we have straightly to oppose the whole to-do, *a part*.
> (Quoted in Stedelijk Museum, 1951, p. 75.)

Van Doesburg was unperturbed. His European peregrination had been designed with propaganda in mind and in this he was aided in 1920 by the publication in Paris,

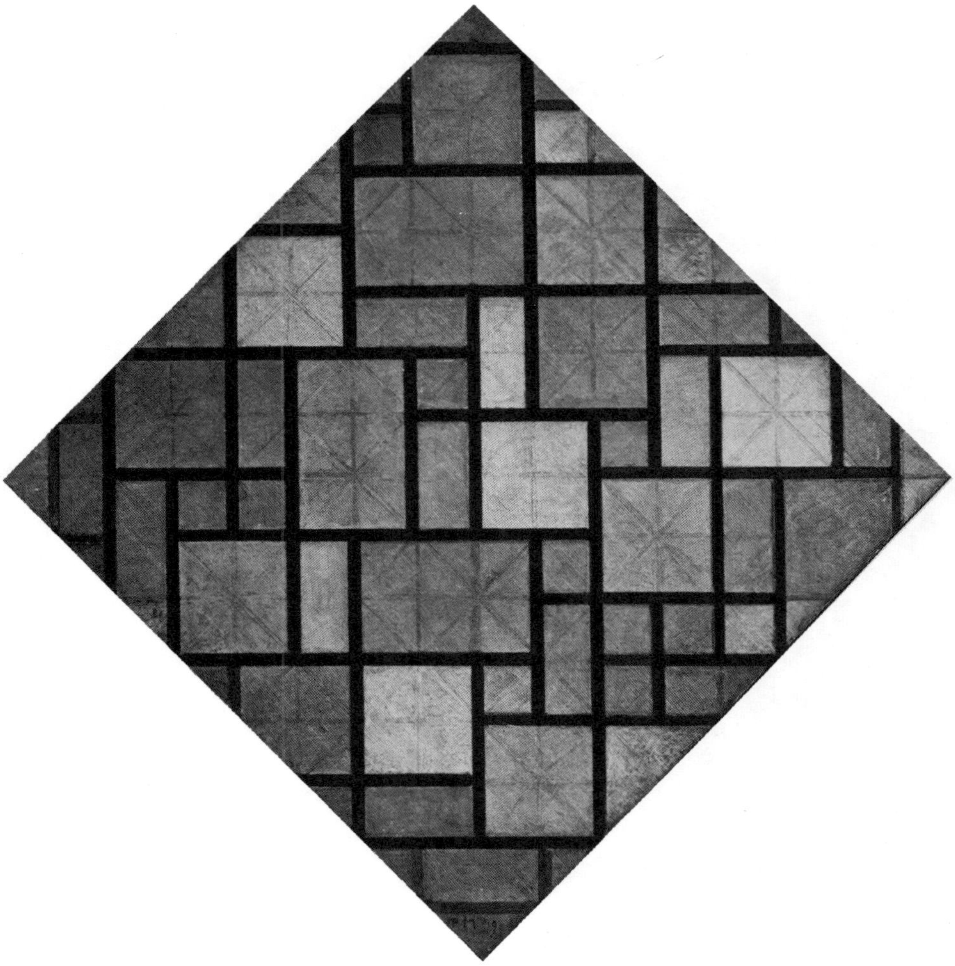

Figure 50 Piet Mondrian, *Composition: Bright Colour Planes with Grey Lines*, 1919, oil, 33½ ins diagonal (Rijksmuseum Kröller-Müller, Otterloo, courtesy Mr Holtzman).

by the emigré Mondrian, of the pamphlet *Le Néo-Plasticisme*[15], under the auspices of Léonce Rosenberg, owner of the Galerie de l'Éffort Moderne. This condensed account of the aesthetics and philosophy of Neo-Plasticism did much to give the group European status which was enhanced by the appearance, also in 1920, of the literary face of *De Stijl*. In April of that year a second manifesto had appeared, this time concerning itself with literature. This time, however, perhaps because of the poor response by English artists to the polyglot appeal to the manifesto of 1918, it appeared only in Dutch, French and German. This strident, iconoclastic document said that

> The organization of our contemporary literature still continues to batten on the sentimentality of a weakened generation. The word is dead.
> (*De Stijl* reprint, 1968, Volume III, p. 49.)

Not only here is there the influence of the destructiveness of Dada, but also a fascinating parallel to the aim of *De Stijl* being the end of art, previously noticed. Even though strength was suggested by this document, *De Stijl* was, in fact, as early as 1920 showing signs of disunity. In a frenzy of activity which preceded decline, Mondrian was independently busy in Paris and van Doesburg was wooing the youth of Germany. The international phase of *De Stijl* was about to begin, and the dissipation of talent and dilution of original purpose which was to end with Mondrian's resignation in 1925 had begun.

Van Doesburg's alter egos and *De Stijl*'s Opponents

Van Doesburg was a typical eccentric: under two pseudonyms—three if you include the name 'van Doesburg' itself—he was able to attack convention and defend the new art in a number of various postures which were not always consistent. As early as 1914, aware even then of the role he wished to create for himself, he had written that

> I imagined myself making a daring, spiritual crusade throughout artistic and intellectual Europe.
> (*Brieven aan Bertha* (*Letters to Bertha*) unpublished manuscript 1914–15; quoted in Baljeu, 1974, p. 10.)

At one time or another—and sometimes simultaneously—van Doesburg was an exponent of *De Stijl*, Dada and Surrealism. In each role, he was always a romantic in the broadest sense; he believed unequivocally in the importance of the aesthetic experience and it is not surprising that he found he needed a number of different identities to express the full richness (and contrariness) of his character which, if all had been advanced under one name, might have dismayed and confused *De Stijl*'s public.

I. K. Bonset was the ludicrous name which van Doesburg employed to project his Dada self. Bonset published his first poem, '*X-Beelden*' ('X-Images') in the issue of *De Stijl* for May 1920. A further version was published in November. The first poem is an extraordinary piece, hinting at the literal interpretation of four dimensions:

> I am penetrated by the room where
> the streetcar slides through
> I am wearing a cap
> the sounds of an organ
> are-within-me and-outside-me
> fall and break behind me.
> (small fragments TIN TIN TIN . . .)

and so on. Although '*X-Beelden*', perhaps a reference to the penetration of X-rays, was Bonset's first appearance in print, it appears that van Doesburg had found it necessary to invent the character some years before. Joost Baljeu has identified an earlier unpublished manuscript called *Nieuwe woordbeeldingen. Kubistische en expressionistische verzen* (*New Word Images. Cubist and Expressionist Poems*): in this manuscript, only the poems written between 1913 and 1915 are signed 'van Doesburg' and the name itself, it seems, was first used by van Doesburg in a letter written to the Dadaist Tristan Tzara in 1918 in which van Doesburg carries out the pretence that Bonset is an active Dutch Dadaist (Baljeu, 1974, p. 38, p. 221 note 3.)

It was quite appropriate that it was Tristan Tzara who was the first to hear of the existence of Bonset, for it was at this time that van Doesburg was being strongly influenced by Dada. Tzara and Hugo Ball seem to have been the chief influences and it was probably an experience of Ball's *Flucht aus der Zeit* (*Flight from Time*) (see Unit 13) that gave Doesburg, or rather I. K. Bonset, the idea to write his *Het Andere Gezicht* (*The Other Face*), an aphoristic piece which has passages like

> After the nocturnal eclipses of the sun had vanished and I had experienced the pleasant sensation of dying, it became clear to me—for the first time in my life—how dependent was the fabric of my being, two unequal parts, which showed no similarity whatsoever to one another.
> (*De Stijl*, Volume XIII, 77, 1926, pp. 66–67; translated in Baljeu, 1974, pp. 162–3.)

which are redolent of the nihilistic spirit of Dada. Clearly, van Doesburg was attracted to Dada because its destructiveness would lead to a vacuum which could be filled as Neo-Plasticism. The complete expression of van Doesburg's attitude to Dada was made in an article entitled 'Is een universal beeldingsbegrip thans mogelijk?' ('Is a universal plastic notion possible today?') (cited in Baljeu, 1974, p. 221 note 7). He said that Dada was good because it was anti-sentimental and healthy because it was anti-art. These qualities, he felt, made Dada necessary to the preparation of the new culture which was to come and, as if in concurrence, *De Stijl* correspondence of this time between van Doesburg, Kok, Mondrian and Oud is distinguished by the word 'dada' added to each signature.

If I. K. Bonset was van Doesburg's Dada persona, then Aldo Camini can be said to have been his philosophical one. Camini gave 'his' name to the Dada philosophy which van Doesburg invented and called 'Camino-scopie', published in *De Stijl* in June 1921. Turning about-face, Camini rejected Hegel—and, almost needless to say, Christianity and other philosophies besides—and proposed an absurd 'philosophy' which said that 'In my belief, art, religion, philosophy, science and alcohol are all consequences of doubt' (translated in Baljeu, 1974, p. 113); the full title of the article in English was 'Caminoscopy, an anti-philosophical view of life without any thread or system'. Camini was the embodiment of van Doesburg's enthusiasm for Futurism, at least in the sense of an admiration for electricity and the like, but it is curious that an exponent of the fairly clearly defined aims of *De Stijl* was able, at the same time, to publicize the cause of philosophical anarchy. However, despite these fruitful exchanges between De Stijl and Dada and Futurism, van Doesburg's connection with other contemporary art movements was not always so amicable or so stimulating.

THE BAUHAUS

Just after the foundation of the Bauhaus in 1919 van Doesburg began to correspond with Lyonel Feininger, the first master whom Walter Gropius appointed to the faculty at Weimar. Furthermore, Gropius's famous Bauhaus manifesto of 1919 was published in *De Stijl*, but it is hard to imagine what van Doesburg saw in it, besides another appeal for the creation of a new world order: van Doesburg, like Vilmos Huszar was to do in 1922, objected strongly to the blatant Expressionist tone of the first phase of Bauhaus activity. However a Feininger painting was published in *De Stijl* and while, like all of Feininger's art, it was clearly representational, van Doesburg hoped that the rigid geometrical structure it displayed would eventually evolve into pure abstraction. It did not.

Neither Feininger nor Gropius had much time for van Doesburg: Feininger was to call him 'claptrap, vain and ambitious' (quoted in Ness, 1975, p. 123) and his association with Gropius was soured by recriminations.

Van Doesburg had been introduced to Gropius in Berlin in 1920 by the Expressionist architect Bruno Taut and there followed an extraordinary series of events. Van Doesburg presumably expected to be invited to teach at the Bauhaus, which at this time lacked any Constructivists on its staff, but the invitation from Gropius never came. Van Doesburg's immediate response was to set up his own *De Stijl* course in Weimar. He told his own version of the story of his association with the Bauhaus in the anniversary number of *De Stijl* in 1927. He wrote that Gropius was impressed by the *De Stijl* photographs which he had shown him and said 'we want something like this at the Bauhaus'.

Van Doesburg continued

> Invitation by Gropius to visit the Bauhaus. January 1921 visit to the Bauhaus, where, in addition to Expressionist degeneration, so-called 'root-compositions' in the manner of Vantongerloo, reproduced by Itten students are found. There are

> also weak imitations of paintings by Mondrian. Gropius puts at the disposal of the editor his complete press archive of the Bauhaus's struggle whilst defending itself against the government of Thüringen. In his turn, the editor (in good faith) places all photographs, booklets, issues of *De Stijl* and so forth at the disposal of the director of the Bauhaus and expresses the wish that the Bauhaus may develop in the same consistent way as *De Stijl* has done in Holland. He offers to support Gropius in his struggle. In the beginning of January, return to Holland. A correspondence between the editor of *De Stijl* and the Bauhaus develops. Gropius and Meyer express the wish to remain in contact with *De Stijl.* Proposals to come over. 17 March 1921, propaganda tour through Belgium, France, Italy and Germany. Lectures with the musical accompaniment of Petro van Doesburg. In April the editor of *De Stijl* is installed at Weimar by Meyer and *De Stijl* adherents. (*De Stijl*, Volume XIV, 79–84, p. 54; translated in Baljeu, 1974, p. 41.)

But Gropius's version of van Doesburg's presence in Weimar was different. In 1953 Bruno Zevi published a letter from Gropius in his *Poetica dell'architettura neo-plastica.* Gropius wrote

> I have never invited van Doesburg to the Bauhaus. He came there of his own initiative because he was attracted by our courses. He hoped to become a professor at the Bauhaus, but I did not give him a position, since I judged him aggressive and fanatic and considered that he possessed such a narrow, theoretical view that he could not tolerate any diversity of opinion.
> (Bruno Zevi, *Poetica dell'architettura neo-plastica*, Milan, translated in Baljeu, 1974, p. 41.)

Gropius as well as other members of the Bauhaus, probably feared that a man with as strong a personality as van Doesburg would take over the Bauhaus, rather as Johannes Itten had done in the years he spent there; but, unlike Itten, van Doesburg represented 'constructivism' and while Gropius was no doubt conscious of the lack of a 'constructivist' component in the Bauhaus teaching at this time, that had to wait until the replacement of Itten by Laszlo Moholy-Nagy in 1923, for van Doesburg's method of self-publicity, determined as he was to spread the 'vermin' of the new order among the Bauhaus students, was not a policy calculated to endear him to a potential employer.

CONSTRUCTIVISM

The third *De Stijl* manifesto, 'Tot een nieuwe wereldbeelding' ('Towards a Newly Shaped World') appeared in August 1921. Quite apolitical in spirit it said that 'Capitalists are deceivers and so are Socialists' (translated in Baljeu, 1974, p. 113), in direct opposition to the predominant political tone of the other constructivists.[16] In the manifesto van Doesburg spoke contemptuously of the recent Communist Internationals and had praise only for what he referred to as the 'International of the Mind'. In October 1921, van Doesburg published in *De Stijl* the Constructivist manifesto of Raoul Hausmann, Hans Arp, Iwan Puni and Laszlo Moholy-Nagy called 'Aufruf zur Elementaren Kunst' ('Call for an Elementary Art'), a harbinger of Functionalism. This, almost in the spirit of Dada (and, after all, both Arp and Hausmann were Dadaists) appeared to be more of a rejection of materialism and sentimentality than an acknowledgment of the future of Functionalism. Also in this spirit was van Doesburg's own 'Der Wille zum Stil. Neugestaltung von Leben, Kunst und Technik' ('The Will to Style. A New Form of Expression of Life, Art and Technology') which appeared in *De Stijl* in two parts in February and March 1922. A long and elaborate piece by the laconic standards which *De Stijl* usuall maintained, it set up the whole of van Doesburg's complex and contradictory aesthetic. (It is translated in Baljeu, 1974, pp. 115–26.)

The International Congress of Progressive Artists, held at Düsseldorf in 1922, gave van Doesburg a further opportunity to express the increasingly Constructivist turn of mind he was developing, but which was, at the same time, serving to isolate Mondrian fron the *De Stijl* group's activities. Much of the material offered at the conference, for instance that of Werner Graeff and El Lissitsky[17], was later to appear in *De Stijl.* Thus giving tacit approval to the aims and methods of El Lissitsky, the compliment was returned when van Doesburg had some of his own writings published in the Constructivist journals *Ma* and *Ves*, *Gegenstand*, *Objet*, but by 1923 van Doesburg was, with characteristic duplicity, attacking the functional ethic of Constructivism, and proposing that painting was still the most advanced form of art. Taking up arms against the artless cadre of Constructivists van Doesburg addressed an article in German called 'Von der neuen Aesthetik zur materiellen Verwirklichung' ('The New Aesthetics and its Realisation') to figures like the architect Mies van der Rohe, prominent in *G*, who was propagandizing for an art devoid entirely of associations. El Lissitsky was not unsympathetic to van Doesburg's aims of creating a form of Constructivism which, in the words van Doesburg used to describe the 'Creative Demands of *De Stijl*' to the International Union of Progressive Artists, were

1 The annulment of exhibitions and the substitution of space in which to demonstrate teamwork.

2 An international exchange of ideas on creative problems.

3 The development of unambiguous, universal means of plastic expression in all the arts.

4 The annulment of the divorce between art and life.

5 The annulment of the divorce between art and mankind.
(*De Stijl*, Volume 4, April 1922, pp. 59–62; translated in Baljeu, 1974, p. 127.)

but late in 1923 van Doesburg and El Lissitsky both left Germany and took with them 'universal' Constructivism, leaving the field open there for the purest expression of purposive Constructivism, the International Style in architecture.

Dynamic Dialectics: Elementarism

The notion of 'elements' in painting of the *De Stijl* group goes back as early as 1917 when van Doesburg said of a Mondrian picture he then much admired that it gave him 'an elementary impression of art'. Van Doesburg may have derived his use of the term from the publications of the art historian Heinrich Wölfflin whose *Kunstgeschichtliche Grundbegriffe* (*Principles of Art History*) (1915), a work inspired in part by theories of pure visibility, laid great stress on the interpretation of art by its different plastic elements.[18] The word was used again in the manifesto 'Aufruf zur Elementaren Kunst' but it was perhaps the event which inspired the word and, in this case, that event was the creation in 1918 by Gerrit Rietveld of his *De Stijl* chair (Plate 12). Any description of it demands the use of the word 'element' for in its design Rietveld had refined the function and appearance of his chair to their basic elements. To van Doesburg, who wrote a poem about it, Rietveld's chair exuded the 'silent eloquence of the machine' (published in Volume III of *De Stijl*). The poem, though, does not mention elements, but instead gives us a valuable clue to an influence on van Doesburg—active around 1920—that of the *Valori Plastici* group, for the poem mentions the painter de Chirico in the same breath as it mentions Rietveld's chair. This was in 1920, and although it took van Doesburg four to five years before he was to paint an Elementarist picture, it was surely the widening of his horizons created by his contacts with groups like *Valori Plastici* from Italy, the *Section d'Or* and *l'Éffort Moderne* in Paris which served gradually to disabuse him of strict adherence to the dogma of Mondrian. This he replaced by a catholic interest in all the manifestations of modern art, and by 1924 when van Doesburg could paint his *Counter Composition V* (Fig. 51) the phase of *De Stijl* painting which was entirely under the influence of Neo-Plasticism was over. This painting was Elementarist.

Of his disenchantment with Mondrian, van Doesburg said

> By the lively and most articulate evolution in the principles, developed mainly by P. Mondrian in *De Stijl*, could not any longer be considered as generally characteristic of the opinion of the group. The realization becoming richer and more manifold, we succeeded in enriching new domains: as a sum of the newly conquered insights and possibilities, elementarism was constituted. In the idea of 'elementary design' everything we had acknowledged in our work as being essential and universally valid, from the very beginning until today was united. (*Neue Schweizer Rundschau*, 1929, p. 540; cited in Jaffé, 1956, pp. 26–27.)

Van Doesburg's departure into the use of the diagonal in his pictures must be seen as a reaction against the dogmatism of Mondrian who believed that in the universal values of the purely vertical and horizontal there was much that was still to be expressed: Mondrian was content to continue refining, as he did, the system of Neo-Plasticism, indeed, his greatest statements in that *genre* were still to be made but by his use of the diagonal, van Doesburg forced a cleavage between the *De Stijl* group and its original aesthetic inspiration.

An Elementarist painting can be distinguished from a Neo-Plasticist one by the presence in the former of lines placed at 45° to the horizontal. The contrast thus achieved, van Doesburg thought, brought an element of dynamism into *De Stijl* art which had hitherto been lacking: he regarded it as a further means of expression while Mondrian (who had, incidentally, already discussed the use of the diagonal component with van Doesburg between 1917 and 1920) regarded it as a corruption of Neo-Plastic purity.

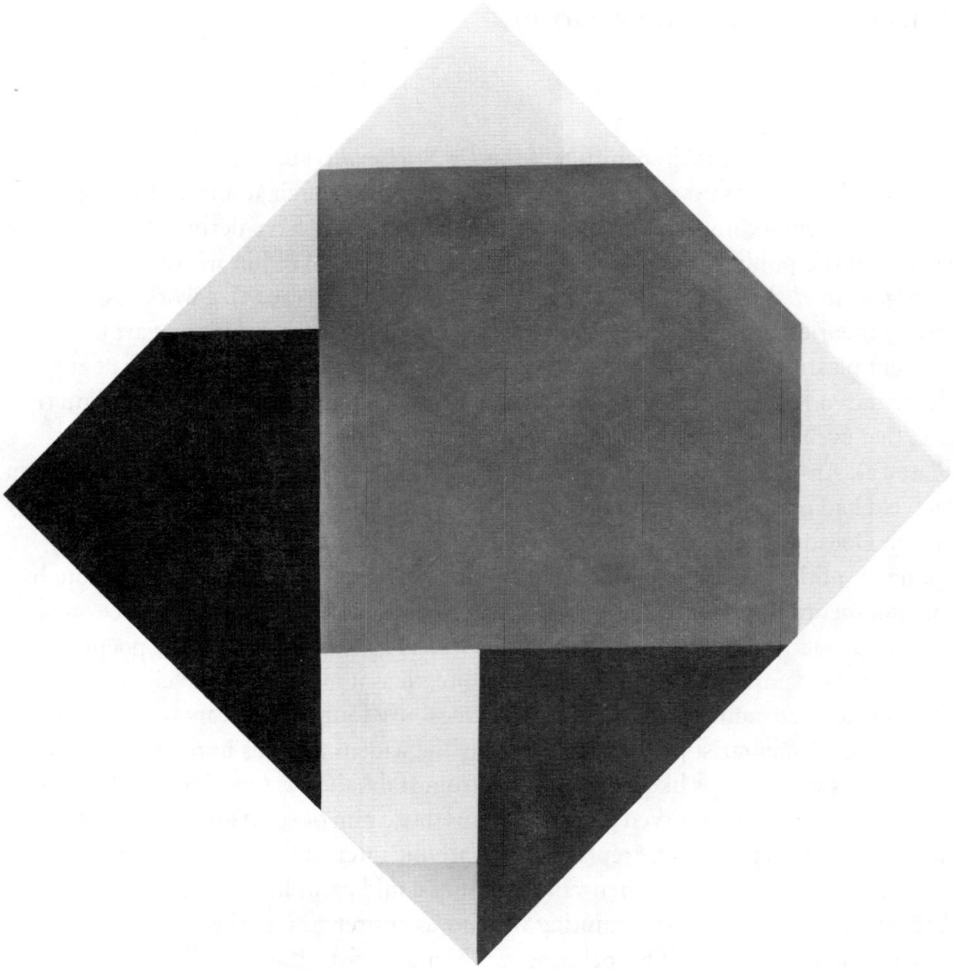

Figure 51 Theo van Doesburg, *Counter Composition V*, 1924, oil, 39 × 39 ins (Stedelijk Museum, Amsterdam).

Exercise

Can you think of a reason why van Doesburg was anxious to introduce a suggestion of dynamism into *De Stijl*?

Discussion

Van Doesburg, as we have seen, was a fiercely ambitious and competitive man. He jealously advanced the cause of *De Stijl* and was always nervously aware of any contemporary advance made by a rival movement. It is possible that he introduced the diagonal into his pictures because his architectural experiments were unproductive and he needed a new innovation to restore his confidence, but I think it is more likely that Elementarism was created as a deliberate attempt to imitate the Futurists' suggestion of motion in their paintings. Van Doesburg had been aware, as early as 1920, that the Futurists had much to offer *De Stijl*, and it was in that year that *De Stijl* began to incorporate Futurist free-form typography and the praise of the machine into its format. By introducing the 'dynamic' diagonal, van Doesburg must have thought that he was putting *De Stijl* on an equal footing with Futurism.

Not realizing the degree of self-parody suggested in his statement, van Doesburg said of Elementarism that it was 'opposed to compromise, to decadence, to contemporary aesthetic confusion'[19] and that 'one must always point in opposition to nature'[20]. Certainly, in a painting like *Contra Composition of Dissonances XVI* of 1925 (Fig. 52) there is a conscious and direct contrast to Mondrian's beloved equilibrium and it would be a brave man indeed who could perceive in this picture any reference whatsoever to the natural world.

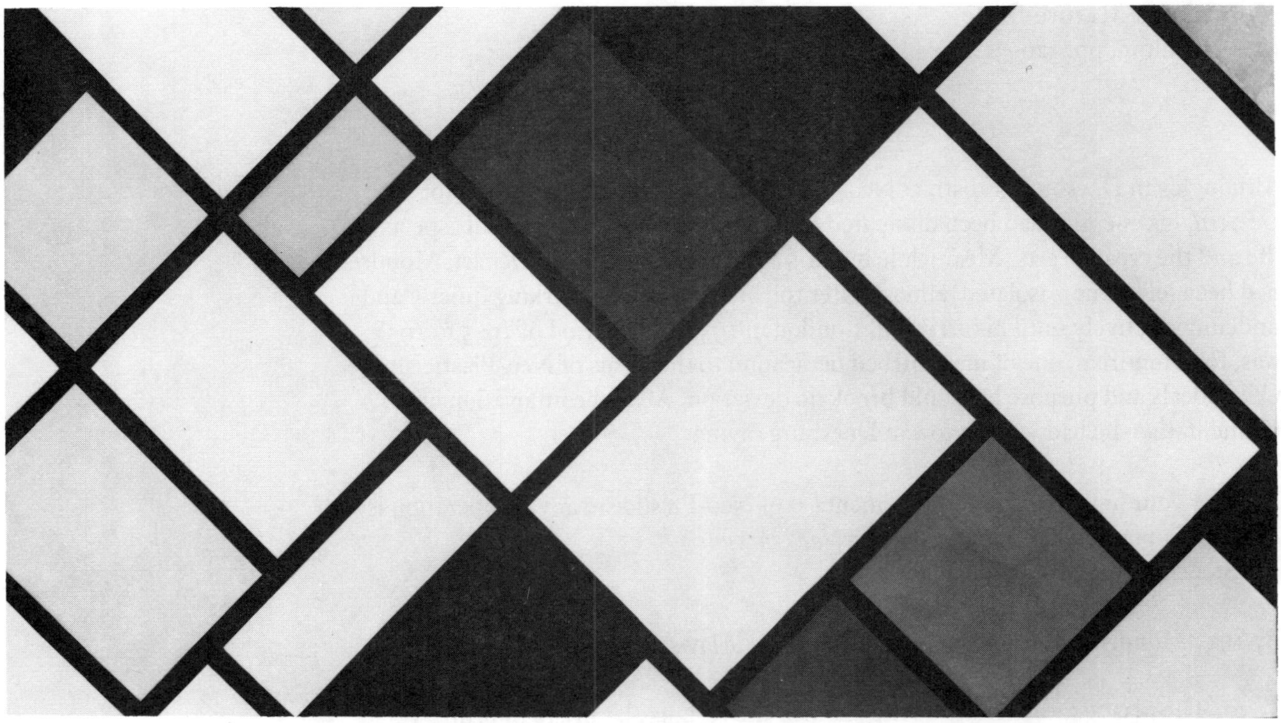

Figure 52 Theo van Doesburg, *Contra Composition of Dissonances XVI*, 1925, 39 × 32 ins (Haags Gemeentemuseum, The Hague).

The conflict in ideology between Mondrian and van Doesburg over the introduction of Elementarism was an intriguing one which resolved itself into the question of whether or not equilibrium was a desirable or an essential element in the art of *De Stijl*. To Mondrian, equilibrium

> reveals that although human life in time is doomed to disequilibrium, notwithstanding this it is based on equilibrium. It demonstrates that equilibrium can become more and more living in us. Reality only appears to us tragical because of the disequilibrium and confusion of its appearances.
> (Piet Mondrian, *Essays*; quoted in Jaffé, 1956, p. 126.)

and was essential to the maintenance of his composed and austere world view, but to van Doesburg equilibrium represented a danger that *De Stijl* might lag behind its rivals. Besides it is clear that van Doesburg believed that *De Stijl* had sacrificed the cause of equilibrium when it had rejected symmetry. He wrote that symmetry

> is associated to our corporal external structure, it would have led in its way to reject rectangular composition as well as the only possible means of expression, as it is associated with our natural organic structure.
> (*De Stijl*, VII, 83; translated in Jaffé, 1956, p. 196.)

The dispute with Mondrian was not, however, entirely new. In *De nieuwe Beweging in de Schilderkunst* (1917) van Doesburg had written that

> It stands to reason, that the new principle in painting will not remain valid for ever. When everything has been expressed on the level which painting as a plastic art has now attached, new aesthetic possibilities will proceed from it.
> (*De nieuwe Beweging in de Schilderkunst*, p. 54; translated in Jaffé, 1956, p. 148.)

In the conflict between van Doesburg and Mondrian over Elementarism there is a remarkable set-piece battle between two very different temperaments: the tortoise and the hare, if you like; the one a restless experimenter, the other a patient researcher. But like the fable, it was the tortoise who travelled farthest.

Mondrian's Mature Style

(See Hamilton, pp. 326–31.)

Although van Doesburg's abstract Neo-Plastic paintings had laid the basis for *De Stijl*, his energies had been dissipated in trying to realize *De Stijl* in all aspects of life and the creative arts. Meanwhile in Paris at his studio 26 rue de Départ, Mondrian had been left alone—isolated, almost, after the break of 1925—working quietly and undemonstratively until his arrival in London in 1938. The period of 1925 to 1938 was, for Mondrian, one of undisturbed dedication to the ideals of Neo-Plasticism. Of its ideals and purpose he would brook no deviation. After the innovation of Elementarism he had written to van Doesburg saying

> After your high-handed improvement (?) of Neo-Plasticism any co-operation is quite impossible for me. For the rest, *sans rancune*.
> (Stedelijk Museum, 1951, p. 72.)

By 1927 Mondrian had developed five Neo-Plastic laws:

> 1 The plastic means must be the plane or the rectangular prism in primary colours (red, blue, yellow) and non-colour (white, black, grey). In architecture, empty space acts as non-colour and volume acts as colour.
> 2 The equivalence of the plastic means is necessary. Although differing in dimension and colour, they must nevertheless have the same value. Equilibrium generally requires a large area of non-colour and a similar area of colour or volume.
> 3 The duality of opposition in the plastic means is equally required in the composition.
> 4 Constant equilibrium is achieved through the relationship of position and is expressed by the straight line (the limit of the plastic means) in its principal opposition.
> 5 Equilibrium neutralises and annihilates the plastic means and is achieved through the relationships of proportion in which they are placed and which creates the living rhythm.
> (*De Stijl*, anniversary number, 1927, pp. 37–38; translated in Jaffé, 1970, p. 226.)

The five Neo-Plastic laws find their complete expression in 'classic'—the word is by no means inappropriate —Mondrian pictures like the *Composition with Red, Yellow and Blue* of 1930 (Fig. 53).

Yet despite the grandiloquence of this magisterial painterly statement of cool purity there is inherent in every picture of Mondrian's mature style a curious anomaly. In reproduction a picture like this of, say, 1930 looks serene, composed, balanced, even in texture and, one imagines, immutable. Yet, on close first-hand inspection the squares can be seen to have been painted in a quite vigorous impasto and the black grid lines, far from having a machine-like finish, overlap each other with a discernible painterly relief.

Exercise

Can you suggest any reason for such an apparent lapse between Mondrian's theory and practice?

Discussion

It is possible that Mondrian felt that, in an art so severely structured, a certain sign of the individual human presence was necessary. Otherwise, it is conceivable that, like

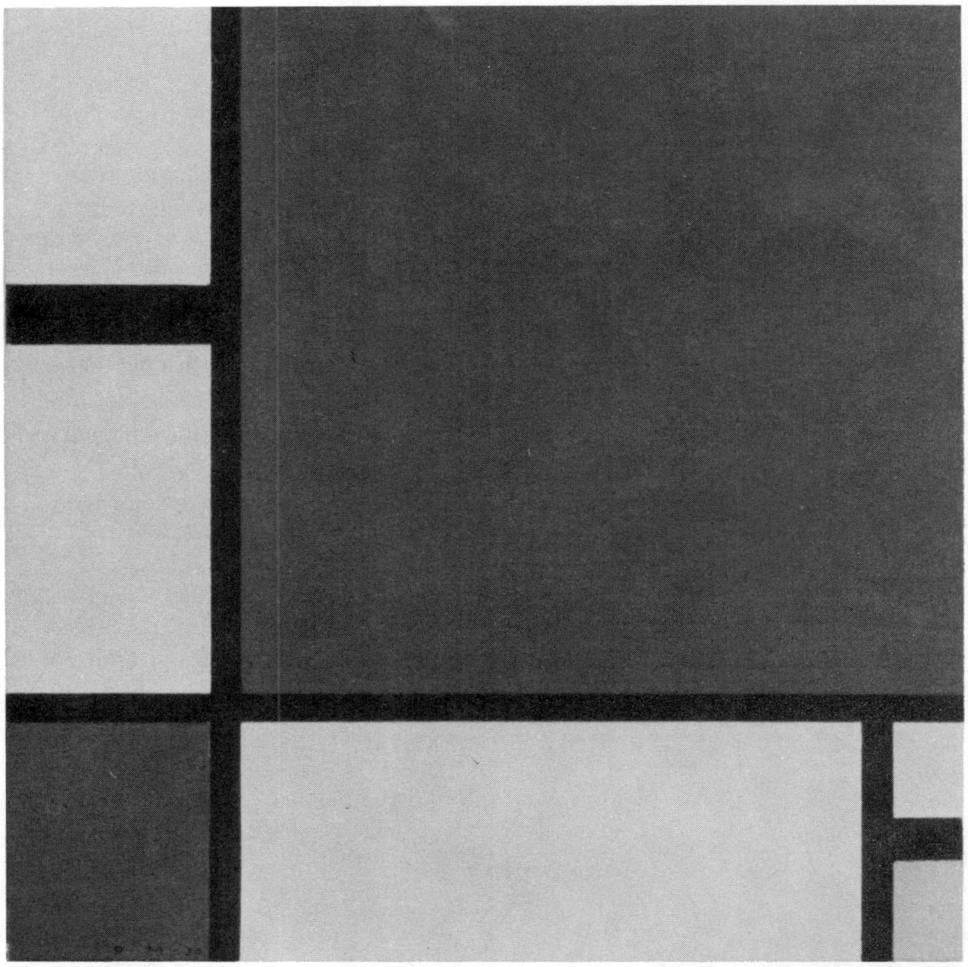

Figure 53 Piet Mondrian, *Composition with Red, Yellow and Blue*, 1930, oil, 18 × 18 ins (Collection Alfred Roth, Zurich, courtesy Mr Holtzman).

the Constructivists, he might have employed mechanical techniques to reduce the human touch almost to zero. By using rules and masking tape, or using spray paint to guarantee a uniformity of line and plane surface, for example, and by abandoning canvas itself with its texture and inescapable connotations, he might have produced an almost totally impersonal object or work of design. It is hard to believe that with the thought and care he characteristically gave to his work, he might merely have been carried along by the force of convention in his choice of materials and techniques. However much Mondrian might have maligned the infatuation of artists with self-expression, it was not the impersonal art of the machine he was concerned with, but, instead, the impersonal art of the humanist merging his individualism with a larger universal spirit.

De Stijl and Architecture

It was Theo van Doesburg's aim that *De Stijl* should penetrate all creative activities and it was only natural that architecture, like painting, should become part of its method. Architecture can be seen to operate on two levels in *De Stijl.*

The first level is a superficial one: a number of writers have made comparisons between abstract-constructivist pictures, such as van Doesburg's own *Composition VIII: The Cow* (Plate 13), the final picture of a series which began with a photograph of a cow, and the International Style in architecture. In 'design' terms, the picture deals with problems familiar to architects: to create the effect of equilibrium from an asymmetric arrangement of lines and masses. The second level is a more fundamental one and is concerned with the problem of time as a fourth dimension which had so perplexed early twentieth-century thinkers. Architecture, with its interpenetration of volume, mass and line, must have seemed to van Doesburg a perfect vehicle for expressing time and change.

One of van Doesburg's first exercises after founding *De Stijl* was to design a tiled floor (Fig. 54) for the house of a friend. At the same time, he was also working on an

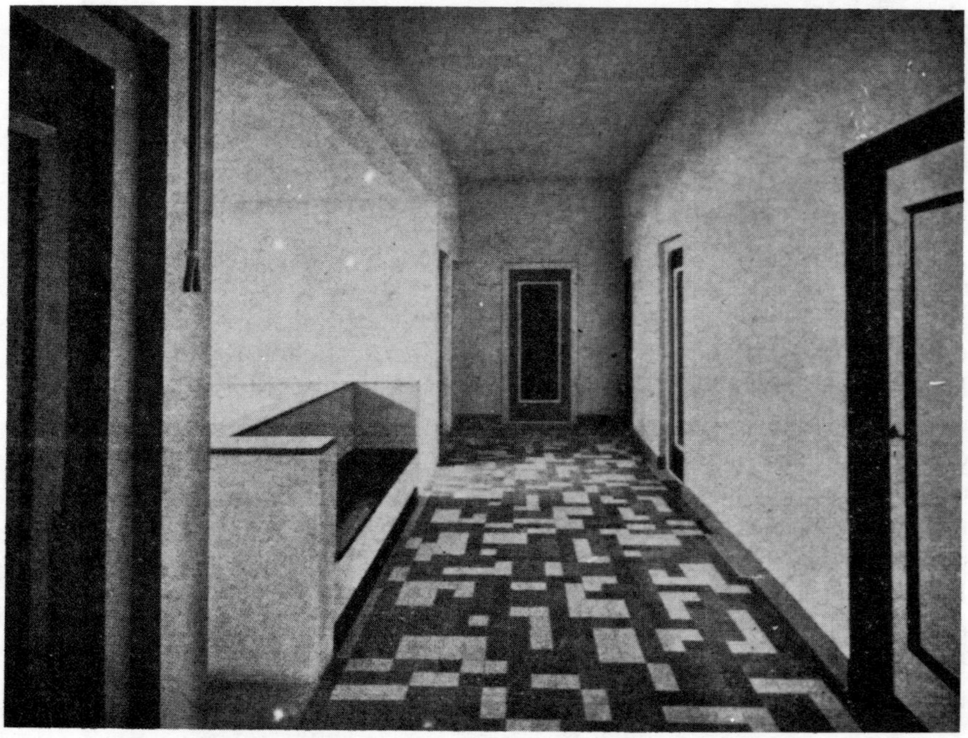

Figure 54 Theo van Doesburg, Tiled floor in the Bart van der Ligt house, Noordwijkerhout, 1918 (*De Stijl*, Volume I, 1, 1918, courtesy Uitgeverij van Gennep).

architectural mosaic and acting as a consultant to the architect, J. J. P. Oud, on colour schemes. After leaving Germany in 1923 van Doesburg had the opportunity to put into practice some of his architectural ideas when he was invited to exhibit at the Galerie de l'Éffort Moderne in Paris. Here he showed designs for a home for the gallery owner Léonce Rosenberg, for a private house, for a studio house and for a spectacular octagonal university hall. In fact, the home for Rosenberg was designed entirely by the architect, Cor van Eesteren. Van Doesburg collaborated with van Eesteren on the design of the second Paris model (Fig. 55). The house was architecturally impossible: the cantilevering defied conventional mechanics, but in his architecture that was what van Doesburg wanted: to defy gravity was to approach a realization of the fourth dimension.

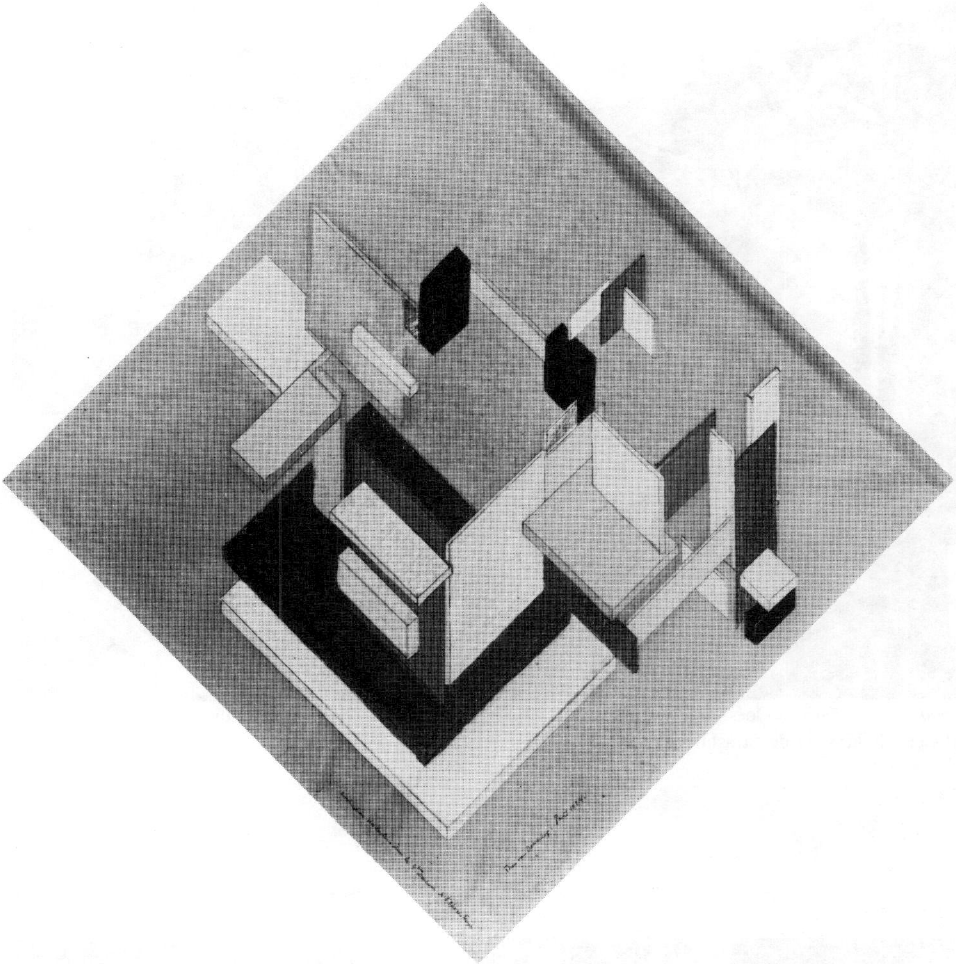

Figure 55 Theo van Doesburg, *Colour Construction in the Fourth Dimension of Space-Time, Axonometric of the Private House 1923*, Paris 1924, gouache on tracing paper, 16 × 16 ins (Stedelijk Museum, Amsterdam).

Van Doesburg's major architectural commission came in 1926 when he was invited to modify the interior of an eighteenth-century restaurant in Strasbourg called L'Aubette. The two years which the work occupied him were filled with activity: in nearly two hundred drawings van Doesburg explored the *minutiae* of the scheme, even down to the designs of ashtrays. L'Aubette was his opportunity to exercise his ideas on Elementarism in an architectural setting, and when a whole issue of *De Stijl* was devoted to L'Aubette in 1928 it included an essay entitled 'Elementarisme et son origine'. Van Doesburg's drawings for the interior show that he intended his work on L'Aubette to express fully the role of colour in architecture, because in the same way that, in van Doesburg's theory, dynamism would introduce into painting the idea of the fourth dimension, so would colour in architecture.

In two of the major rooms of L'Aubette van Doesburg experimented with the different effects of Neo-Plasticism and Elementarism applied to architecture. In the cinema and dance hall (Fig. 56) Elementarist requirements have left the planes in high relief so that there was an effect of painting *becoming* architecture. On the other hand, in the Festivity Hall (Fig. 57) van Doesburg used a more Neo-Plasticist design, with the planes depressed, to emphasise immutability. Unfortunately, these decorative designs have been destroyed. Just after the Second World War L'Aubette was remodelled again to conform to contemporary taste.

Van Doesburg's last architectural project was the studio Meudon-Val-Fleury, near Paris, which he had intended to make the new centre of Elementarist activity (Fig. 58). The house was intended for his own occupation and, despite Le Corbusier having insulted *De Stijl* a few years before, it shows much of his influence. The house was

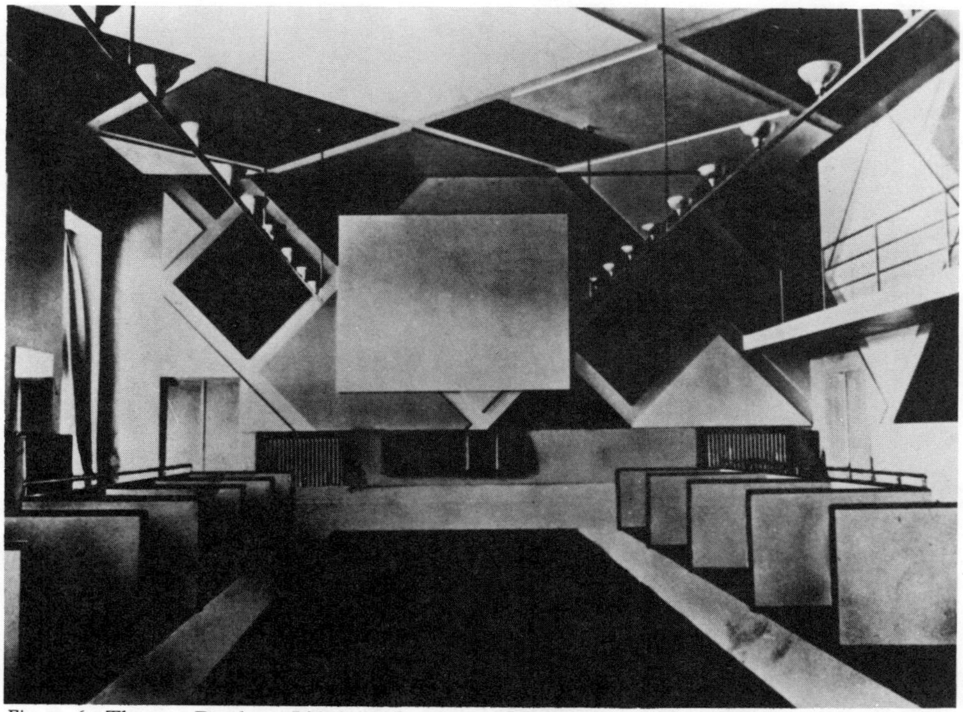

Figure 56 Theo van Doesburg, L'Aubette, Strasbourg, cinema and dance hall, 1926–28 (destroyed; photo: Musées de la Ville de Strasbourg).

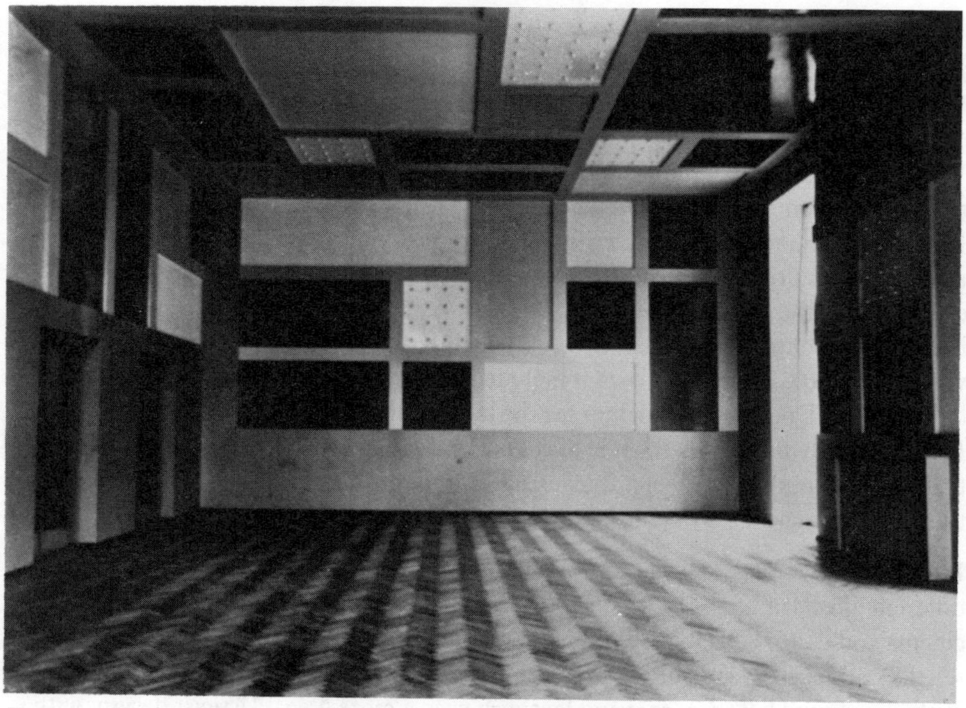

Figure 57 Theo van Doesburg, L'Aubette, Strasbourg, Festivity Hall, 1926–28 (destroyed; photo: Musées de la Ville de Strasbourg).

hardly lived in by van Doesburg. He died in March 1931. He had moved the centre of *De Stijl*'s operations away from Holland and, without him, the movement and the magazine lost momentum. The last issue of *De Stijl* to appear was a memorial volume dedicated to its founder.

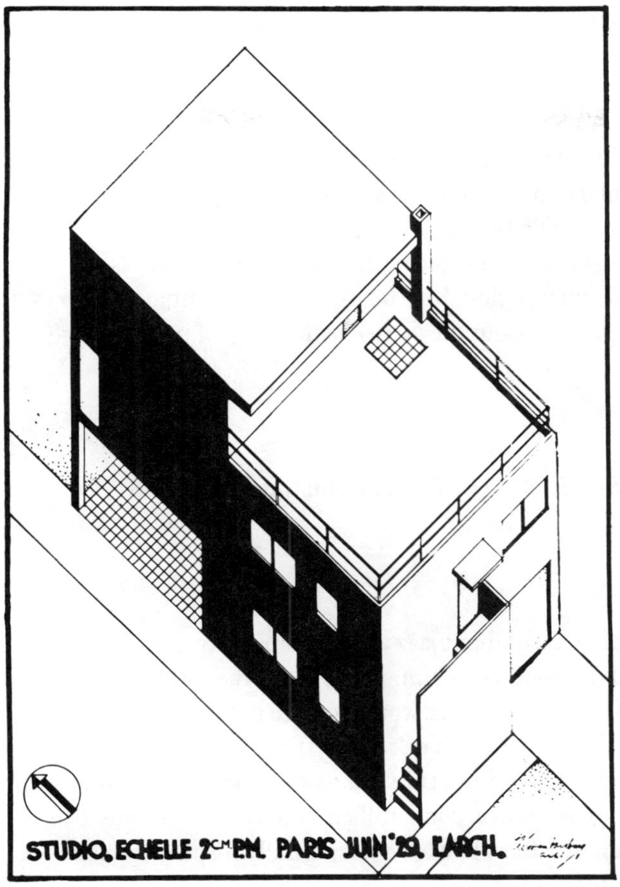

Figure 58 Theo van Doesburg, Studio House, Axonometric project (*De Stijl*, last issue 1932, courtesy Uitgeverij van Gennep).

Mondrian's Late Development

After a brief period in London, Piet Mondrian moved to the United States. His New York works suggest an extraordinary change of character. He was seventy when he painted his *Broadway Boogie-Woogie* (Plate 14). Like everything else in his career, this painting was an advance over what had preceded it. The composition is as restless as his immediately post-Cubist period, but the riot of colour employed shows that Mondrian was no longer dogmatic about the Neo-Plasticist use of primary colours.

Exercise

Look at Mondrian's *Broadway Boogie-Woogie*. What do you think might have suggested this picture to him?

Discussion

We know that Mondrian was enthusiastic about jazz and perhaps it was, as the title suggests, music which suggested this picture to him. However, if the right angle is still a persistent theme reminding us of his earlier work, is there not in the dynamism of this picture a reference to the vitality of New York City? If this is so, and if *Broadway Boogie-Woogie* is an almost literal interpretation of the skyscrapers and streets of Manhattan, then does not the wheel come full circle and suggest to us also that Mondrian's early pictures might, after all, have been partially inspired by the order and serenity of the Dutch landscape?

Postscript

De Stijl was over when van Doesburg died, even if Mondrian did continue his own painting. We value *De Stijl* today because of its prominence among those movements which sought to expand and redefine art. But the moment was not right for them: 'The old culture', van Doesburg had written

> ... of Jean-Jacques Rousseau, the culture of the heart, the uncultured culture of a petit-bourgeois intelligentsia and its hairy apostles, Morris and Ruskin; the concentric culture, the culture of 'I' and 'mine' is not yet completely a corpse. (*De Stijl*, Volume II, p. 103; translated in Jaffé, 1956, p. 150.)

De Stijl had been looking for order after confusion and a heaven on earth after the promise of too many utopias. Theo van Doesburg and his colleagues had wanted to rediscover the foundations of art in order to build upon them a new edifice owing nothing to the past, but their's was a utopia too.

Notes

1 '*De Stijl*' is, simply, the Dutch expression for 'The Style'.

2 The Dutch have a proverb which says 'God made the earth, but the Dutch made Holland'.

3 Schoenemaekers' *Het nieuwe wereldbeeld* (*The New Image of the World*) was published at Bossum in 1915, and his next book, *Beginselen der beeldenden wiskunde* (*Principles of Plastic Mathematics*), was published there a year later.

4 In any discussion of *De Stijl* there is always the problem of taxonomy—*De Stijl* was the name given by van Doesburg to his magazine and the group which revolved around it from 1917–31. The name derives from the usage given the word *style* by the Dutch architect, H. P. Berlage, whose *Gedanken über stil* (*Thoughts on Style*) had acquired its own title from the influence of Gottfried Semper's *Der Stil in den technischen Künsten* (*Style in Technical Art*). Although van Doesburg had used the Dutch version of the term 'Neo-Plasticism' in his 1919 publication, *Three Lectures on the New Plastic Art*, it was Mondrian who used the term first in 'De Nieuwe Beeldung in de Schilder Kunst' which appeared in the first issue of *De Stijl* in October 1917. The term 'Neo-Plasticism' was coined by Mondrian in his French publication *Le Néo-Plasticisme* of 1920. Both van Doesburg and Mondrian used the German version, *Neue Gestaltung*, in their respective Bauhaus books, *Grundbegriffe der neuen gestaltenden Kunst* (*Principles of Neo-Plastic Art*) and *Neue Gestaltung* (*Neo-Plasticism*).

5 Throughout the publication of *De Stijl*, the authority of, for instance, Aristotle and Plotinus is also cited to support aesthetic opinions.

6 It was after van Doesburg had the temerity to paint abstract rectilinear forms *diagonally* that Mondrian left *De Stijl*.

7 In their own terminology, the 'brown' world of sentimental late Cubism was to be replaced by a 'white' world which drew inspiration from the examples of Cézanne and Van Gogh.

8 It is worth noting that the dates of *De Stijl*, from 1917 to 1931, correspond almost exactly to the period which spans that spectacular period of European history from the October Revolution to the burning of the Reichstag.

9 Van Gogh also had a school of his own, which included the painters Jan Sluijters, Kees van Dongen and Leo Gestel.

10 The family name was 'Mondriaan', but the painter dropped the second 'a' from his name in Paris in 1919–20. Most paintings are signed with the initials P. M. but from 1913 some pictures are signed 'Mondrian'.

11 There is little to read on Toorop, except J. B. Knipping's 'Jan Toorop' in *Palet-Serie, een reeks monografieën over Hoolandse en Vlaamse Schilders* (*c.* 1948). See also, for a brief account, Schmutzler, 1964, and Hamilton, p. 132.

12 A journal whose title means 'unity', reflecting Berlage's familiar dictum that harmony is '*eenheid in veelheid*' ('unity in plurality').

13 This was similar in intention to the Futurist ethic.

14 Van Doesburg's 'Introduction to Volume II of *De Stijl*' is translated in Chipp, pp. 324–25.

15 This was later to become Mondrian's *Bauhausbuch*, *Neue Gestaltung* (1925).

16 Such as Laszlo Moholy-Nagy whose 'Constructivism and the Proletariat' was published in *Ma* in May 1922.

17 The whole of the double issue of *De Stijl*, 10/11, 1923, was devoted to the work of El Lissitsky.

18 Wölfflin's book is available in English translation as *Principles of Art History*, George Bell, 1932.

19 *De Stijl*, Aubette issue, Volume XV, 87–89, pp. 20–25; translated in Baljeu, 1974, p. 171.

20 *De Stijl*,van Doesburg issue, January 1932, pp. 17–19; translated in Baljeu, 1974, p. 184.

References and Recommended Reading

The following books should be readily available in most good libraries and provide further discussion and references concerning issues raised in this unit:

Baljeu, J. (1974) *Theo van Doesburg*, Studio Vista.
A well informed monograph (with a number of minor inaccuracies) but rather unimaginatively compiled and tedious to consult.

Banham, R. (1960 and subsequent editions) *Theory and Design in the First Machine Age*, The Architectural Press.
A book of fundamental importance, dealing with the interrelation of painting and architecture in the first decades of the century.

Elgar, F. (1968) *Piet Mondrian*, Thames and Hudson.
Rather a poor book.

Jaffé, H. L. C. (1970) *De Stijl*, Thames and Hudson.
A useful collection of translated documents with an introductory essay.

Overy, P. (1969) *De Stijl*, Studio Vista.
A compact survey of *De Stijl* influences in painting, architecture and sculpture.

The following group of books are more difficult and will also present some difficulties in location. It is by no means necessary to consult them, but they are included here to provide sources for detailed references in this unit:

Bonset, I. K. (1975) *Nieuwe Woordbeeldingen, De gedichten van Theo van Doesburg* (*New Word Pictures, The Poetry of Theo van Doesburg*), edited by K. Schippers, Querido, Amsterdam (in Dutch).

De Stijl (complete reprint 1968) edited by Ad. Petersen, in three volumes, Athenaeum, Amsterdam.

Feltkamp, W. C. (?1955) *Bart Antonij van der Leck: Leven en Werken* (*Bart van der Leck: Life and Work*), Leiden (in Dutch).

Jaffé, H. L. C. (1956) *De Stijl 1917–1931, The Dutch Contribution to Modern Art*, J. M. Meulenhoff, Amsterdam (in English).
A masterly study, the most thorough treatment of *De Stijl* there is; unlikely to be superseded.

Ness, J. L. (ed.) (1975) *Lyonel Feininger*, Allen Lane.

Stedelijk Museum (1951) *De Stijl*, exhibition catalogue, Stedelijk Museum, Amsterdam.
The most complete exhibition catalogue and a valuable source of documentary information.

Stedelijk Museum (1963) *150 jaar Nederlandse Kunst: Schilderjen, beelden, tekenningen grafiek, 1813–1963*, Stedelijk Museum, Amsterdam (in Dutch).
The only survey of nineteenth and twentieth-century Dutch art. Very well illustrated.

Utrecht Central Museum (1972) *Het nieuwe wereldbeeld: het begin van de abstrakte kunst in Nederland 1910–1925*, exhibition catalogue, Utrecht Central Museum (in Dutch).

Unit 12 Artists of the Bauhaus

Introduction to Unit 12 115

Part I *Weimar—The Emergence of the Artists from a Background of Art Nouveau and Expressionism* 116

Art in Germany before the Founding of the Bauhaus 116

Lyonel Feininger and the Foundation of the Bauhaus 117

Johannes Itten 124

Oskar Schlemmer 129

The Bauhaus Exhibition of 1923 131

Part II *Dessau* 132

Mysticism: Klee and Kandinsky 132

Technocracy: Moholy-Nagy 138

Bauhausbücher—The Art Theory of the Bauhaus 142

Part III *Berlin and After* 151

Conclusion: Art in Political Eclipse 153

Introduction to Unit 12

(See Hamilton, pp. 331–33.)

'The Bauhaus' said its last director, the architect, Mies van der Rohe, 'was an idea'.[1] The idea was given form by another architect, Walter Gropius, who, deriving influence from both the practicality of his predecessor at Weimar, Henry van de Velde, and from the heady, emotional spirit of post-war Germany, created, first of all, the Staatliches Bauhaus in Weimar and then the famous Bauhaus which he designed and built in Dessau, 1925–26. After the closure of the Berlin Bauhaus by the Nazis in 1933, the idea was carried to the United States by Laszlo Moholy-Nagy where a New Bauhaus was founded in Chicago and, changing its name to the Chicago Institute of Design, still exists today.

What Mies meant when he said that the Bauhaus was an idea was that, despite the fame of the Dessau building and of the painters who worked there, the spirit of the enterprise transcended any temporal or physical limits. The Bauhaus was not, in his view, so much the vehicle upon which the new art and design rode into the century, but a unique synthesis of ideas aimed at achieving a new unity and direction in the visual arts, and by these means to change society as well.

To his Bauhaus Gropius managed to attract a distinguished group of painters to serve as members of staff. Although exponents of a traditional genre, the artists of the Bauhaus made fundamental contributions to the development and reputation of the institution. Some showed more enthusiasm than others for the Bauhaus ideal, but to all who worked there the years at the Bauhaus formed the central part of their careers.

PART I *Weimar—The Emergence of the Artists from a Background of Art Nouveau and Expressionism*

Art in Germany before the Founding of the Bauhaus

Immediately after the war Gropius had been involved in the radical utopian Expressionist movements, the *Novembergrüppe* ('November Group') and the *Arbeitsrat für Kunst* ('Workers' Council for Art'). He brought with him to the Bauhaus much of the inheritance from these groups. However, despite their part in the creation of the Bauhaus, you should not assume that the avant garde, which historians tend to emphasize, was the sole front on which art was active, for in Germany more than any other country in Europe, the federal nature of the nation produced a scope and diversity of artistic activity unequalled elsewhere. The foundation of the Bauhaus in 1919 was just one manifestation of a nervous national activity in the arts and it would be false to suggest that the Bauhaus of 1919 represented a more respected or more successful movement at that time than its now more obscure rivals.

Berlin, always a cosmopolitan city, became around 1920 the centre of much avant-garde experimentation in the arts. In 1910 the serious concern felt for the arts was characterized by the foundation of the *Sturm* publishing house and journal by the entrepreneurial Herwarth Walden.[2] These were followed by the opening in 1912 of Walden's *Sturm* gallery. As his chosen title for his enterprises suggests, Walden's interests were at first affected by the concerns of Expressionism, but this was not to prevent him later broadening his scope to embrace constructivism as well: indeed, *Der Sturm* was among the first journals to publish the work of Moholy-Nagy.

However, not all artistic activity in Germany was so advanced. One has only to recall Hamilton's anecdote regarding the Kaiser's dismissal of Hugo von Tschudi, the director of the Berlin Museum, on the basis that he bought too many French paintings, to realize that, even as late as 1908, while the battle for the acceptance of Impressionism had long since been fought and won elsewhere, its result was not certain all over Germany where in many places, conventional bourgeois taste was still supreme.[3]

Concerning another avenue of art, Hamilton also stresses the influence in Germany of the materialistic aesthetics which began with Gottfried Semper, but were most influential in the work of the aestheticians Conrad Fiedler and Theodor Lipps and the art historian Heinrich Wölfflin. These men provided the theoretical justification for the acceptance of an art which did not rely on literary content. Fiedler had advanced the theory of 'pure visibility', the idea that art begins where the literary content of a painting ends and is dependent on form. As an art historian Wölfflin had, particularly in his book *Klassische Kunst* (*Classic Art*), applied similar principles to the art of the Renaissance. These ideas were influential in speeding the acceptance of non-objective art in Germany, for if painting devoted purely to visual sensations, such as Impressionism, could be justified by theory then the basis for a new art was established.

Yet it was on the basis provided by Expressionism that the achievements of the Bauhaus painters were built: in that quintessentially Expressionist organization, the *Arbeitsrat für Kunst*, Gropius had known artists such as Erick Heckel, Karl Schmidt-Rottluff, Gerhard Marcks and Lyonel Feininger. Gropius knew what he wanted at the Bauhaus, his aims of reforming the art school curriculum, basing education on craftsmanship and synthesizing the arts were all developed from the declared objectives of the *Arbeitsrat*, in which he had been a crucial figure, and when Gropius came to decide who was to help him create the Bauhaus he chose members of the *Arbeitsrat* as well: the first was the American-born painter Lyonel Feininger.

Lyonel Feininger and the Foundation of the Bauhaus

Walter Gropius invited Lyonel Feininger to Weimar in 1919; he was the first painter to be hired by the Bauhaus. Feininger was followed by Johannes Itten in the same year, Georg Muche, Itten's disciple, in 1920, Paul Klee and Oskar Schlemmer in 1921, Wassily Kandinsky in 1922 and Laszlo Moholy-Nagy in 1923. Gropius was evidently in no great hurry to employ painters in Weimar: the last vacant post was only filled in 1922 with the arrival of Kandinsky, but Gropius's plans might have been delayed by the presence of staff he inherited at Weimar.

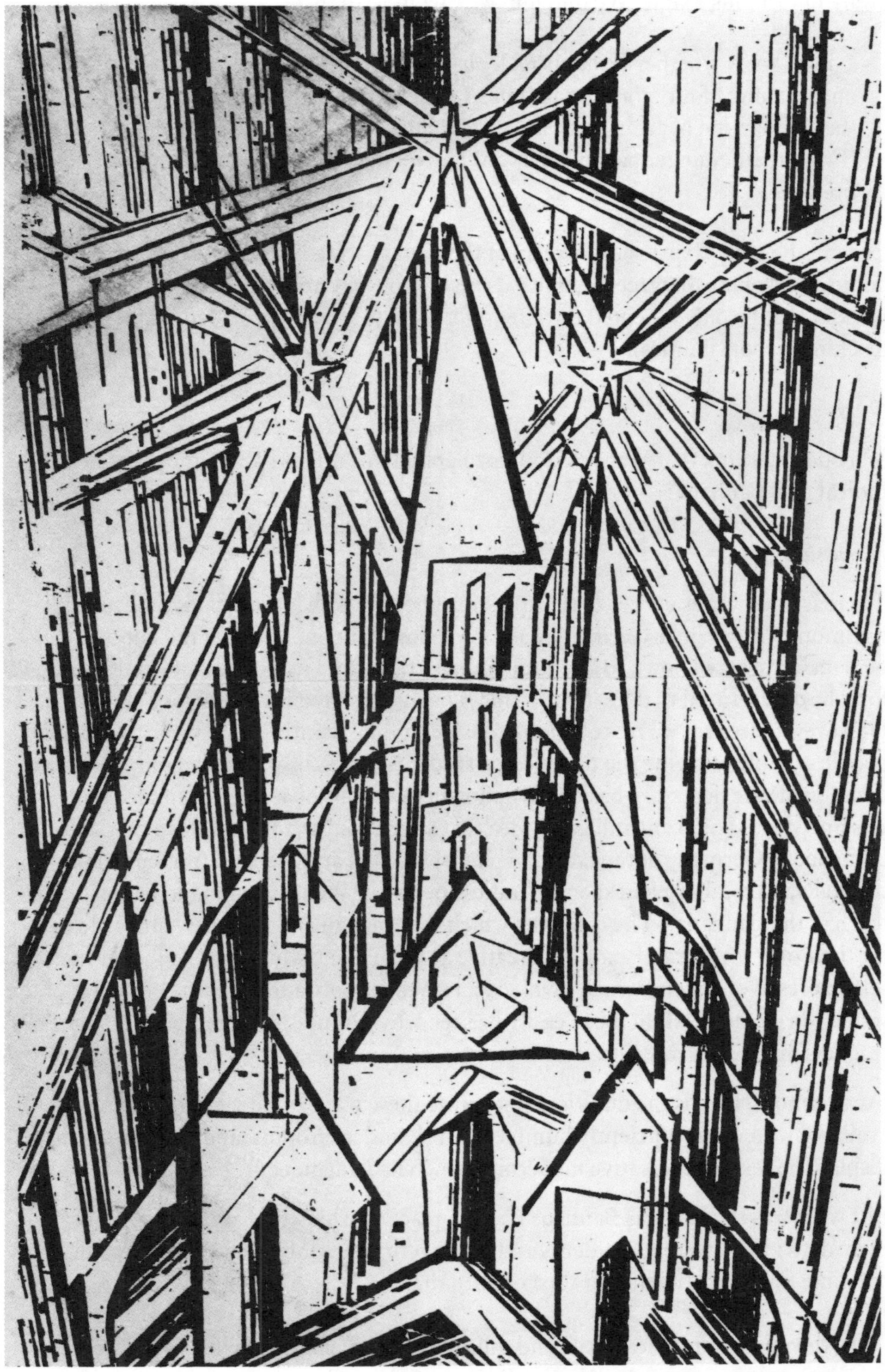

Figure 59 Lyonel Feininger, *Cathedral*, 1919, wood engraving for cover of the Bauhaus Manifesto (Bauhaus Archiv, Berlin © ADAGP Paris 1976 © Cosmopress, Genève).

The specific character of Feininger's work is discussed later in this section, but first I want to establish the character of the Bauhaus itself on its foundation.

First of all, there was the conflict between Gropius's declared intention, born out of the vision of the *Arbeitsrat für Kunst*, to create a unity in the arts, and the fact that he appeared—both explicitly and implicitly—to be quite willing to tolerate fine artists at the Bauhaus and allow them to treat it almost as an old-fashioned art academy. Perhaps Gropius only regarded artists as useful so long as they were men of vision; if so, then Lyonel Feininger would hardly have qualified. Throughout his presence at the Bauhaus, which in his case more than anybody else's besides Itten's was anomalous, Feininger appears to have missed the point entirely and to have been only peripherally aware of Gropius's aims. We find him writing in 1919 that:

> I don't know whether Gropius really has any contact with a deeper, spiritual art in our meaning of the word. Sometimes I almost think his efforts are directed toward the subjugation of art in the service of architecture.
> (From the Feininger papers, Harvard University; cited in Franciscono, 1971, pp. 170–71.)

Even in the early Expressionist years of the Bauhaus, Feininger found the technocratic atmosphere disagreeable and was insensitive to Gropius's larger design. It is no wonder that he only accepted the later offer to go to Dessau provided that it carried no teaching responsibilities.

Question

Why do you think that Walter Gropius tolerated fine artists like Feininger at his radical new Bauhaus?

Discussion

There is one simple answer to this question and that is that the artistic and cultural community in Weimar Germany was a very close-knit one; most of the famous personalities were known to a central figure like Walter Gropius and it would, therefore, be only natural that he invite to his Bauhaus talented men of his acquaintance. However, there are two more serious considerations: painters were perhaps the only people capable of giving the uneducated students (many of whom had only just been demobbed) the necessary basic instruction in questions of aesthetics and formal design. More significant still is the idea that after about 1920 there was a marked influence in Germany of the radical new art of Russia and Holland (remember, Unit 11, that van Doesburg had spent a fruitless period in Weimar hoping to be invited to teach at the Bauhaus). The concerns which the Russian and Dutch avant garde took for their own involved placing the creative artist in a role which was no longer merely self-expressive, but one which involved an investigation into the basic grammar of the visual world. In this light it can easily be seen why Gropius favoured painters as teachers in the Bauhaus.

Furthermore there is the question of whether there were architects and designers available who were sufficiently humble to work under Gropius, and at the same time, display the aesthetic–creative modernity which he demanded.

But what was the Weimar Bauhaus like as a place in which to live and work in its early days? Who were its students and what were their ambitions? Alfred Arndt, a one time Bauhaus student, recalled of 1919 that:

> In the midst of political strife and unimaginable economic plight, young people, mostly men, came to the Weimar Bauhaus. The majority wore soldiers' uniforms which the girls made look 'civilian' by dyeing them and removing the collars.

> Many came from the 'Wandervogel' movement, wore long hair which to everyone's amusement, they had cut off later at a Bauhaus dance.
>
> Usually a pot was put over the person's head and the hair cut off around it. Some had their hair shaven off completely. The baldness stimulated ideas, such as painting one's shaven head with black squares for a party.
>
> . . . for practical reasons, most of them had Russian-type smocks and carpenter's pants . . . there was still a type of uniform worn by the 'mazdaznaners': pants that were wide at the top and narrow at the bottom, a jacket with a belt and narrow, 3-centimetre high collars . . . the mazdaznaners . . . ate much garlic and gargled often.
> (Alfred Arndt in Neumann, 1970, p. 311.)

When Arndt took over the studio which had belonged at one time to a student adherent of the Mazdaznan cult (see p. 126), he found a straw pallet on the floor and a blue painted circle on the wall five feet in diameter. To the Mazdaznaners, the circle served as an aid to concentration; the significance or function of the straw pallet was not explained.

Arndt's graphic description, even if it only concerns people and not art, gives us an idea of why one modern historian has written that 'Expressionism, though it protested strongly against academies, had one of its own—the Bauhaus in Weimar' (Pehnt, 1973, p. 107). Yet life in the early days of the Bauhaus was not all that colourful: for the first public viewing in 1919 Gropius had to borrow pictures from resident Weimar artists like Robert Michel, Johannes Molzahn, Ella Bergman and Karl Peter Röhl to liven up the bare walls! Gropius had, at first, even been obliged to take over some of the older, conservative teachers such as Walter Klemm, Richard Engelmann and Max Thedy. These masters' works were of a traditional academic character: a caricature of the sterility in art which the Bauhaus painters were determined to oppose (Fig. 60). Thus Lyonel Feininger's stay at the Bauhaus began in an atmosphere of

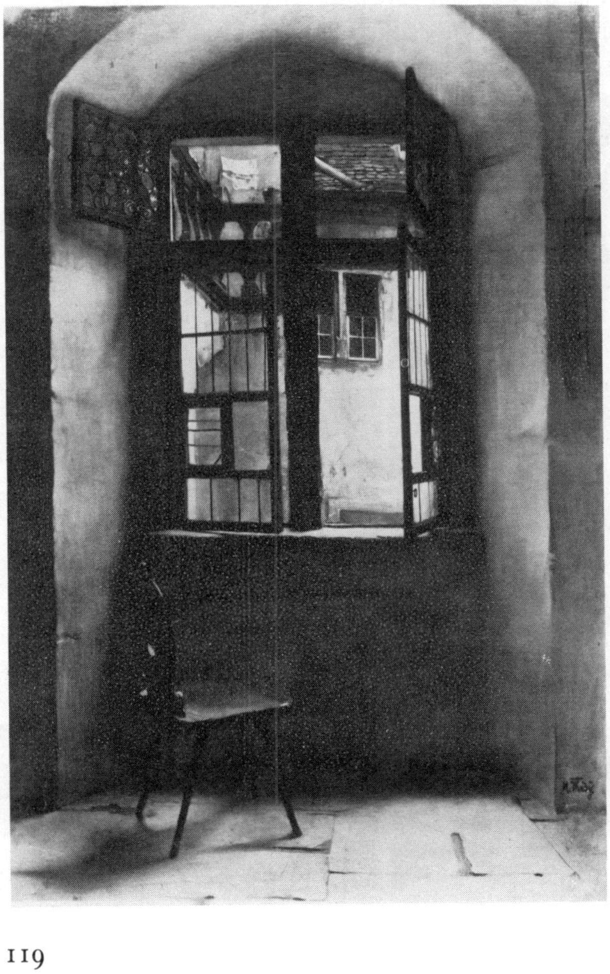

Figure 60 Max Thedy, *Interior Study*, watercolour, $39\frac{1}{4} \times 27\frac{1}{8}$ ins (Museum der Bildenden Kunst, Leipzig; photo: Deutsche Fototek Dresden).

confused purpose, exuberant excess and austerity. An independent master, his work was hardly at all affected by external conditions.

LYONEL FEININGER
(See Hamilton, p. 334.)

Feininger's first interest had not been painting, but music; he was himself a fine violinist and the influence of the discipline of that art was consistently present throughout his career. He began his career in the visual arts as a successful cartoonist for publications like *Humoristische Blätter*, *Ulk* and *Lustige Blätter*, only slowly coming round to the idea of taking painting seriously; like Kandinsky, he was no longer very young when he created his first significant oil painting, a picture of a china monkey, painted in Paris in 1907 when he was thirty-six. It was the experience of Paris, and subsequently the impression of seeing the paintings of Turner in London —Feininger visited England in 1908—which were the influential forces on the development of his personal style.

The critical year was 1913 when, having synthesized the experiences of Paris and London and wedded them to his own technique which he had developed as a cartoonist, Feininger was introduced, through the intervention of Franz Marc, to the circle of Herwarth Walden and of progressive art in Germany. In the same year Feininger began his series of paintings of the villages around Weimar, where he had been living since 1911, and whose names—Neppermin, Gelmeroda, Gaberndorf, Zirchow—his paintings have made famous. Throughout his career in Germany Feininger, to use a musical analogy, exposed, developed and recapitulated the images which these villages gave him.

Feininger's mature style, seen in a picture like the *Barfüsserkirch in Erfurt I* of 1924 (Plate 15), is among the most readily recognizable in all modern European art. With few exceptions Feininger's themes, like those of his heroes, J. M. W. Turner and Caspar David Friedrich, are landscapes, seascapes or architectural settings.[4] Look at his *Clouds over the Sea* of 1923 (Fig. 61) and compare it to Friedrich's *Monk on the Sea Shore* (see Unit 1, Plate 1), and you can see a community of spirit and intention between the nineteenth-century Romantic and the Bauhaus master. Feininger's

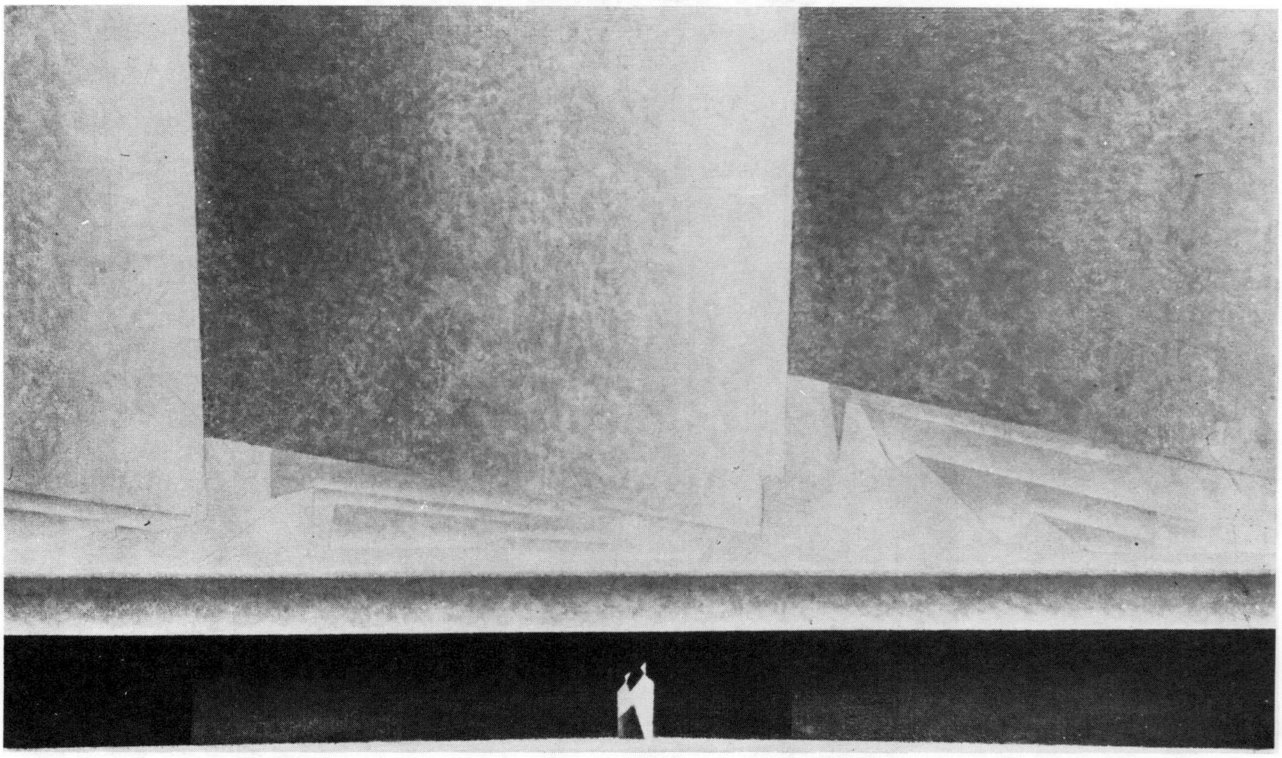

Figure 61 Lyonel Feininger, *Clouds over the Sea*, 1923, oil, $14\frac{1}{8} \times 23\frac{1}{2}$ ins (Altonauer Museum, Hamburg © ADAGP Paris 1976 © Cosmopress, Genève).

mystical approach to the simple scene—which must have impressed the visionary side of Gropius—was enhanced by his careful, meditative system of composition and creation.

Feininger's works owe something to both Expressionism and Cubism. Certainly, he was aware of the metaphysical content of Expressionism, but Cubism was the more significant influence and the label by which he came to be known. In Paris in 1911 he had declared with enthusiasm that in Cubism he had seen the light, but in Weimar in 1919 this discovery was his damnation: righteous horror was expressed in a letter from von Fritsch to Wilhelm von Bode that Gropius could appoint so devilish a painter as the *Cubist* Feininger, for, if Impressionism had not been acceptable in Berlin in 1908, then, in 1919, Cubism was certainly not welcome in the more conservative Weimar (Wingler, 1969, p. 33).

Indeed, although Feininger's Weimar years were blighted by poverty and the overt antagonism of most of the Weimar population (in May 1919 some politicians in the *Landtag* had published a brochure called 'Bolsheviks in Art' aimed directly at the Bauhaus; after this Gropius discouraged political activity among his staff), nothing could fundamentally disturb his dedication to the careful processes which comprised the preparation of one of his pictures.

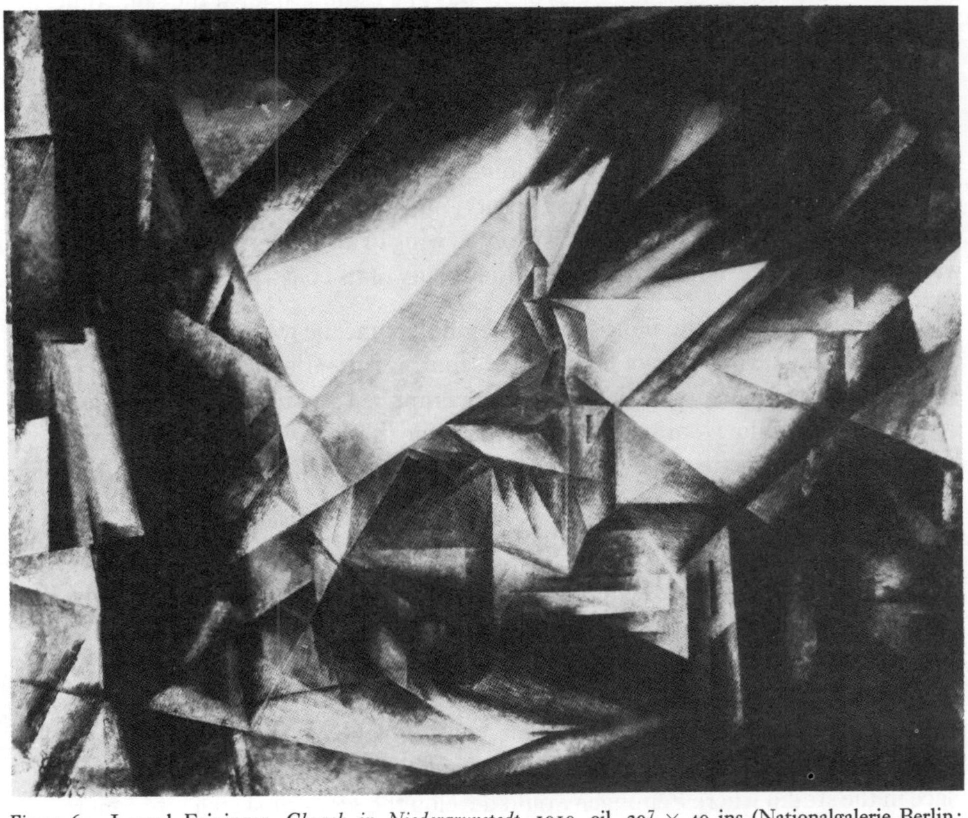

Figure 62 Lyonel Feininger, *Church in Niedergrunstedt*, 1919, oil, $39\frac{7}{8} \times 49$ ins (Nationalgalerie Berlin; photo: Bildarchiv Preussischer Kulturbesitz © ADAGP Paris 1976 © Cosmopress, Genève).

Look at Figure 62, Feininger's painting of the church in Niedergrunstedt. In a letter to his wife of September, 1919, the artist has left us a valuable insight into the process of accretion and experimentation which culminated in the finished picture:

> Yesterday and today I worked with intensity at Niedergrunstedt. Yet in the end it struck me as clumsy and ignoble. Therefore, with my well-known determination to get to bed-rock I washed off the entire thing and reconstructed it completely. Still not satisfied today, I had to repeat the whole procedure, thus preparing a very good surface to paint on. I shall be on my guard, building up forms according to the original conception and paint carefully, 'with air' to keep it soft. I have com-

> posed a piece flooded with light, so to speak not dissected or harsh anymore. It is growing naturally now. . . .
> (Quoted in Ness, 1975, p. 111.)

This picture might, after trial and error, have grown 'naturally', but it is clear that, despite his obvious talent, Feininger did not consider himself a 'natural' painter. His results were achieved by studious application and continuous study of his motif. For instance, moved to despair at the slow progress of a painting of the village of Gaberndorf, Feininger cut it up. Explaining this dire act to his wife, he wrote:

> The cut-up *Gaberndorf* was the worst thing of that sort I ever did. The longer I look at it the more content I am at having cut it up. In the end there was no truth or life in it any more, just handicraft. As a picture it was dead. Paying too much attention to manual skill may become dangerous. . . .
> (Quoted in Ness, 1975, p. 137.)

a testament to his belief that painting is an activity whose results are more than the mere demonstration of physical skills.

Feininger's attitude to broader issues of art was not a simple one: at the same time, he could suspect Itten's religiosity, encouraging van Doesburg to come to Weimar to dispel the smug atmosphere of mysticism by incisions of cold *De Stijl* insight, while detesting any idea of Gropius's that art might be useful; his opposition to Gropius's new Bauhaus creed of 1923 that 'Art and technics equals a new unity' is well known. Yet while there are few references in Feininger's pictures to mechanical devices or motifs, he was able to appreciate their beauty; on one occasion in Dessau, for instance, he was very struck by seeing a part dismantled wing of a Junkers flying boat and wrote to tell his wife of his experience of the beauty of its construction.

These complications could flourish because, all the time, he was singlemindedly dedicated to the furtherance of his art. The same rapt attention which Feininger paid to the development of an individual picture was applied also to series of pictures of the same motif. Unwilling—or unable—to exhaust the full reservoir of meaning from a subject in a single picture, the subject would be developed in series. Look at three of Feininger's pictures of Gelmeroda: numbers IV and IX (1915 and 1926) are illustrated in Figures 63 and 64, while number XII is shown as Figure 198 in Hamilton.

Each painting was developed out of a similar process. First of all, at the beginning, Feininger would make sketches of the subject with a soft lead pencil and make notes about the colours on site. Feininger favoured, like the Romantics, gloomy days: 'there is something depressing', he wrote, 'in sun-drenched hills under a cloudless sky' (quoted in Ness, 1975, p. 244). Once made, the original sketches would be discarded for perhaps years at a time. The next stage of a picture's development would take place in the studio where Feininger would develop the *plein-air* sketch into a more finished version using first of all charcoal and then indian ink for the lines, and the effect of charcoal on paper's grain to build up mass. Again, the subject is filed away to be used later as the starting point for a watercolour. To Feininger charcoal gave him the opportunity of creating *space*, while the watercolour allowed him to create the effects of solid light which he sought.

Despite this sophisticated process, for the final oil painting Feininger would return to the charcoal sketch, which, as in the case of the Gelmeroda series, would apply time and again, the source for pictures which explored with successive vigour the action of light on forms and the painter's reaction to it.

Feininger had—unlike many of the other Bauhaus masters—no programme to his art. Perhaps it was for this reason that, with the spirit of the Bauhaus getting more and more purposeful, in a technocratic sense, by 1926 with the move to Dessau, he gave up teaching there and was happy to accept Gropius's offer of the unpaid post of artist-in-residence.

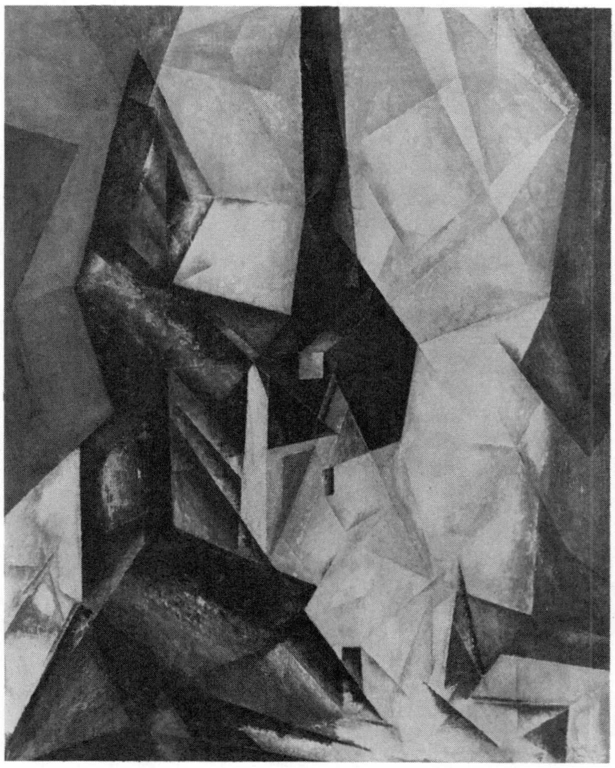

Figure 63 Lyonel Feininger, *Gelmeroda IV*, 1915, oil, $39\frac{1}{8} \times 31\frac{1}{4}$ ins (Solomon R. Guggenheim Museum, New York © ADAGP Paris 1976 © Cosmopress, Genève).

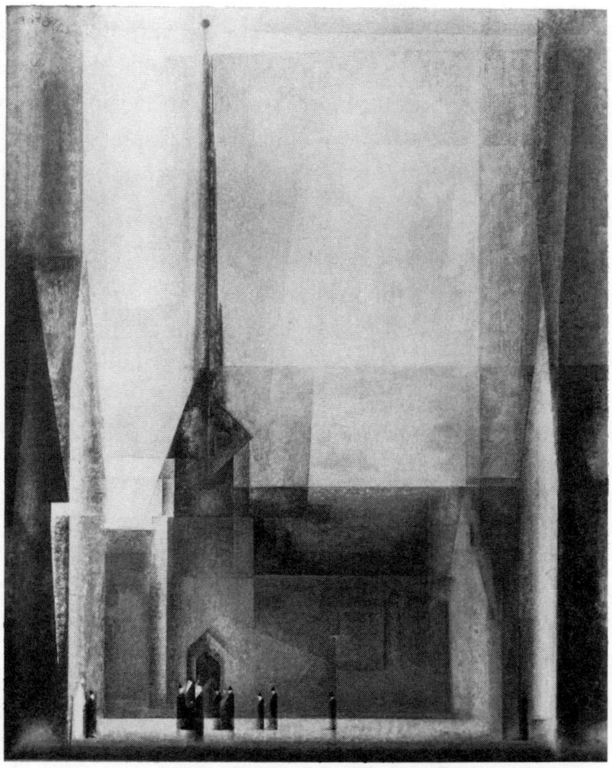

Figure 64 Lyonel Feininger, *Gelmeroda IX*, 1926, oil, $39\frac{3}{8} \times 31\frac{1}{2}$ ins (Folkwang Museum, Essen; photo: Liselotte Witzel © ADAGP Paris 1976 © Cosmopress, Genève).

Johannes Itten

(See Hamilton, p. 333.)

Johannes Itten was the second master to join the Bauhaus staff. Although an accomplished painter, Itten is remembered most of all not for his art, but for his educational method and the extraordinary strength of his personality which drew to him, in the four years he spent at the Weimar Bauhaus, most of the young students thirsty for some mystery in the austere post-war era, and at the same time, much of the ire of other Bauhaus staff.

Itten was Swiss, born in Zurich in 1888. First of all he trained as a secondary school teacher in Bern where he knew Klee's father and then went to train as a painter in the studio of Adolf Hölzel, where he met the painters Oskar Schlemmer, Willi Baumeister and Ida Kerkovius as fellow students. In 1916 he exhibited his first abstract picture at Walden's *Der Sturm* gallery and afterwards moved to Vienna, where he exhibited in an exhibition organized by the architect Adolf Loos. In 1919 Itten met the popular wife of Gustav Mahler, Alma, and through her was introduced to her second husband, Walter Gropius. His appointment to the Bauhaus was made in 1919.

In the early years of the Bauhaus, Itten appears to be a living symbol of all that the technocrats were later to reject from its curriculum: hope in the mysterious, energy for the unusual, exercises for the soul and the gratuitous development of the inner man.

An ex-Bauhaus student recalled:

> Intuition! The Unconscious! These were the master keys of Itten's teaching. Before long we would all be using the jargon of Freud and Jung, but in 1920 and 1921 we were all trying to read the works of the mystics. Meister Eckhardt, Suso and Tauler were our constant companions.
> (Von Erffa, 1957, p. 104.)

So much did Itten's attitude to life depend on intuition that it was said that his method of interviewing prospective students was merely to subject them to the impassive scrutiny of an existing student whom Itten felt to be highly sensitive. The student, eyes unfocused and staring into the distance, would, if the newcomer was approved, merely nod to indicate approval and subsequent acceptance for the course.

Itten's world view, in its broad sense, may have been influenced by his teacher Adolf Hölzel (1853–1934) who, if no mystic, was keen to encourage originality in his pupils. Hölzel developed a science of colour and an understanding of pictures on the basis of two-dimensional analysis. His style of 1902 can be seen in Figure 65, *Landscape with Birches*. His style is one where colour and effects of light have precedence over form. The picture is a severely limited composition with three broad, horizontal bands painted in soft focus, with the highlights of the silver birch trees indicated by the vertical marks left by dragging a heavily loaded brush lightly over the surface of the canvas. The effect was to dissolve solidity, but by the later twenties Hölzel, having given himself over to a form of Orphic abstraction, had found a better way of achieving the same effect.[5]

Itten's own painting became abstract in 1915–16. Before, he had been painting scenes of religious subjects such as *The Good Samaritan* of 1915 (Fig. 66) in a Cubo-Futurist style. *Horizontal–Vertical* (Fig. 67) and *Ascent and Rest*, 1915–16 and 1918–19 respectively, are examples of his pure abstract style. Around 1918, however, Itten—perhaps under the influence of Chinese art or, perhaps, under the influence of Freud—discovered automatism.[6] This may have been the key to the ever more curious

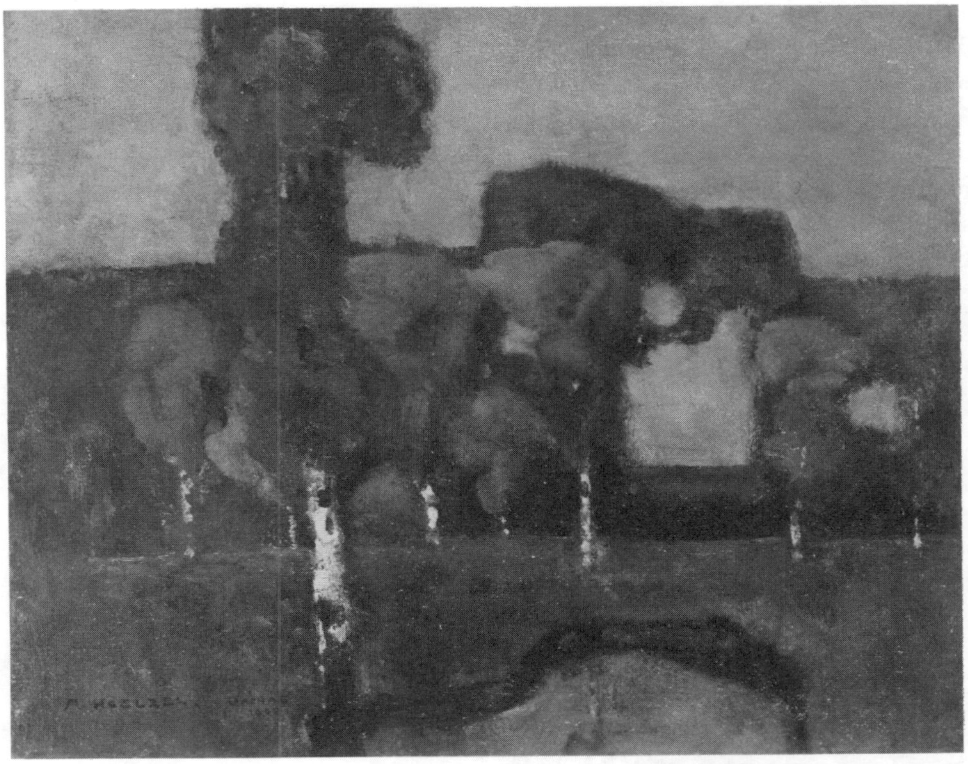

Figure 65 Adolf Hölzel, *Landscape with Birches*, 1919, oil, $15\frac{3}{8} \times 19\frac{1}{4}$ ins (Mittelrheinisches Landesmuseum, Mainz, courtesy Mrs Dieckmann-Hoelzel).

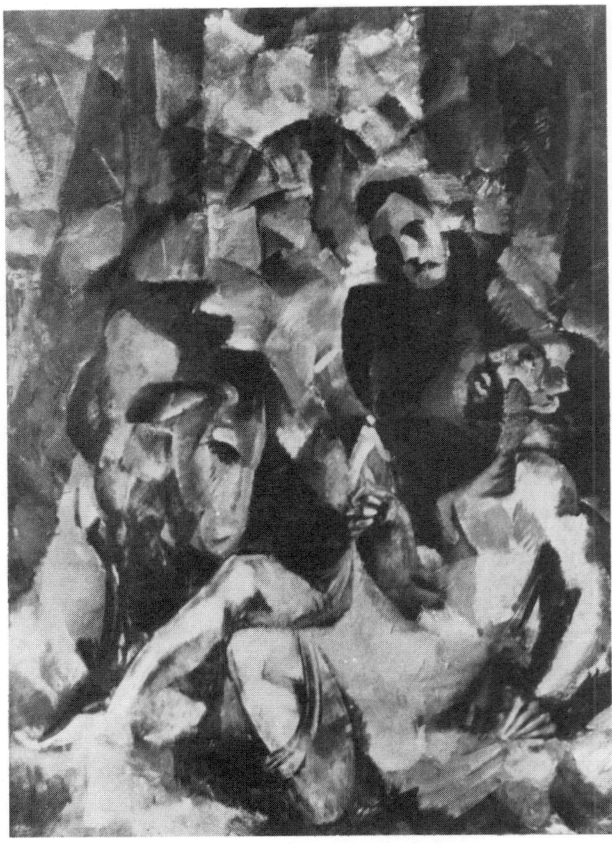

Figure 66 Johannes Itten, *The Good Samaritan*, 1915, oil, $78\frac{1}{2} \times 59$ ins (Collection Anneliese Itten).

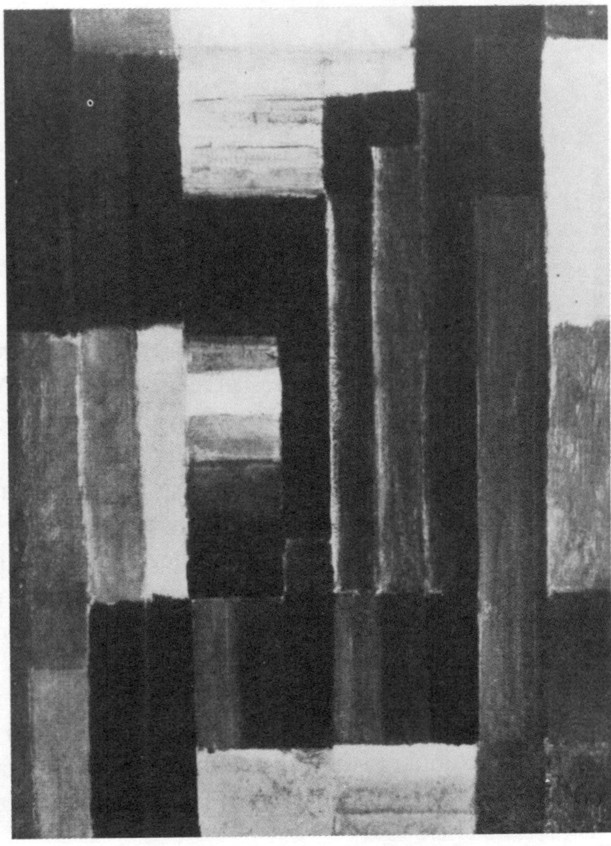

Figure 67 Johannes Itten, *Horizontal–Vertical*, 1918/19, oil (Kunsthaus, Zurich).

mystical activities which Itten participated in. His mysticism was not only fired by the example of the Orient, but also by the European Middle Ages. His interest in the structures of mediaeval paintings (Fig. 68 shows his analysis of Meister Francke's *Adoration*) is well known. While Gropius was intent on organizing lectures on anatomy for serious-minded students, under the influence of Itten a man called Werner Henser, dressed in a black robe and with a full black beard, gave the students lectures on Thomas à Kempis's *Imitation of Christ*. Gropius was so inflamed by this errant romanticism that he threatened expulsion to any students too busy finding their inner selves to be bothered to attend classes in mid term; in fact, some students did leave the Bauhaus in order to follow Henser.

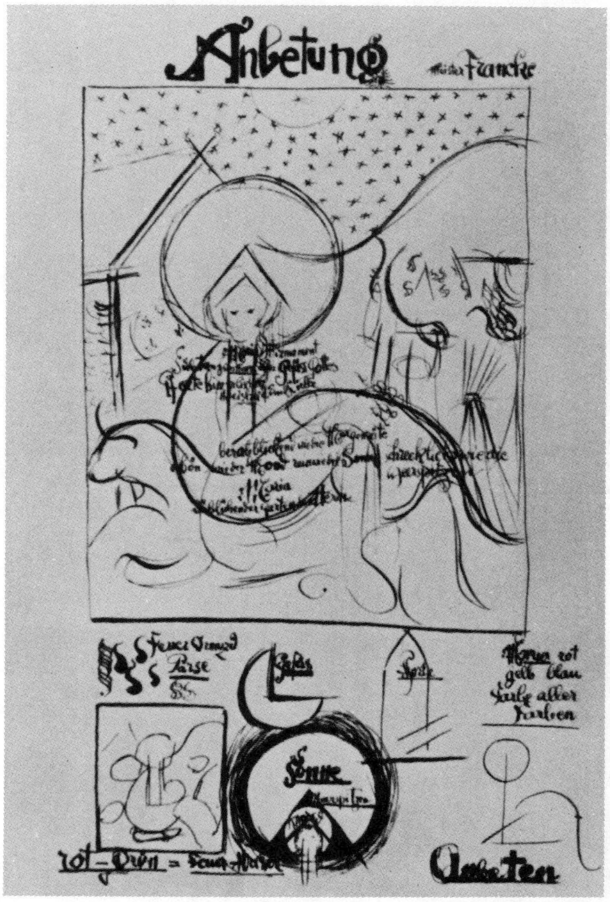

Figure 68 Johannes Itten, analytical sketch of *The Adoration* by Meister Francke, published in *Utopia —Dokumente der Wirklichkeit*, 1921 (Bauhaus Archiv, Berlin).

However, by far the greatest influence on Itten and on the whole Bauhaus before about 1923 was the imitation Persian religion known as Mazdaznan. Itten's pedagogy demanded a system and Mazdaznan provided it. It was only one of the curious religions which sprang up in Europe after the First World War: Mazdaznan was a corrupt form of the ancient Persian Zoroastrianism, a dualistic religion believing essentially in the goodness of light and the evil of the dark. The modern Mazdaznan was founded by a German-American typographer who, finding his name of Otto Hänisch unconvincing for his role as Zoroastrian priest, decided to be known as Dr Othoman Zar-Adusht Ha'nisch, a gallant but inaccurate attempt at a Persian identity.

Itten was indoctrinated to Mazdaznan immediately after the beginning of the foundation course, no doubt to the indignation of Gropius, by taking some months away to visit Ha'nisch's Mazdaznan centre at Herrliberg in Switzerland. Paul Citroen, the artist, recalled that

> Itten knew how to inflame us, shake us up, break down all the dikes and plunge us into a veritable frenzy of production. . . . There was something demonic about Itten. As a master he was either ardently admired or just as ardently hated by his

> opponents. . . . At all events it was impossible to ignore him.
> (Citroen, in Neumann, 1970, pp. 44–45.)

The Mazdaznan cult included devotion to health

> Still, most of us did not look blooming. This must be ascribed to the fact that in Germany, disintegrating in economic inflation, sufficient and decent food was available only at great cost . . . I, [it is Paul Citroen writing] who was naturally sallow, could look green and grey, whenever my innards were upset, which was often enough.
> (Citroen, in Neumann, 1970, pp. 44–45.)

It is no surprise that the weaknesses of Citroen were exposed by the rigid cult of Mazdaznan. Their Easter celebrations began by bathing in well water, being vigorously dried and then drinking wine. This, and the long walk which preceded the eating of undisclosed numbers of eggs, symbolized the end of a fast.

(The rigours of the fast may explain something of the temporary nature of the popularity of Mazdaznan: the fast began with a strong laxative, followed by hot fruit juices and a symbolic weeding of the cult's own orchard on a hillock near Weimar. Hot baths were followed by a brisk rubbing down with charcoal to cleanse the skin of its impurities; if the cathartic effect of this action proved insufficient, then the Mazdaznaners would prick their skin and rub the abrasions with the oily laxative with the intention of causing the formation of pustules. The pustulating limb would then be bound with bandages to absorb the expelled impurities. The success or failure of these methods is not recorded, but what is known is that their implementation had a divisive effect on the Bauhaus.)

After his return from Herrliberg, Itten was increasingly at odds with Gropius, even if he enjoyed the support of many of the students. Similarly, the Mazdaznan cult also served to make its student adherents impatient with those who were uninitiated.

Itten's popularity with the students and his extraordinary behaviour alienated him from the other members of the Bauhaus. Oskar Schlemmer, who had never liked him even when they were students together in Hölzel's studio, wrote to his friend Otto Meyer-Amden of Itten's position in the Bauhaus:

> I think I can see two ways in which Itten seeks to dominate. He is dictatorial and shows a complete lack of consideration for others. In addition, he indulges in a scholarly pedantry which drives the students to protest.
> (Schlemmer, *Briefe und Tagebücher*, p. 195; cited in Roters, 1969, p. 47.)

Itten was just as unpopular with Lyonel Feininger. Even before he joined the Bauhaus staff, Feininger was on his guard: 'Itten arrived from Vienna today', Feininger wrote in a letter to his wife, Julia in June 1919

> I am curious to meet him. It seems as though he has made up his mind to join the staff here. I had hardly written the sentence above when there was a knock on my door and Gropius came to see me to introduce Itten, who made a good impression on me and seems to be clever.
> (Quoted in Ness, 1975, pp. 104–5.)

But by November 1921, when Itten had exhibited the worst excesses of his eccentricity Feininger was less tolerant:

> Yesterday I had a visit from van Doesburg. . . . He at least is very real and healthy flesh and blood. He was rather explicit on Monsieur Itten. It seems this champion

> of Theosophy[7] at times does not act up to the role. He is said to have ripped down my work and to have left hardly a shred of my person, which is gratifying. Anyhow he did it publicly—he should come to grips with me and we might get even. (Quoted in Ness, 1975, p. 112.)

Itten, too, was getting intolerant of the Bauhaus and when Gropius announced his decision to hold the major Bauhaus Exhibition in 1923, the preparations brought the crisis between Gropius and Itten to a head. Itten was not prepared to tolerate what Gropius wished the Exhibition to make manifest, that is to say, a real wedding of art, design and commercial production, and accordingly left to found his own School of Painting, Graphics, Photography and Architecture in Berlin. This was followed by directorships in schools of art and craft and museums in Krefeld and Zurich.

Oskar Schlemmer

(See Hamilton, pp. 334–37.)

Oskar Schlemmer was born in Stuttgart in 1888 and died at Sehringen in 1943. While working on the sets of Kokoschka's *Mörder—Hoffnung der Frauen* (*Murder—Hope of Women*; see Unit 8, Fig. 85) and Franz Blei's *Das Nusch-Nuschi* at the Stuttgart State Theatre he met Walter Gropius who, impressed with his work, invited him to join the Bauhaus staff. In December 1920, Schlemmer subsequently taught at the Bauhaus until 1929 when he left to work for the Breslau Academy.

Schlemmer began his training as an artist under Landenberger, F. von Keller and Adolf Hölzel. Schlemmer's art is a difficult one at first to understand apparently owing little to either his teachers or his contemporaries. Far more subtle and complex than the simple, often crudely painted forms of his pictures would suggest, Schlemmer's whole philosophy of art was, of all the Bauhaus masters, perhaps the one which came most convincingly near to embracing the ideals of universal art. Through reducing human forms to their simple essence—which he did both in the dance and in painting[8]—he could do honour to the aesthetic of abstraction, while at the same time retaining human reference in his art. Hamilton's illustration of Schlemmer's *Abstract Figure* of 1921 (Fig. 200) is perfectly illustrative of Schlemmer's method applied to sculpture. Similarly, in his painting, *Group of Fourteen Figures in Imaginary Architecture* (Hamilton Fig. 199) the human form is immediately recognizable as the source of the motif, even if the contortions which Schlemmer makes it perform have little to do with everyday perceptual reality. In both works Schlemmer's interpretation of the human theme has been governed by what, in his view, was the necessity of making nature bend to the needs of his own aesthetic requirements.

What Hamilton calls the 'multi-dimensional irrational space' of Schlemmer's paintings was a characteristic of his paintings influenced by his work in the theatre and in dance. After his taking over of the theatre workshop, the theatre was Schlemmer's major contribution to Bauhaus activity in the years that he was there. The period included the best of both Weimar and Dessau, in which his works in theatre and painting represent, perhaps the fullest expression of the Bauhaus's original intentions.

So much did Schlemmer devote his time to the theatre that for much of the 1920s his output of paintings was low. However, the metaphysics of the dance were, to him, not at variance with the aims of painting. One of the diagrams from his *Bauhausbüch*, *Die Bühne am Bauhaus* (*The Theatre of the Bauhaus*) is a beautiful evocation of his vision of the human figure in a chaotic world upon which the artist has imposed order (Fig. 69). In his paintings, this sense is combined with the use of the affecting formal arrangement of the human body: *Tänzerin—Die Geste* (*Dancer—The Gesture*) (Fig. 70) and his *Konzentrische Gruppe* (*Concentric Group*) (Plate 16) remind us that, like many of his contemporaries, the roots of Schlemmer's inspiration were tapping the bed of nineteenth-century Romanticism.

Puppets were an important motif in German romantic literature and the image of the puppet performing tasks dictated from another source is similar in principle to Schlemmer's drive to determine laws by which human form and movement were governed. All his art was grounded in the theatre; Schlemmer believed in a metaphysics of the human body, but when Hannes Meyer took over the directorship of the Bauhaus on Gropius's resignation in 1928 his arid, purposive philosophy had no sympathy for metaphysics. Shortly afterwards the Bauhaus theatre was disbanded and Schlemmer left for Breslau.

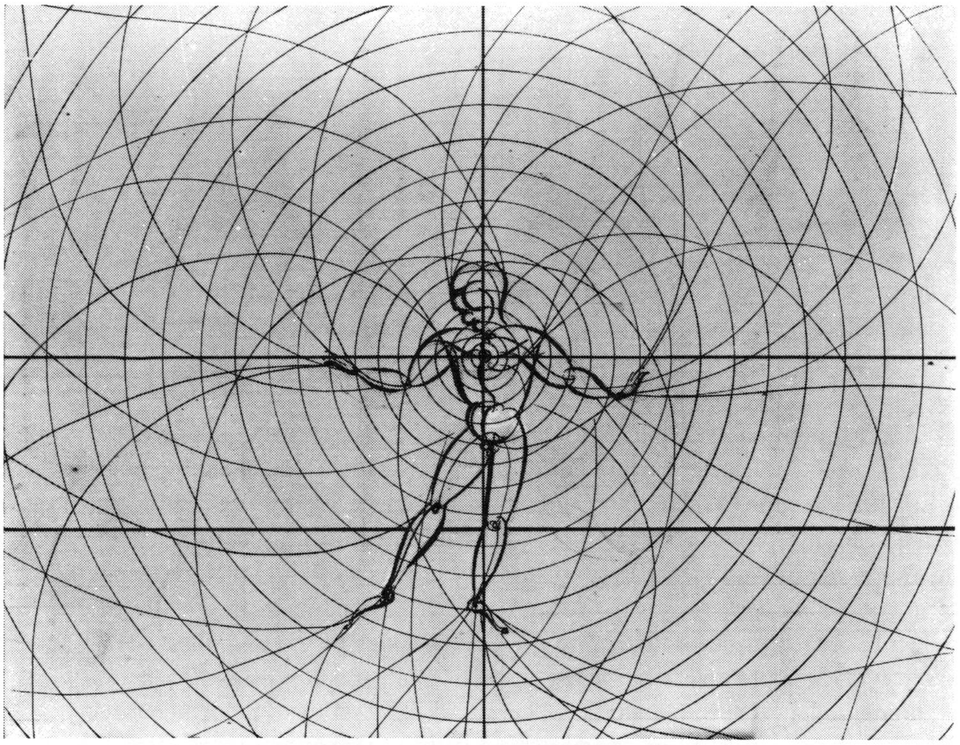

Figure 69 Oskar Schlemmer, 'The laws of man place him in the centre of an imaginary spatial relationship resulting from man's movements and his radial emanations', from 'Mensch und Kunstfigur', in *Die Bühne am Bauhaus*, 1925 (Schlemmer Archiv, Staatsgalerie Stuttgart).

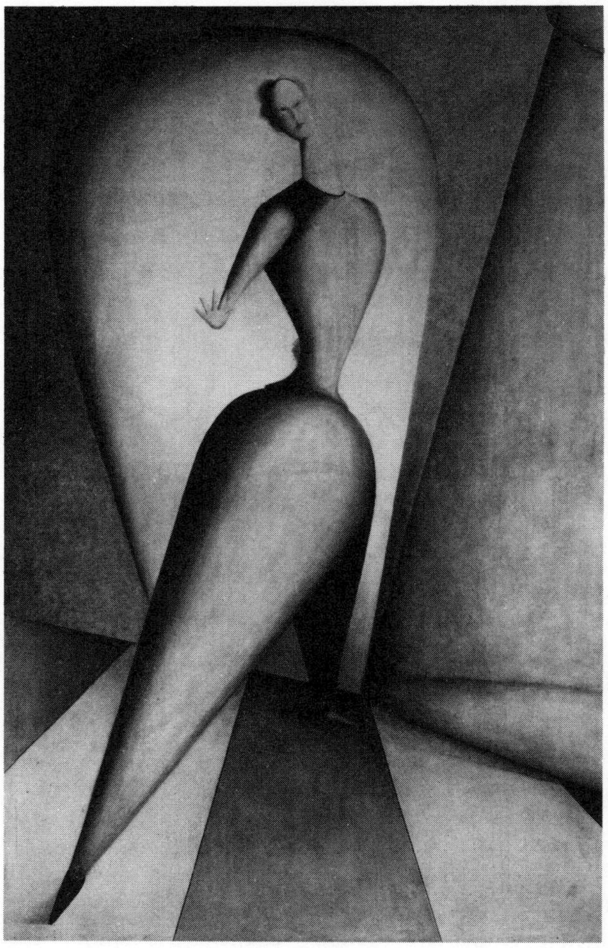

Figure 70 Oskar Schlemmer, *Dancer—The Gesture*, 1922/3, oil and tempera on canvas, $78\frac{3}{4} \times 51\frac{1}{8}$ ins (Neue Pinakothek Munich; photo: courtesy Staatsgalerie Stuttgart).

The Bauhaus Exhibition of 1923

By 1923 the flavour of modernism was moving away from Expressionist excess towards a more utilitarian attitude to art. The First International Congress of Progressive Art had taken place in Düsseldorf in 1922, in which van Doesburg had been influential, and this may have encouraged Gropius to alter the direction of the Bauhaus.

It was in 1923 that Johannes Itten left and Laszlo Moholy-Nagy arrived, but perhaps a more important symbol of the change in emphasis was the organization of the Bauhaus Exhibition of July–September for which Joost Schmidt designed a poster (Fig. 71) of uncompromising clarity, announcing that now the Bauhaus intended to show itself to the world. However, the publicity gained from the exhibition was not altogether beneficial: conservative thinkers in the *Landtag* had been offended and a scurrilous brochure attacking the Bauhaus had been issued. Legal action taken by Gropius had little effect and by September 1924 state aid was withdrawn from the Weimar Bauhaus. Gropius was forced to move.

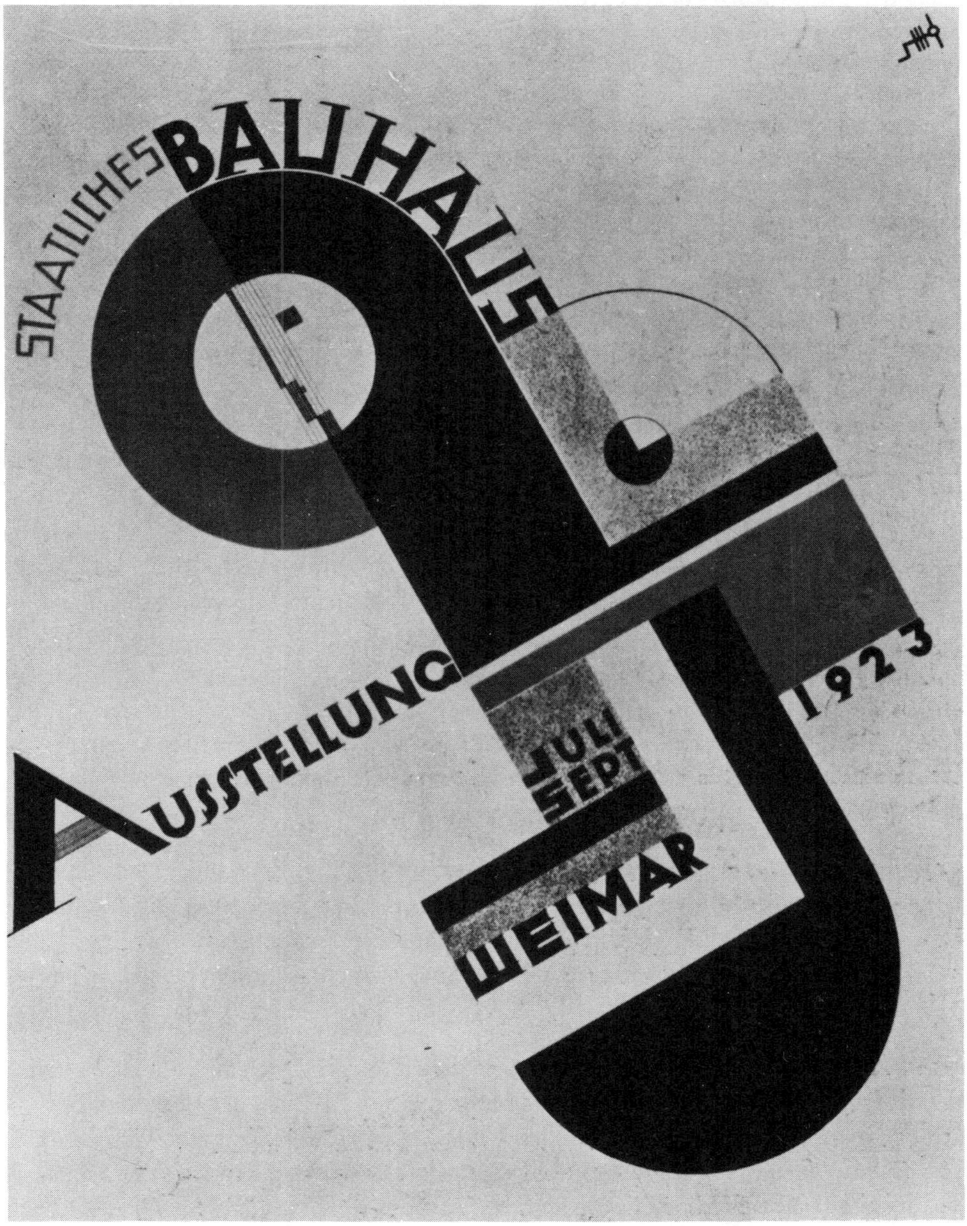

Figure 71 Joost Schmidt, Bauhaus exhibition poster, 1923 (Bauhaus Archiv, Berlin).

PART II *Dessau*
Mysticism: Klee and Kandinsky

Expressionism was central to Gropius's original conception of the Bauhaus, but in retrospect it appears that his own Expressionist sympathies were short-lived. Like others after the war, Gropius was caught up in the drama of Expressionist utopia, but soon his own mature, sober, rational plans for the future of art began to emerge. These plans had been symbolized by the organization of the Bauhaus Exhibition of 1923. However, even if after 1923 the direction of the Bauhaus began to change, painters still held sway and it is significant that the two greatest painters associated with the Bauhaus, Paul Klee and Wassily Kandinsky, flourished during both the Weimar and Dessau periods.

For both Klee and Kandinsky, the Bauhaus was a central part of their careers in which they gave themselves fully to the exploration and legislation of the visual world and the spirit. Somewhat negligent of the functional aims of the Bauhaus, both were professionally unassailable and above criticism, because of their supremacy in their art. Their theories of art have much in common (the two men were close friends and must often have discussed matters of mutual concern)[9] but take physical form in entirely unmistakable ways.

Despite their somewhat anomalous position in the production-orientated Bauhaus of the Dessau years Gropius understood the generative importance of painting to design.[10] To cover himself, though, he ascribed to these painters less ethereal roles: Klee was in charge of the book-binding and glass-painting workshop while Kandinsky took charge of mural painting.

PAUL KLEE

(See Hamilton, pp. 494–99.)

Klee's teaching, which followed on from Itten's *Vorkurs* ('Preliminary course'), was apparently difficult. In it he developed a theory of form and of art which had some debts owed to German Romanticism. In his *Diary* he once wrote.

> In this world, I am not really comprehensible. I dwell both with the dead and with the unborn. A little closer to the heart of creation than most people. And yet not close enough.
> (Quoted in Roters, 1969, p. 95.)

Klee's obsessive interest in physiognomy may also have been indebted to German Romanticism, but regardless of its source, is expressive of his anxiety to understand more than mere surface appearances.

Different in character to the metaphysics of Kandinsky, Klee's art theory was almost wholly concerned with the process of describing our deepest responses and reactions to primeval nature. In his most famous single statement on the nature of art he said that 'Kunst gibt nicht das Sichtbare wieder sondern macht sichtbar',[11] a statement of almost mystic intensity.

Klee's theorizing about art was somewhat more whimsical than Kandinsky's. In his drawing illustrating his essay 'Wege des Naturstudiums' ('Paths of Nature Study'), 1923 (Fig. 72), Klee illustrates his belief that the microcosm reflects the macrocosm, but despite the impressive grandeur of the scale of the drawing's conceit there is a quality about the draughtsmanship and the notations which impresses us that Klee did not set about this demonstration of his philosophy with a heavy heart.

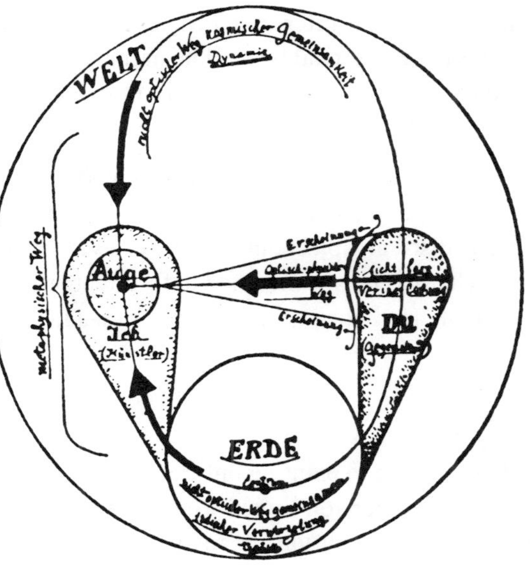

Figure 72 Paul Klee, 'Paths of Nature Study', from 'Wege de Naturstudiums', published in *Staatliche Bauhaus Weimar 1919–1923* (Bauhaus Archiv, Berlin © SPADEM Paris 1976).

To Klee, both in his everyday life, his theory and his art, everything was tentative and equivocal. It is said that he would not mediate between Kandinsky and his students in a dispute over aesthetics; his statements on art are whimsical or ironical and often open to numerous interpretations.

To him the world and the spirit represented a common source of imagery and artistic possibility and he would often juggle with the two. His *Leaf of Memory* (Hamilton Fig. 291) and his *Precious Container for Stars* (Hamilton Fig. 292) are proposals of what might be, and the equivocation is expressed in the titles. The dalliance between the heart, the head and the eye sometimes gives Klee's paintings an irritating, precious quality; sometimes they are so fine that the viewer's senses almost squeak while other pictures like *Villa R* (Plate 17), painted just before his arrival at the Bauhaus, have a certain vigorous crudeness which is missing from his later works.

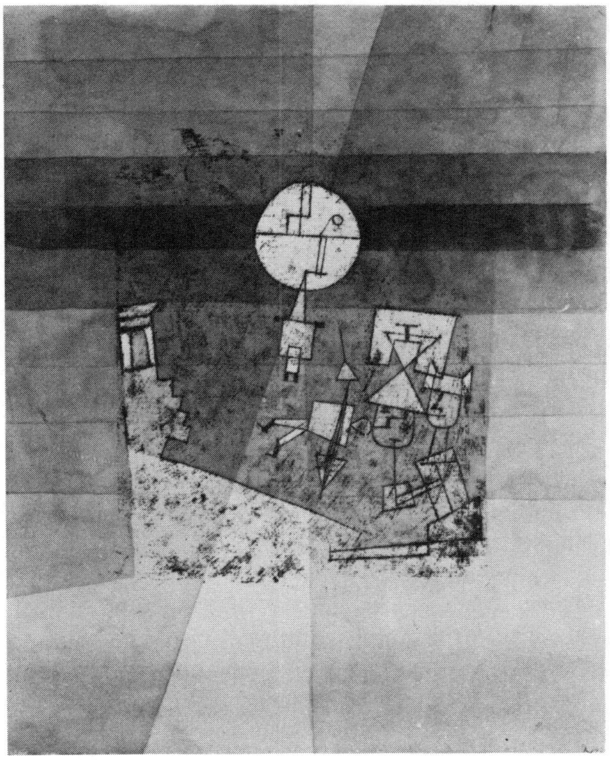

Figure 73 Paul Klee, *Moongame*, 1923, watercolour, 20 × 15½ ins (Staatliche Museen Preussischer Kulturbesitz, Nationalgalerie Berlin West; photo: Anders © SPADEM Paris 1976).

Moongame (Fig. 73), a watercolour painted in 1923, shows Klee's growing interest in relating bands of colour and tone combined with his interest in physiognomy, shown here by the delicate, notional assemblages of geometrical form. The natural starting point has been lost sight of entirely and the whole picture is reduced to a sensitive *proposal* of the nature of reality.

Klee's work was, briefly, lauded by the Surrealists (his name was mentioned in Bréton's Manifesto of 1924), but while the field of the irrational was, to Klee, susceptible to interpretation, it was, to the Surrealists, an object only of awe and veneration. Essentially, they had little in common. Klee was most concerned to formulate the rules of the visible world; a discussion of his art theory appears on pp. 142–44.

WASSILY KANDINSKY

(See Hamilton, pp. 337–40.)

Kandinsky, it must always be remembered, came to painting only late in life. He arrived in Munich in 1896 (where he studied under von Stuck) when he was already thirty years of age, with a career in law and administration already behind him.

Kandinsky is an artist of the greatest stature, at once a great theoretician and aesthetician, a great teacher and an innovating painter. Perhaps the most fascinating feature of Kandinsky's *oeuvre* is the combination of tensions in his work which demand attention both from our intellect and from our emotions. At the same time Kandinsky erected an elaborate structure to justify his artistic experiments, a structure which wants for nothing in complexity and difficulty, but painted pictures which, even if our response to them is restricted without an understanding of the principles which guided their creation, make a blatant —if controlled—appeal to our emotions. 'Kandinsky', said his biographer, Will Grohmann, had a heart which 'lay in the realm of the head' (in Royal Academy, 1968, p. 217) and was compulsively driven to maintain order both in his own being and in the world of painting and aesthetics which he determined to make his own.

When Kandinsky joined the staff of the Bauhaus in Weimar he was fifty-six years old, significantly older than Klee, whom he already knew from his *Blaue Reiter* period, and, earlier than that, from studio days with von Stuck in Munich. The age tells us much about the man; few people start new careers in their fifties and even fewer set about them with the single-minded determination of Kandinsky.

Although Kandinsky's art derives much of its power from the spiritual and emotional responses which it evokes, he was himself a man who kept total control over his feelings. Georg Muche recalled that in conversation Kandinsky had been accused of being so cold and aloof that it was as if he was seven versts distant from his friends. 'Ah', Kandinsky replied, 'but seven *versts* is no distance between friends!'[12]

Throughout the Bauhaus period Kandinsky refrained from any emotional outbursts and viewed with distaste any such performance from other people. No photograph shows him smiling, he was all the time playing the role of 'professor', which title he was anxious to keep, even when the new Bauhaus styles were introduced. Looking more like a banker than a painter, there are photographs which show Kandinsky painting one of his vivid, frenetic, sizzling pictures with a fine brush in slow, deliberate and measured strokes, dressed in an immaculate pin-striped suit. This equanimity which he maintained throughout his life made him a cornerstone of the Bauhaus, even though the united front of Bauhaus production for consumption made his position in the school appear irrelevant after 1923.

From his arrival in 1922 Kandinsky took over the mural-painting workshop in Weimar, which had previously been the province of Itten and Schlemmer. It was here that he further developed his ideas of form and colour which he had first essayed in his *Über das Geistige in der Kunst* (*Concerning the Spiritual in Art*) of 1912 (see pp. 145–47). Kandinsky, perhaps influenced by his legal training, was not afraid to be dogmatic about his pronouncements on art and his convictions, although constantly developing, were at any one time inflexible.

Many factors influenced the development of Kandinsky's art. He had had an upbringing in Russia, surrounded at once by images from the Orient, the hypnotic presence of icons and a tradition of painting which had only recently come across the central perspective which had been the foundation of European art since the Renaissance. There were psychological components of his personality, too, which encouraged his artistic development. Kandinsky was both *eidetic* and *synaesthetic*.[13] Being eidetic means that a person has the ability of total recall and synaesthesia is the ability to perceive one sense experience through a stimulus to any entirely different sense. It was no doubt partly through fear of the potential anarchy which these two characteristics could produce that Kandinsky inflicted his harsh discipline upon himself. However, the synaesthesia was what encouraged him to conceive of his first abstract pictures as well as enabling him to conceive of a series of woodcuts, published by Reinhold Piper in 1913, called *Klänge* (*Sounds*) and to write a play, with proposed music by Schoenberg, called *Der gelbe Klang* (*The Yellow Sound*). This cross referencing is a vital clue to the nature of Kandinsky's art. His paintings are written in a special language and can be read as such. In *Über das Geistige in der Kunst* Kandinsky cited Delacroix's attitude to painting as an important percursor to his own, both men believing that musical sound corresponded exactly to certain feelings. However, despite the invocation of the great French Romantic, Kandinsky eschewed any superficial or literary Romanticism in his art. In a letter written to Will Grohmann in 1925 he wrote

> I only wish people would understand what is behind my painting . . . and not just content themselves with pointing out the fact that I use triangles or circles. I know the future belongs to abstract art, and I am distressed at the undue importance other abstract painters attach to mere questions of form. . . . Form is for me only a means to an end, and I spend much time and intensive effort on the theory of form because I want to penetrate its inner mysteries. . . . I do not want to paint tears for tear's sake, nor do I like sickly sweetness, but Romanticism goes far, far beyond the boundaries of tears. Today there is a new Objectivity (Neue Sachlichkeit): there should also be a new Romanticism. I once felt like writing about this subject, and had thought of devoting one chapter of the new edition of *Concerning the Spiritual* to Romanticism. . . . What I do know is that modern man has a sub-conscious longing for Romanticism. . . . The circle [see Hamilton Fig. 129A] which I have been using so often of late, is nothing if not Romantic. Actually, the coming Romanticism is profound and beautiful—the hackneyed word 'beautiful' must be used if it is meaningful, joy-giving—it is a block of ice with a burning flame inside. Too bad if people can only feel the ice and not the flame.
> (Grohmann, 1958, pp. 180*ff.*)

While at the Bauhaus, Kandinsky kept a record of the paintings he had done. The years of greatest activity were 1926, 1929 and 1930 (49, 52 and 54 paintings respectively); the years of least activity were 1922, 1923 and 1932 (3, 19 and 13 paintings respectively). This systematic recording of his activity is reflective of the man: perfection, orderliness and objectivity were his ideals. The precision appears, also, in the titles of his paintings: *No. 58* (*Bow and Point*) of 1923 (Fig. 74) and *Throughgoing Lines* (Fig. 75) are straightforward enough, at least in nomenclature, but in other pictures Kandinsky attempted to find a visual equation for fine, subtle feelings such as his famous *At Rest* and his *Pink Sweet* of 1929 (Plate 18).

Uninterested, or, at least, unperturbed, by all that was going on around him, Kandinsky stayed on at the Bauhaus through all the vacillations of its progress in its

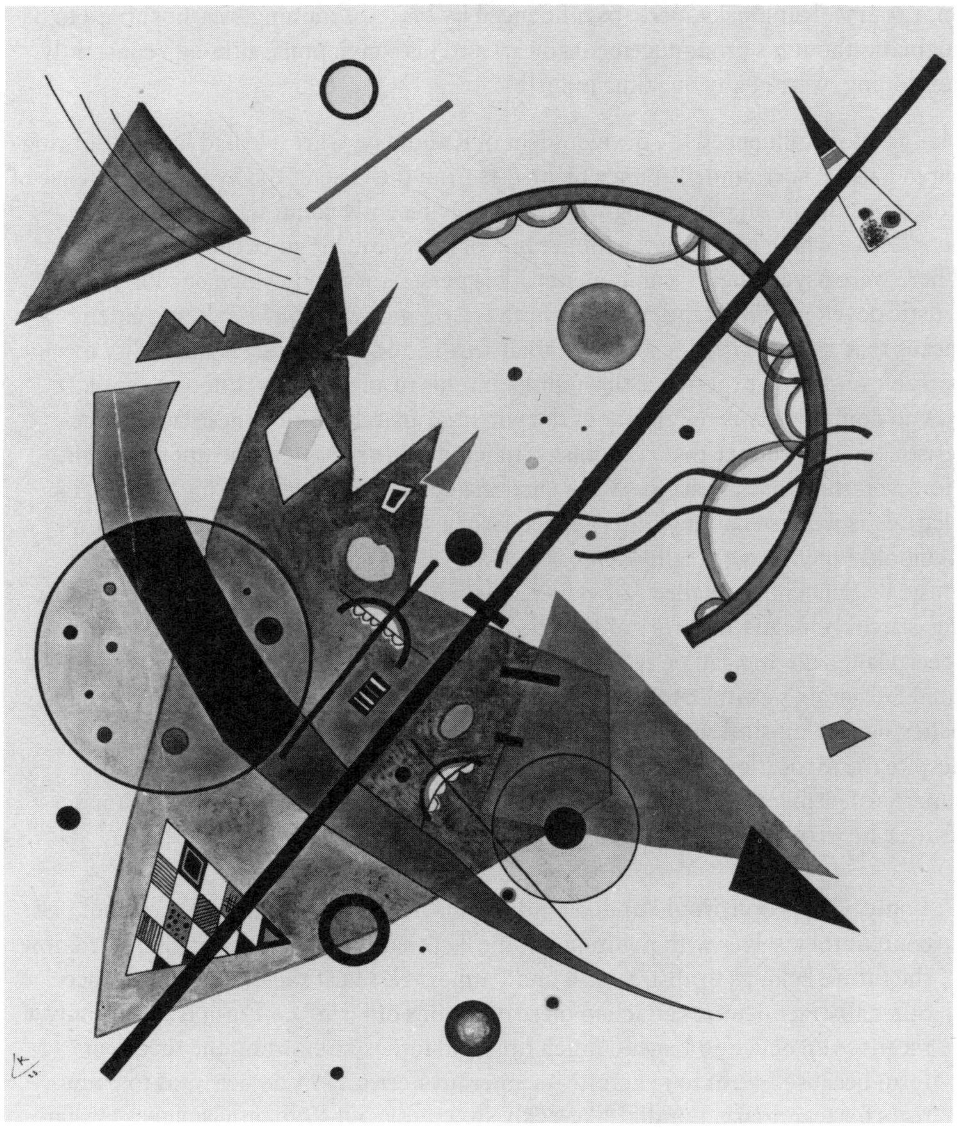

Figure 74 Wassily Kandinsky, *No. 58* (*Bow and Point*), 1923, watercolour and ink, $18\frac{1}{4} \times 16\frac{1}{2}$ ins (Solomon R. Guggenheim Museum, New York © ADAGP Paris 1976).

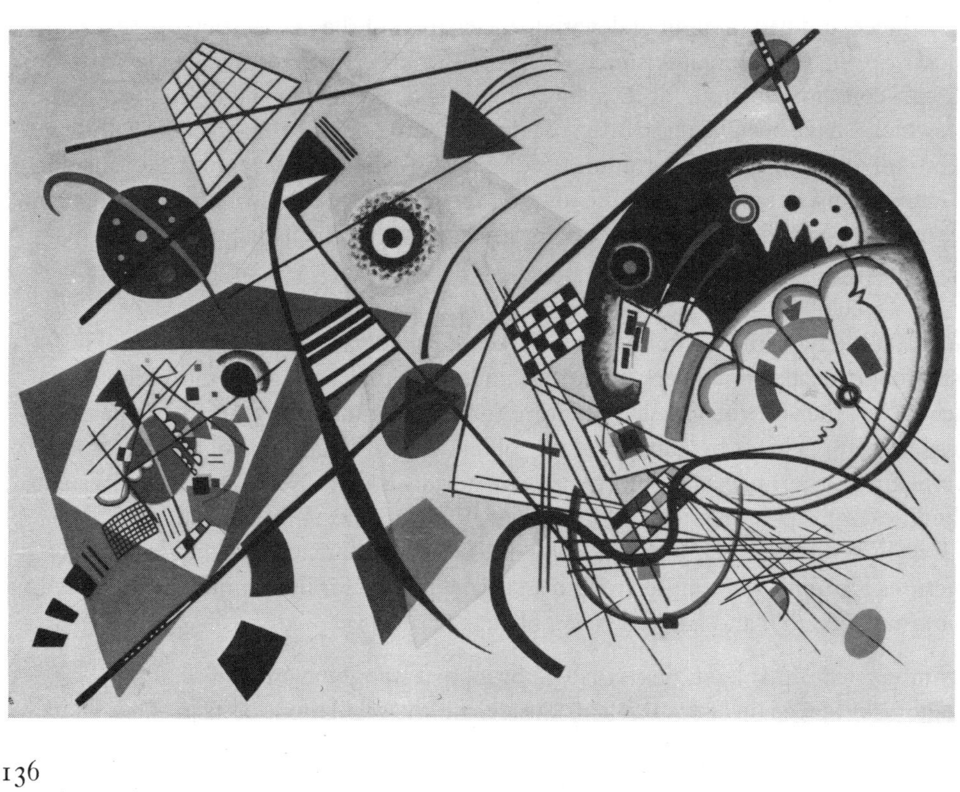

Figure 75 Wassily Kandinsky, *Durchgehender Strich* (*Throughgoing Lines*), oil, $55\frac{3}{8} \times 79\frac{3}{4}$ ins (Kunstsammlung Nordrhein-Westfalen, Düsseldorf © ADAGP Paris 1976).

later years; he was the only painter to serve under all three Bauhaus directors and when the Berlin Bauhaus was forced to close down by the Nazis in 1933 he considered continuing his teaching on a private basis, but decided, instead, to settle at Neuilly-sur-Seine in Paris where he lived, doing no more theorizing but making many experiments in painting, until his death in 1944.

Technocracy: Moholy-Nagy

(See Hamilton, pp. 340–42.)

To better effect some kind of economic recovery after the disastrous inflation of the early twenties, when the groceries had to be paid for with a wheelbarrow full of bank notes, the far-sighted mayor of Dessau, Fritz Hesse, had enticed the embattled Weimar *Bauhauslers* to shift the seat of their operations to his city.

This gave Walter Gropius his greatest opportunity to demonstrate his real faith in the idea of the unity of the arts which he so cherished and to which he gave such monumental form in the new building of the Dessau Bauhaus (1925–26), the most famous building of the International Style in architecture. The man chosen by Gropius to show that art could be taken off its high horse and still remain creative and rewarding was Laszlo Moholy-Nagy.

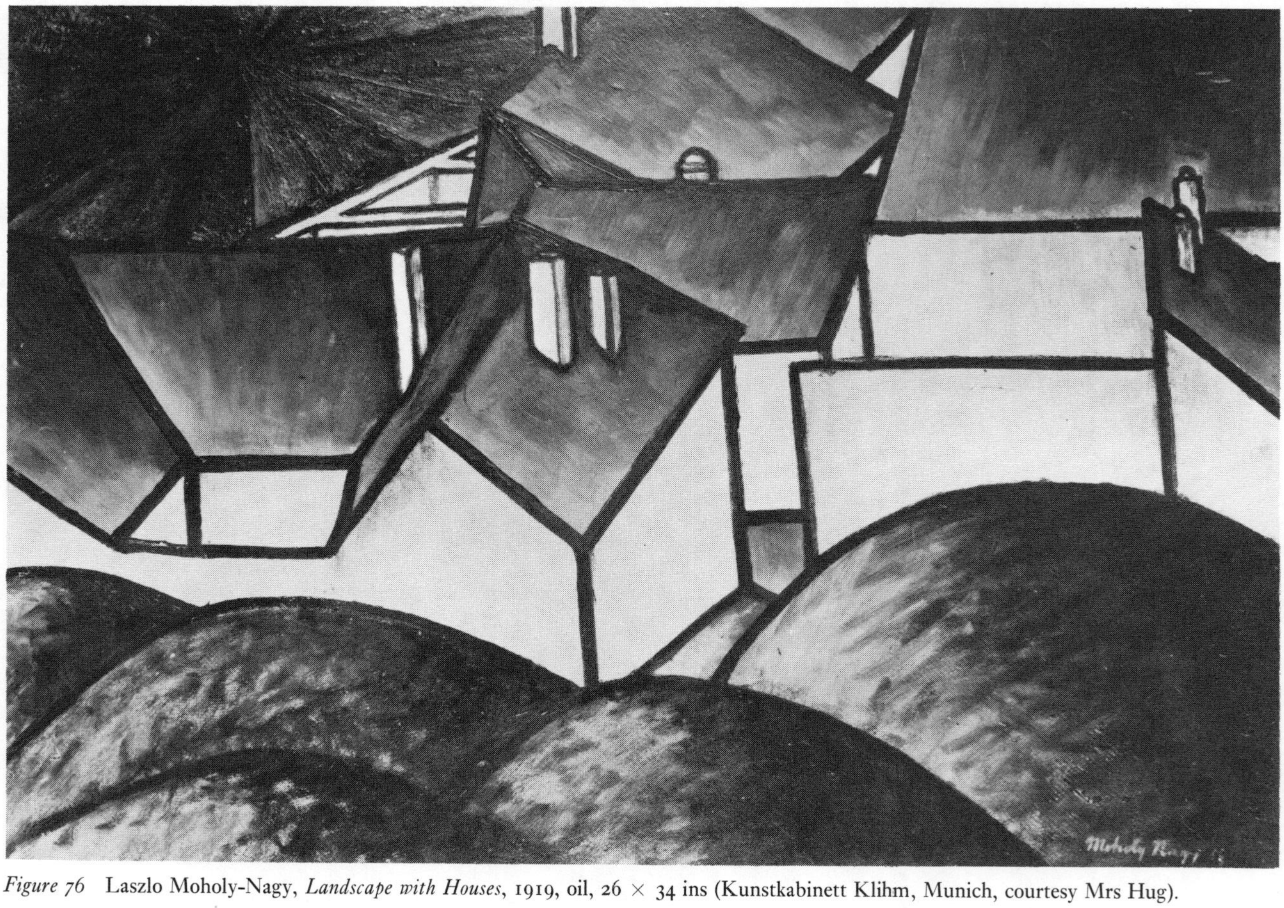

Figure 76 Laszlo Moholy-Nagy, *Landscape with Houses*, 1919, oil, 26 × 34 ins (Kunstkabinett Klihm, Munich, courtesy Mrs Hug).

Ernst Kallai, a fellow Hungarian, wrote in 1920 of Moholy's strong, cubistic landscapes which, he felt, showed a 'serious stasis of a timeless space perception'. Such a picture is illustrated in Figure 76, *Landscape with Houses* of 1919. A comparison with a contemporary painting by Oskar Kokoschka (for instance Hamilton Fig. 289) is instructive. Kallai felt that the two painters represented two different generations and that he saw

In Moholy-Nagy the artistic expression of an objective, crystal hard life positivism based on highest intelligence and will power; and on the other side Kokoschka, his art a symbol of a decadent, only in nerve substance and extravagant vibrations living super culture.[14]
(Quoted in Kostelanetz, 1971, p. 30.)

What did Kallai see in this painting of Moholy-Nagy's? Does the picture show an 'objective, crystal hard life positivism'? It is a simple picture where the elements of landscape (the hills and houses) are reduced to an elementary visual code. Plastic form is given to the objects by crude brushwork which changes in tone to suggest the passage of light across both hillock and cottage roof. Only barely 'cubistic', this painting shows Moholy in 1919 to be developing towards abstraction but you should remember that at this time Kandinsky had been painting abstract pictures for over six years. Indeed, in a way, Moholy's landscape is not unlike Kandinsky's early Murnau pictures with their expression purged and the vigour replaced by simplicity. Pictures like this and some of Moholy's highly Expressionist drawings made during the First World War must be understood before it is possible to appreciate how Moholy could so suddenly begin to create pictures like *Composition No. 19* of 1919 (Fig. 77), characteristic of his early non-objective style but lacking the simple clarity

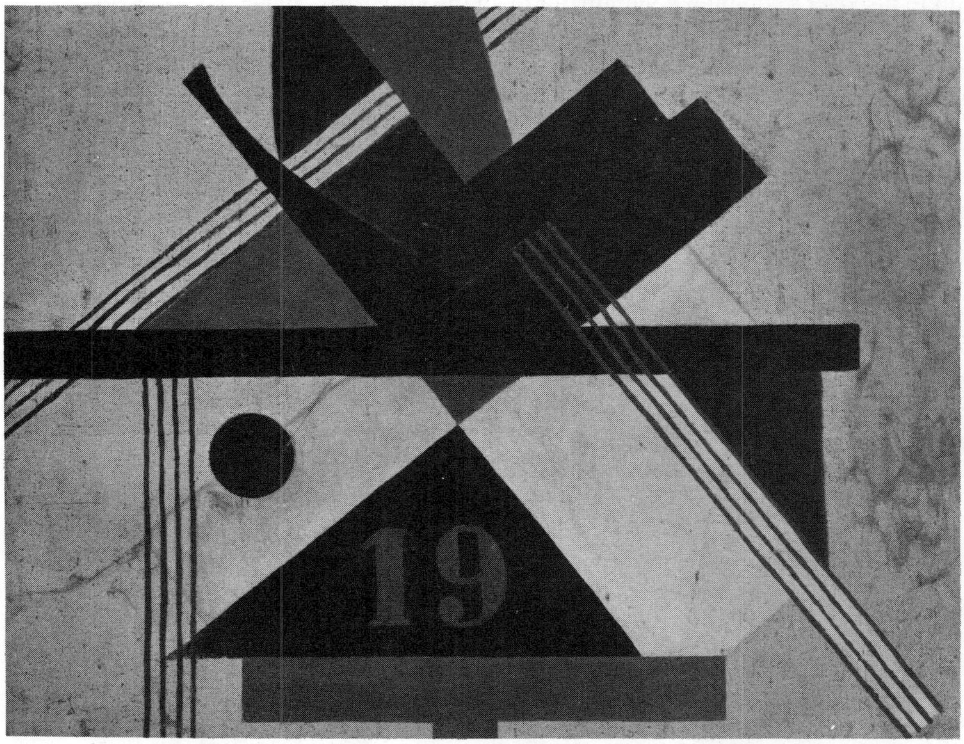

Figure 77 Laszlo Moholy-Nagy, *Composition No. 19*, 1919, oil, 44 × 36½ ins (Busch-Reisinger Museum, Harvard University, gift of Mrs Sybil Moholy-Nagy, courtesy Mrs Hug).

of his compositions of *c.* 1923. Writing of his paintings in this period Moholy recalled that they

. . . became completely freed from all elements reminiscent of nature. Their genesis was determined by a complete liberation from the necessity to record. I wanted to eliminate all factors which might disturb their clarity—in contrast for instance with Kandinsky's paintings which reminded me of an undersea world. My desire was to work with nothing but the peculiar characteristics of colours, with their pure relationships.
(*Abstract of an Artist.*)

Yet some of his paintings still have evocative titles like *Large Emotion Meter*, an uncharacteristic title for a man who was later to claim that emotion had no place in art.

In the years just after 1920 Moholy was feeling his way towards total abstraction, a pursuit perhaps aided by his not then being attached to any group of artists and being tied to neither manifesto nor programme: his research and progress could be pure.

It is extraordinary that this unattached country man from rural Hungary could speak of a new art employing a 'Dynamic-Constructive Energy-System'. In this piece of writing he shows a characteristic naive enthusiasm for what sounds 'scientific':

> We must . . . replace the *static* principle of *classical art* with the *dynamic* principle of universal life. In practice: instead of static material-construction (relationships of material and form) we have to organise dynamic construction (vital constructivity, energy relationships), in which the material functions solely as a conveyor of energy.
> (Quoted in Kostelanetz, 1971, p. 29.)

Someone holding these views, with the facilities of the Bauhaus before him, would not, like Moholy, forever go on producing paintings, but in the meantime Moholy set out to discover a common denominator of all the visual arts. Believing as he did that photography had destroyed the usefulness of imitative art, it is no surprise to learn that Moholy's experience of El Lissitsky at the *Erste russische Kunstaustellung* ('First Exhibition of Russian Art') held at van Diemen's Gallery in Berlin in 1922 gave him the final push towards his own unique form of Constructivism which, embracing as it did constructions with transparent materials, photography, film and non-functioning machines known as light-space modulators, had as its common denominator that inevitable, elemental phenomenon: light.[15]

Immediately before Moholy joined the Bauhaus an event occurred which has become part of the apocrypha of modern art. The story goes that in order to demonstrate the

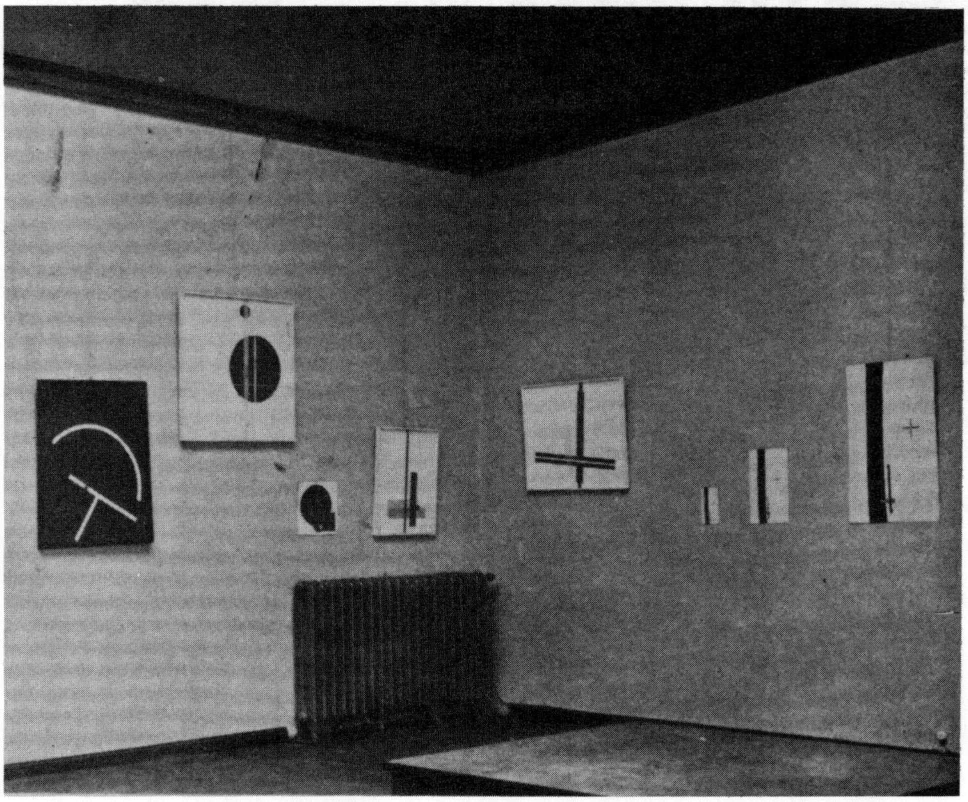

Figure 78 Laszlo Moholy-Nagy, telephone pictures as exhibited at the *Der Sturm* exhibition, Berlin 1922 (Taken from Moholy-Nagy, 1969, p. 31).

role of technology in the creation of art and to underline the possibilities of the modern age Moholy ordered some pictures over the telephone in conversation with the foreman of an enamelling factory. These so-called 'telephone pictures' were exhibited in the *Der Sturm* gallery in February 1922 (Fig. 78).[16]

The purpose of the exercise was to experiment with different colours and forms in different sizes; in the exhibition, as you can see in the figure, three identical pictures were produced in three different sizes in order to test the response to each different format. Now, contradicting the conventional story, Lucia Moholy, the artist's first wife, has recently refuted the traditional interpretation. She writes

> When the panels, carried out in an enamel technique on a metal base, among them three different sizes of identical colours and composition, were finally delivered, Moholy-Nagy was satisfied, more than satisfied, he was enthusiastic. His wishes had been complied with, his ideas had taken tangible form, his self-assurance had received a new uplift. His buoyancy exceeded all bounds. I had not seen him in a comparably exalted state for a long time. . . . It did not surprise me, therefore, when, overcome by emotion, he exclaimed—I distinctly remember the timbre of his voice on this occasion—'I might even have done it over the telephone'. (Moholy, 1972, pp. 75–76.)

How the suggestion that Moholy had ever actually ordered these pictures over the telephone came about is something of a mystery[17] for Moholy himself, in an article in *Der Sturm* in February 1924, enthusing about the perfect precision made possible in the period of industrial production with the help of graph paper and Ostwald's colour chart, only ever claimed that the exercise 'might even be done over the telephone'. But critics and historians, anxious to seize upon this icon of modernism, have changed what was a wistful subjunctive into a positive assertion.

Moholy was not very active as a painter during his years at Dessau. *A XX* (Plate 19) of 1924 is typical of his paintings in his early Bauhaus period: it represents an attempt to transfer onto canvas effects of transparency which Moholy had detected in earlier constructions created under the influence of the Dadaists in Berlin at the beginning of the decade.

Two later examples of Moholy's work are illustrated in Hamilton: the *Light-Space Modulator* of 1922–30 (Fig. 204), used in the film *Lichtspiel Schwarz-Weiss-Grau*, and the *Space Modulator* (Fig. 203). Again, both 'machines' show a fascination with the manipulation of light for aesthetic effect. But does, as Hamilton suggests, Moholy's propagandist drive to make art available to all help produce cold, anonymous and undemonstrative works? Perhaps, but seen as battles in the campaign for a new vision and as components of what Moholy called a 'socialism of the mind', they are masterly exhibits of orderly constructivist art.

Bauhausbücher—The Art Theory of the Bauhaus

The *Bauhausbücher* were not really published by the Bauhaus at all, but appeared under the imprint of the Albert Langen-Verlag in Munich who, with sponsorship from the Bauhaus, published the fourteen texts between 1925 and 1929. Of the fourteen works which actually appeared eight were directly concerned with painting, while the others were on architecture or theatre. The *Bauhausbücher* by painters and about painting were: Paul Klee, *Pädagogisches Skizzenbuch* (*Pedagogical Sketchbook*), 1925; Piet Mondrian, *Neue Gestaltung* (*New Design*), 1925; Theo van Doesburg, *Grundbegriffe der neuen gestaltenden Kunst* (*Principles of the New Art*), 1925; Laszlo Moholy-Nagy, *Malerei, Fotographie, Film* (*Painting, Photography, Film*), 1925; Wassily Kandinsky, *Punkt und Linie zu Fläche* (*Point and Line to Plane*), 1926; Kazimir Malevich[18], *Die Gegenstandslose Welt* (*The Non-Objective World*), 1927; Albert Gleizes, *Kubismus* (*Cubism*), 1928; and Laszlo Moholy-Nagy, *Von Material zu Architektur* (*From Material to Architecture*), 1929.

The *Bauhausbücher* were jointly edited by Walter Gropius and Laszlo Moholy-Nagy. Planned to appear in 1924, but held up by the economic recession in Germany at that time, they represented the first real fruits of the new ideology of the Bauhaus. Gropius and Moholy-Nagy did not always enjoy the best of relations with one another but their united effort served, as Sybil Moholy-Nagy put it, 'to annihilate the beaux-arts spirit' (S. Moholy-Nagy, 1969, p. 38) and must now be considered one of the greatest of all the achievements of the Bauhaus.

In the *Bauhausbücher* an individual identity and a novel format were given as a mouthpiece to the creators of the new art, wherever they were, and this constituted a major achievement in art publishing; the *Bauhausbücher* were not the products of critics or historians, but were the authentic works of the most advanced and the most influential artists working in Europe. Although not widely distributed (they were not all translated until after the war), in many cases the *Bauhausbücher* were the first publications to give a degree of availability to the theories of the new art.

One of the reasons why the *Bauhausbücher* were so distinctive is the innovations in layout and typography which Moholy-Nagy pioneered in them (Fig. 79a–h). By the time Moholy joined the Bauhaus his first wife, Lucia, had become thoroughly familiar with the theory and practice of printing which she willingly passed on to her husband. The novelty of the typography and the layout can, however, be overstated: despite the world-wide identity of lower-case sans-serif type with Bauhaus publishing, in fact, only two of the *Bauhausbücher* were set without capital letters and, after Moholy's departure, his typography was substantially modified by Herbert Bayer who gave it a lighter, more flexible form which is still in wide use today.[19]

Although fourteen *Bauhausbücher* have become famous, the original plans were much more ambitious aiming to produce no less than fifty titles. If these books had ever been published—if, indeed, they were ever written—the history of twentieth-century art might have been written a little bit differently.

The first *Bauhausbuch* by an artist was by Paul Klee:

(a) Paul Klee, *Pädagogisches Skizzenbuch*
The cover of this book (Fig. 79a) was designed by Farkas Molnar and the book itself as its title suggests, is an abstract of Klee's teaching method. By induction, Klee makes analogies between the abstract and the concrete (brain, muscle and bone are compared to active, medial and passive moods) and between the microcosm which, in Klee's view, always illustrates the greater issues of the macrocosm.

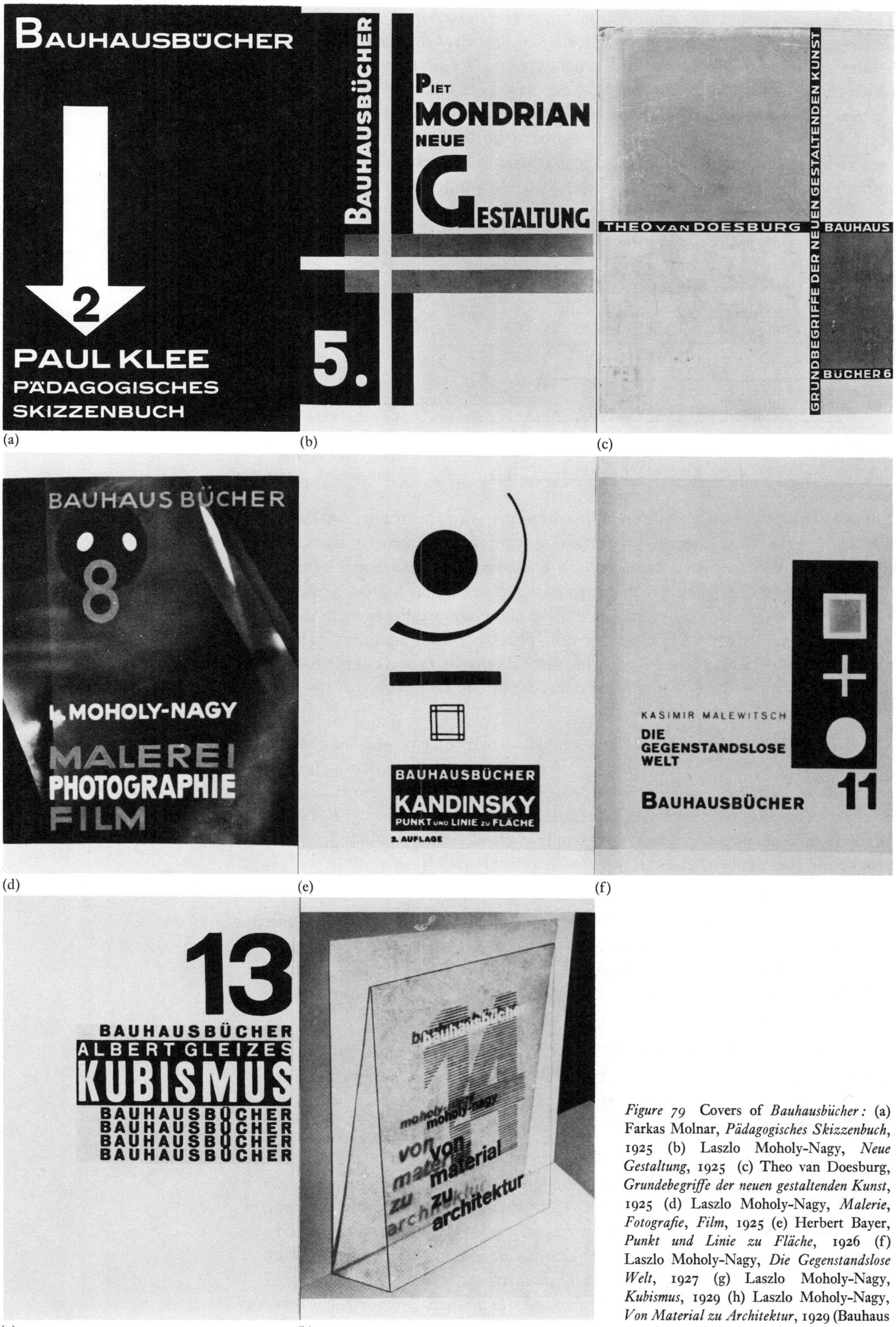

Figure 79 Covers of *Bauhausbücher:* (a) Farkas Molnar, *Pädagogisches Skizzenbuch*, 1925 (b) Laszlo Moholy-Nagy, *Neue Gestaltung*, 1925 (c) Theo van Doesburg, *Grundebegriffe der neuen gestaltenden Kunst*, 1925 (d) Laszlo Moholy-Nagy, *Malerie, Fotografie, Film*, 1925 (e) Herbert Bayer, *Punkt und Linie zu Fläche*, 1926 (f) Laszlo Moholy-Nagy, *Die Gegenstandslose Welt*, 1927 (g) Laszlo Moholy-Nagy, *Kubismus*, 1929 (h) Laszlo Moholy-Nagy, *Von Material zu Architektur*, 1929 (Bauhaus Archiv, Berlin).

There is clear evidence throughout the *Pädagogisches Skizzenbuch* of the influence of *Gestalt* psychology which was, in the 1920s, a new branch of science which seemed to offer new insights into the nature of artistic creation. Look at Figure 80, a drawing which Klee uses to illustrate his section 'Nochmals die Senkrechte' ('Once More the Vertical'). It is employed to underline one of the basic principles of perceptual psychology: we see buildings as they are shown in the drawing, but compensate for the strangeness by, in fact, distorting them so that they look 'real'. You should ask yourself whether this principle might be applied to any other aspect of Klee's art.

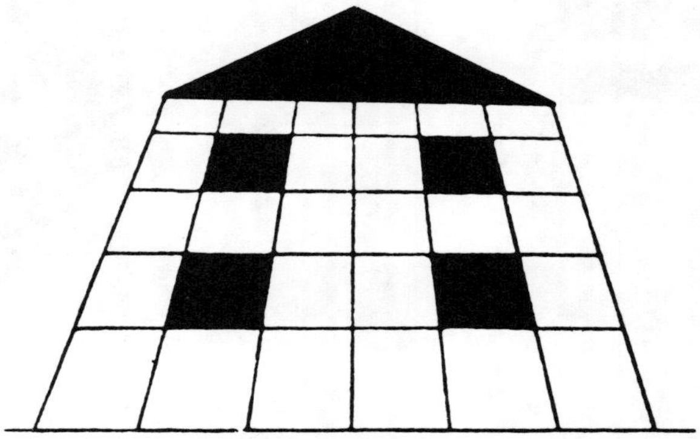

Figure 80 Paul Klee, 'Once More the Vertical', II, 20, from *Pädagogisches Skizzenbuch*, 1925 (Reprinted by permission of Faber and Faber Ltd).

The book, which is mostly made up of line drawings, is an attempt to reveal some of the basic laws of visual language by illustrating events and phenomena familiar to us all from everyday experience: balances with uneven weights and stones for building towers are shown side-by-side with stairs and the trajectories of bullets. The arrow had, for Klee, a special significance. 'The father of the arrow is the thought' he writes, 'How do I expand my reach? Over this river? This lake? That mountain?' and added, wistfully, 'The contrast between man's ideological capacity to move at random through material and metaphysical spaces and his physical limitations, is the origin of all human tragedy' (Klee, 1953, p. 37).

The *Pädagogisches Skizzenbuch* is divided into four parts each of which is concerned with a different potential of line: sections are concerned with, for instance, line as a point progression, line as mathematical proportion, line as optical reason, line as energy projection and line as a symbol of will and infinity. The multifarious intricacy of Klee's examination of line, this most simple of the elements of painting, offers an insight into the deeply mysterious world which Paul Klee inhabited.

(b) Piet Mondrian, *Neue Gestaltung*

The cover (Fig. 79b) of this *Bauhausbuch* was designed by Moholy-Nagy. Mondrian's aesthetic philosophy has been summarized in Unit 11. (*Neue Gestaltung* was a translation of Mondrian's first piece of theoretical writing, *Le Néo-Plasticisme*, which was published in Paris in 1920 by Léonce Rosenberg.)

(c) Theo van Doesburg, *Grundbegriffe der neuen gestaltenden Kunst*

Van Doesburg designed the cover of his own *Bauhausbuch* (Fig. 79c). Van Doesburg's art theory was the subject of much of Unit 11. (*Grundbegriffe* ... was a German translation of articles by van Doesburg which were originally published in *Tijdschrift voor Wijsbegeerte* in 1919.)

(d) Laszlo Moholy-Nagy, *Malerei, Photographie, Film*

His *Bauhausbuch*, crammed with 102 illustrations between covers which, naturally, he designed himself (Fig. 79d), gave Moholy the first large-scale opportunity to explain himself and to make elaborate claims for the potential of the new vision of which he considered himself to be the protagonist. Besides the idea of progression the title itself suggests that, to Moholy, the status of painting in the new order was to be neither greater nor lesser than that of movie and still photography: each was a part of a total visual continuum.

It is an *apologia* for constructivist film, for the argument of still photography as art, for abstract painting and the idea of absolute visual experience. In it Moholy writes:

> Until photography was invented, painting combined within itself the missions of representation and expression in colour. . . . Now since the division, one field embraces pure *colour* composition, the other representational composition.
> (L. Moholy-Nagy, 1969, p. 8.)

Experience of colour had to be restricted to light shows like those Schwerdtfeger and Hirschfeld-Mack had experimented with, and organization of static colour had, in 1925, to be the province of painting alone. Movie film did, however, even in monochrome, offer new possibilities for both form and content:

> Film practice has so far been largely restricted to reproducing dramatic action without, however, fully utilising the potentialities of the camera in an imaginatively creative manner. The camera as a technical instrument and the most important productive factor in film-making copies the objects in the world around us in a manner that is 'true to nature'. . . .
> (L. Moholy-Nagy, 1969, pp. 33–34.)

Moholy senses the nearness of a unity in the arts to be achieved through the delegation of different roles to painting, photography and film. Soon, he thought, everyone would recognize that 'photography was one of the most important factors in the dawn of a new life' (L. Moholy-Nagy, 1969, p. 15) and in his second *Bauhausbuch*, *Von Material zu Architektur* Moholy developed further his theme away from the purely visual concerns of *Malerei*, *Photographie*, *Film* and, as if to give impetus to the original Bauhaus ethic, he devoted the volume to the genesis of building out of the new vision which photography had helped to create.

(e) Wassily Kandinsky, *Punkt und Linie zu Fläche*

The cover of *Punkt und Linie* was designed by Herbert Bayer (Fig. 79e). *Punkt und Linie zu Fläche* (*Point and Line to Plane*) was what Kandinsky called an 'organic continuation' of his first major treatise of personal art theory, *Über das Geistige in der Kunst* (*Concerning the Spiritual in Art*). In fact, although it was not published until 1926 it was written in Switzerland as early as 1914. A further attempt to make art into a science, the very title itself reflects the investigative nature of Kandinsky's researches: as if to emphasize the experimental nature of his writing, his *Bauhausbuch* implies the debt of art to scientific method.

Kandinsky's intention was to relate colour to form and to quantify his results so that the precise nature of human response to art could be formulated. To Kandinsky, form and colour carried precise meanings: the direction of a line could suggest, for instance, temperature values. Verticals were warm, while horizontals were cold. Similarly, black to Kandinsky was a silent colour which expressed the horizontal, while white, while also being silent, expressed instead, the vertical. You will see that Kandinsky's own synaesthetic personality must have had an effect on these responses and, while they were, perhaps, more personal than objective interpretations Kandinsky was not afraid to represent them as timeless, incontrovertible truths. It is his dogmatism which adds to the difficulty of fully appreciating the complete burden of meaning which Kandinsky attached to his painting.

In Kandinsky's researches into the science of art, as in Klee's, there can clearly be seen the influence of *Gestalt* psychology. Put at its basest, *Gestalt* psychology is the science which seeks to understand the nature of human perception. Like the *Gestalt* psychologists, Kandinsky, time and again, stresses the importance of seeing the whole as more than a sum of its constituent parts and his emphasis on the relevance of the figure–ground relationship and the law of 'strong form' (where the dominant feature in a pattern asserts itself) all support the thesis that he was, at one time, influenced by experiments in this new science. Certainly, Kandinsky could have read the publications on perceptual psychology which were appearing in the early 1920s which emphasize similar ideas.

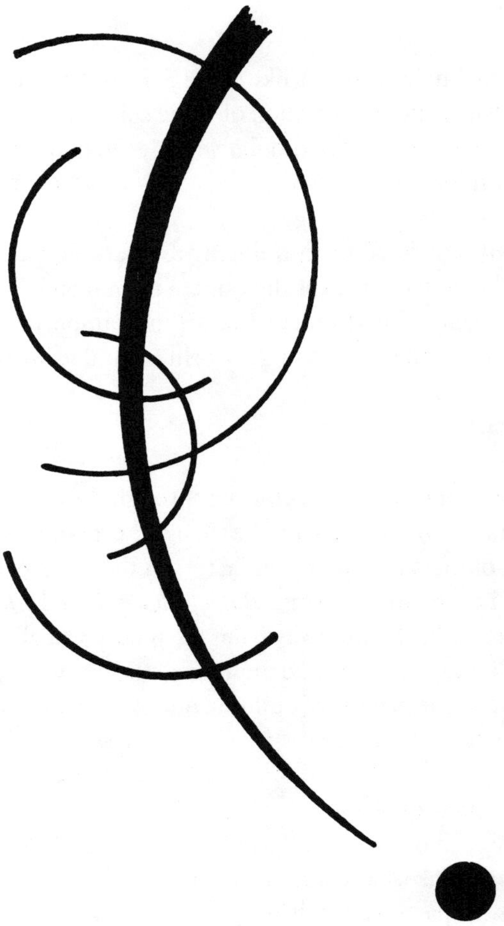

Figure 81 Wassily Kandinsky, 'Free curve versus point with resonant geometric curves', Plate 15 from *Punkt und Linie zu Fläche*, 1926 (Bauhaus Archiv, Berlin © ADAGP Paris 1976).

Look at Figure 81, Plate 15 from *Punkt und Linie*. In Kandinsky's terminology this is a free curve with resonant geometric curves. In the following passage Kandinsky is speaking of art in general, but the description can be used to apply to this individual drawing:

> In fact, the content of a work of art is not determined by the outer forms but by the living forces alive in these forms—tensions. If these tensions were to disappear suddenly at the wave of a magic wand, or die, then the living work itself would be dead at once. If this were so, any accidental combination of forms would be a work of art. The content of a work is expressed in the composition, i.e. in the internally organised sum of its tensions. This seemingly simple statement is of great significance: its acceptance or refusal divides not only the artists but all men of today into two camps: 1. Those who acknowledge the existence of the non-material or the spiritual, as well as the material, and 2, those who do not want to recognise anything beyond the material. For the second category, art cannot exist and therefore, these people negate even the word art itself, and try to find a substitute for the word.
> (*Punkt und Linie zu Fläche*, p. 27; translated in Roters, 1969, p. 142.)

Such theories are profound and moving, but do you not think that an illustration from *Punkt und Linie* such as reproduced in Figure 82 (Plate 9 from the book) suggests an influence on Kandinsky separate from the broader issues of the cosmos? Surely, there is in this drawing called 'Thin lines hold their own against the heavy point' not only a mystical interpretation of geometry but also a clear debt to the revolutionary graphics of El Lissitsky whose '*Beat the Whites with the Red Wedge*' (Unit 10, Fig. 26) this drawing so clearly resembles?

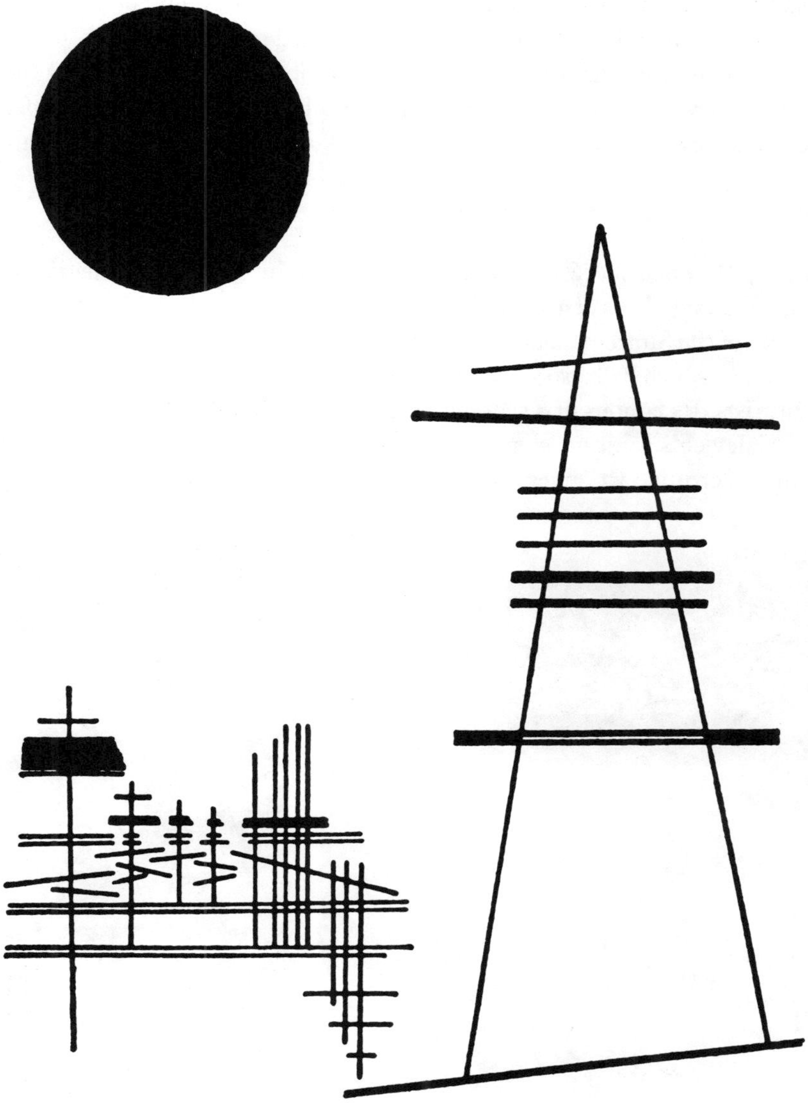

Figure 82 Wassily Kandinsky, 'Thin lines hold their own against the heavy point', Plate 9 from *Punkt und linie zu Fläche* (Bauhaus Archiv, Berlin © ADAGP Paris 1976).

(f) Kazimir Malevich, *Die Gegenstandslose Welt*

Although Malevich never had an official connection with the Bauhaus in any of its roles or locations his work, which attracted attention at the Van Diemen show, was considered of such central importance to the development of modern art (for instance his influence on Moholy-Nagy appears to have been substantial) that his treatise was one of those few works by artists who were not Bauhaus members of staff actually to see the light of day: in the days of heady optimism, many had been promised, but only Mondrian, van Doesburg, Gleizes and Malevich survived the initial enthusiasm of the *Bauhausbücher* programme. We must assume that Moholy's role as joint editor must have influenced the appearance of Malevich's treatise; certainly it was no coincidence that it was Moholy who designed the cover of *Die Gegenstandslose Welt* (Fig. 79f).

Malevich's *Bauhausbuch* contained two essays: the first was called 'Einführung in die

Theorie des additionalen Elementes der Malerei' ('Introduction to the Theory of the Additional Element in Painting') and the second, and better known, part: 'Suprematismus' ('Suprematism'). Malevich only left Russia once, in 1927, to visit Germany for the exhibition of his paintings at the Grosse Berliner Kunstaustellung. In his Introduction to the Theobald edition of the book, Ludwig Hilbersheimer recalled that

> In 1927 Kasimir Malevich came to Berlin and I got to know him personally. . . . Malevich came to Berlin for two reasons. He wanted to show his work, pre-suprematist and suprematist, as well. The exhibition, which took place at the *Grosse Berliner Kunstaustellung*, was made possible by the Novembergruppe. Malevich's second reason to get his book, *The Non-Objective World*, translated and published.
> (Ludwig Hilbersheimer in Malevich, 1959, p. 9.)

As we know, Malevich succeeded. The second half of the book, 'Suprematism', is Malevich's abstract ideals of art laid bare. Figure 83 shows Malevich's illustration of 'The Reality of the Suprematists' the third in a series of illustrations from *Die Gegenstandslose Welt*, which had also shown the reality of the Academicians, and the reality of the Futurists. Its famous first sentence, seemingly completely at odds with the reality of Malevich's painting, 'Under Suprematism I understand the supremacy of pure feeling in creative art' gives the lie to all the theorizing and the principle sug-

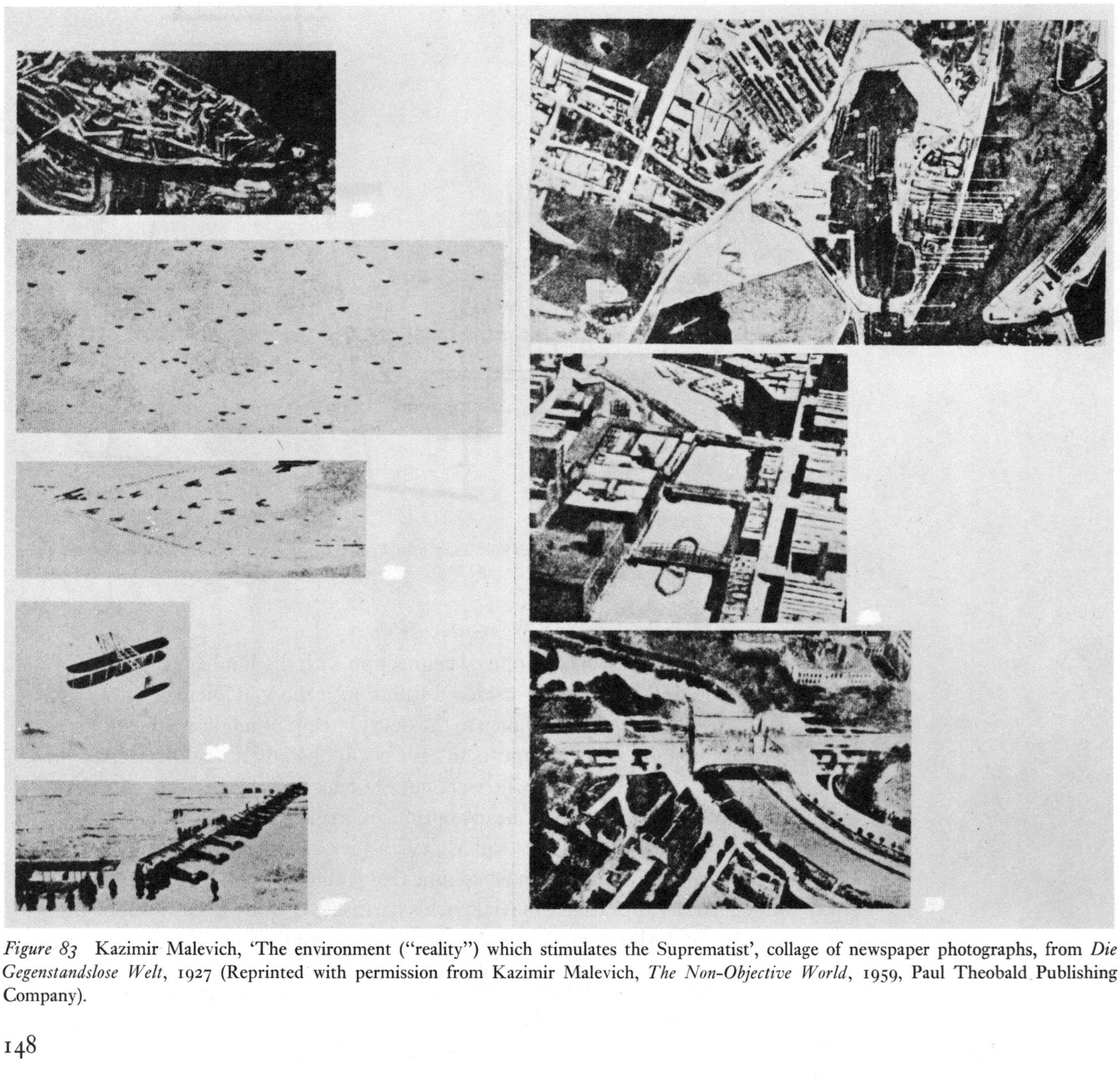

Figure 83 Kazimir Malevich, 'The environment ("reality") which stimulates the Suprematist', collage of newspaper photographs, from *Die Gegenstandslose Welt*, 1927 (Reprinted with permission from Kazimir Malevich, *The Non-Objective World*, 1959, Paul Theobald Publishing Company).

gested in this part are applied in the first. Indeed, one of the characteristics of Malevich's work which brought him closer to German interests was that almost alone among Russian artists he did not deny the emotional content of painting.

(g) Albert Gleizes *Kubismus*
(See Chipp, pp. 207*ff.*)
If the presence of Malevich's *Bauhausbuch* in the Albert Langen-Verlag lists could be explained by the community of interests shared by him and the leading Bauhaus figures, the place on the lists of Gleizes' defence of Cubism is somewhat less easy to explain. (Fig. 79g shows the cover of *Kubismus*, designed by Moholy-Nagy.)

Kubismus was translated from the original French which Gleizes had published with Jean Metzinger in 1912, immediately before the *Section d'Or* exhibition of that year. With Appollinaire's *Les Peintres Cubistes*, *Kubismus* represents the major theoretical text of the movement. In a sense Braque and Picasso, the leading figures of the Cubists, were content to let lesser lights like Gleizes and Metzinger speak for them, and it was no surprise that when the two men formed a group with Le Fauconnier and Delaunay it excluded from its membership both Braque and Picasso.

The curious inclusion of *Kubismus* in a list of *Bauhausbücher* otherwise largely given over to social and spiritual concerns must be seen in conjunction with the planned inclusion of books by Kurt Schwitters (on Merz), F. Wichert (on Expressionism), Marinetti and Enrico Prampolini (on Futurism) and by Tristan Tzara (on Dada). Plainly Moholy-Nagy and Gropius, as editors, wished to demonstrate the artistic inheritance of the Bauhaus. It seems that not only were the *Bauhausbücher* to expand the Bauhaus's own philosophy, but they were also, by extension, to wed to their own purpose the broader aims of modern art. Nevertheless, despite the curtailed ambitions of the publishing enterprise the editors must have been pleased to find that a *freie künstler* readily espoused opinions such as 'the ultimate end of painting is to reach the masses', for in the implied extension of time and space which was a necessary part of Cubist theory there was a direct analogue with the universalist intentions of the Bauhaus.

(h) Laszlo Moholy-Nagy, *Von Material zu Architektur*
It was quite fitting that the man who had done so much to create the *Bauhausbücher* should have written what was to be the last of the series, *Von Material zu Architektur*. Just as Kandinsky used the literary formulation 'From . . . to . . .', to suggest a science of painting so Moholy used the same formula to suggest the ethic of the Bauhaus (Fig. 79h).

In his introduction to the American edition of the book (1946), Walter Gropius wrote that 'Moholy has observed and registered light with the eye of the camera from the perspective of the frog and the bird', using the strange imagery to suggest the novelty and variety of Moholy's vision. *Von Material zu Architektur* gave Moholy the opportunity to summarize his whole artistic credo, an extension of his Bauhaus teaching between 1923 and 1928.

The efficacy of Gropius's imagery is borne out by Moholy's continual emphasis on the search for a biological interpretation of art. Art, Moholy feels, must be neither unique nor esoteric; specialists are scorned as perpetrators of alienation and the artist is seen as one who must be in sympathy with industrial processes. The cause of art, he states time and again, will not be served by opposition to technical progress, but by flirtation with it. In *Von Material zu Architektur* Moholy adapted all the advances of technique which the century had seen to the purpose of teaching, of educating the student's eyes in the possibilities of the 'new vision'. In Moholy's view, everyone was talented: the camera was a device which served to reduce the discriminating tyranny of manual skill but it was this attitude which brought some conflict with Gropius who, throughout his life, continued to maintain a rather romantic view of creative activity which owed much to the old idea of genius.

Moholy was able to use *Von Material zu Architektur* as a means of expressing his whole world view. He writes:

> The injuries caused by a technical civilisation can be combated on two fronts:
> 1 By a purposeful observation and a rational safeguarding of organic, biologically conditioned functions—through art, science, technology, education, politics.
> 2 By relating the single results to all human activities.
>
> We need Utopians of genius . . . not to sketch the broad outlines of an easily imaginable technical Utopia, but to prophesy the existence of the man of the future.
> (L. Moholy-Nagy, 1946, p. 18.)

He was singlemindedly dedicated to sweeping away all the accretions of the past which hindered the development of a new art, in the interests of creating a whole new existence where life and art were integrated; indeed the original title of the book was to have been *Von Kunst zu Leben* (*From Art to Life*).

Although the Dessau period looked as though it was the beginning of the establishment of the Bauhaus as a functioning institution with a list of important publications behind it, some of the world's most famous painters and designers on the payroll and its first batch of students recently become masters,[20] by 1928 there was a crisis in the air. Walter Gropius, overworked and anxious to concentrate on his own architectural practice, offered his resignation to the local government. The decision dismayed the students, who had come to respect the quiet competency of Gropius's leadership.

As his successor Gropius wanted to appoint the young Swiss architect, Hannes Meyer, the director of the architecture department at the Bauhaus. Meyer took over the directorship after Gropius's resignation was accepted by the authorities on 1 April 1928. With the Nazi storm on the horizon, Gropius's selection of Meyer was not a happy one. During his directorship Gropius had forbidden political activity by his students in order not to arouse the attentions of the authorities, but Meyer was a practising Marxist. His presence at the Bauhaus, which gave avant-gardism a positive political face, did not endear the Bauhaus to the tremulous local government.

Meyer had an aridly functional attitude to work, life and art. Life, he thought, enamoured of recent discoveries in biochemisty, was nothing more than a striving for oxygen, carbon, sugar, starch and protein and because of this, he felt that good design should respond only to needs. This attitude was reinforced by Marxist doctrine and although Meyer himself was by no means insensitive to art, in his official role his posture was designed to suggest that the intervention of taste or aesthetics could be nothing other than disruptive or irrelevant to the cause of the school.

Although Meyer's presence as director of the Bauhaus in Dessau was fated to be short-lived, in some senses his period there saw the fullest realization of the original ideals of the institution. Besides broadening the curriculum to include courses on psychology and sociology, under Meyer the workshops were more productive than they had ever been before. The criticisms Meyer made of the Bauhaus on notification of the termination of his contract show just how great the distance was between the imperative of production for needs (which he represented) and the reality of the institution. Meyer attacked Kandinsky for lazing on Adriatic beaches while there was work to be done, and was generally contemptuous of the activities of the individualists (by which he meant 'painters') at Dessau. Many of his remarks sound very up-to-date and are similar to modern criticisms of inconsistencies at the Bauhaus: 'A "Cathedral of Socialism" in which a medieval cult', he wrote to the Lord Mayor of Dessau in August 1930,

> was being followed by the revolutionaries of prewar art with the assistance of a younger generation which cast sly glances at the Left yet simultaneously hoped some day to be canonized in the very same temple. . . . Art stifled life everywhere. . . . As Director of the Bauhaus I fought against the Bauhaus style. I fought constructively through my teaching. . . . It became my aim to place design on a scientific basis and the educational structure of the institute underwent important changes: the industrial consultant joined the structural engineer.
> (Wingler, 1969, pp. 164*f.*)

Although Meyer was probably quite justified in calling the Bauhaus an 'aesthetic amusement park', his hard-line puritanism gained him few admirers. Even Moholy-Nagy, whose views might be thought to have been superficially similar to Meyer's, resigned soon after Gropius.

Under Meyer the Bauhaus became a vocational training school. Although Meyer's motives were of the highest, he was, in fact, playing into the hands of the conservative authorities who had all the time opposed the original Bauhaus idea of integrated education in favour of the development of specialist skills with the end in view of more profitable production. By 1930 the ethic had been lost.

Meyer's militancy had caused disruption both inside and outside the Bauhaus. When asked to suggest a replacement for Meyer Gropius put forward the name of the architect, Ludwig Mies van der Rohe, who had made his reputation at the Weissenhof Housing Exhibition at Stuttgart and at the International Exhibition in Barcelona. Mies's architecture exemplified the man: he once said that he did not care if his buildings were not interesting as long as they were good and to him, quality, almost in a Platonic sense, was the highest good and the end and aim of all activity. His love of beauty emphasized the difference between the Bauhaus under Mies and the Bauhaus under Meyer. Between 1928 and 1930 collectivization, utilitarianism and production had been the guiding principles, but under Mies the Bauhaus became a school of architecture.

As for the painters, Klee had left for the Düsseldorf Academy in 1930 and it was only presence of Kandinsky which assured the continuation of the art classes. By 1932 the the Nazis[21] had gained a majority in the Dessau local government and, thus given new strength, they moved in under the aegis of the *völkisch* architect and writer, Paul Schultze-Naumberg, to close down the Bauhaus, which they considered to be a hotbed of dissent, communism and degeneration. Mies managed, by a legalistic ploy, to assure the continuation of the master's salaries and then contrived to make the Bauhaus his own responsibility by moving it to a disused telephone factory near his own offices in Berlin-Steglitz.

Although the move to Berlin won for the remaining *Bauhauslers* a temporary respite, Hitler's eventual seizure of power in 1933 meant that the Dessau government was unable to continue to pay the salaries and although the Bauhaus was able briefly to continue on income brought from the sale of licenses to manufacturing concerns, it was finally closed by the SS in April 1933.

From West-Deep in the Baltic, Lyonel Feininger wrote to his wife in May of that year

> Yesterday I wrote to Gropius for his birthday. I felt almost with pain the cruelty of what he has to go through now. He who was one of the first to assemble what was left in Germany after the war by way of spiritual and constructive potentiality, to build up methods of new development in a concentrated effort, who never faltered or was side-tracked, he is now suspected and hunted down.
> (Quoted in Ness, 1975, p. 235.)

Conclusion: Art in Political Eclipse

Under the Nazis any sort of artistic activity—beside the empty adulation of mythical Aryan stereotypes—was impossible. Individuality was branded as '*Kunstbolschewismus*' ('artistic bolshevism') and free expression was held in contempt. But what *was* the precise attitude which the Nazis had to art?

The Nazi view of modern art had been very much influenced by the work of Max Nordau, a psychologist who had attacked modernism in the arts. As a study of the psychopathology of philistinism Nordau's writing makes fascinating, if uncomfortable, reading. Nazi art theorists owed him great debts because he supplied them with a pseudo-scientific framework on which to base their attack on *Kunstbolschewismus*. Nordau dedicated his book *Entartung* (*Degeneration*) to Cesare Lombroso, an Italian psychologist who had made his name by suggesting identities between physiognomy and personality. In his introduction Nordau wrote that

> Degenerates are not always criminals. . . . Some among the degenerates in literature, music, and painting have in recent years come into extraordinary prominence, and are revered by numerous admirers as creators of a new art, and heralds of coming centuries.
> (Max Nordau, *Degeneration*, 1895.)

Nordau's assessment of the contemporary malaise of 1895 was strikingly similar in its details to the Nazi attack on modern art of forty years later. Nordau blamed *mysticism* (the expression of the inaptitude for attention), *egomania* (an effect of faulty transmission by the sensory nerves, of obtuseness in the centres of perception) and *false realism* (confused aesthetic theories . . . the irresistible tendency to licentious ideals) as the cause of the degeneration of artistic standards.

After April 1933 events moved quickly. In may of that year Berlin students, led by their Professor of Political Pedagogy, gathered in the Opernplatz to burn the works of Heinrich Mann and Sigmund Freud. In September, the *Kulturkammer* ('Culture Chamber') system, which required artists to group themselves into easily controlled units under the wing of Goebbels's Propaganda Ministry, was set up. Meanwhile, Gropius, Moholy and Mies fled the country.

However, Nazi attitudes to art were by no means clear cut. Throughout the Nazi period, Classical architecture (which was not, after all, indigenous to Germany) was preferred to the north European vernacular and, astonishingly, in his novel *Michael*, Goebbels had written that 'we are all Expressionists today'. Furthermore, Goebbels, who had a taste for such things, was prepared to borrow paintings by Emil Nolde to hang in his own office.[22]

The style of painting favoured by that Nazi aesthete found its most luxuriant expression in the work of Professor Ziegler, who became known as the 'Master of the Pubic Hair' because of his amply exercised taste for painting naked women in pictures whose mawkish allegorical themes (*Noble Blood* and *Maidenhood* are typical titles) were not impaired by the admixture of a crude and insensitive lubricity.

It was Ziegler who inaugurated the Nazi *putsch* against modern art by arriving at the Mannheim Kunsthalle with a letter from Goebbels empowering him to confiscate all paintings executed after 1910 which he considered to be degenerate. Confounded by the enormity of his task, Ziegler eventually made a collection of 16,000 works which, by any standards other than his own, would have been considered a discriminating selection of the finest modern works in the Reich's museums.

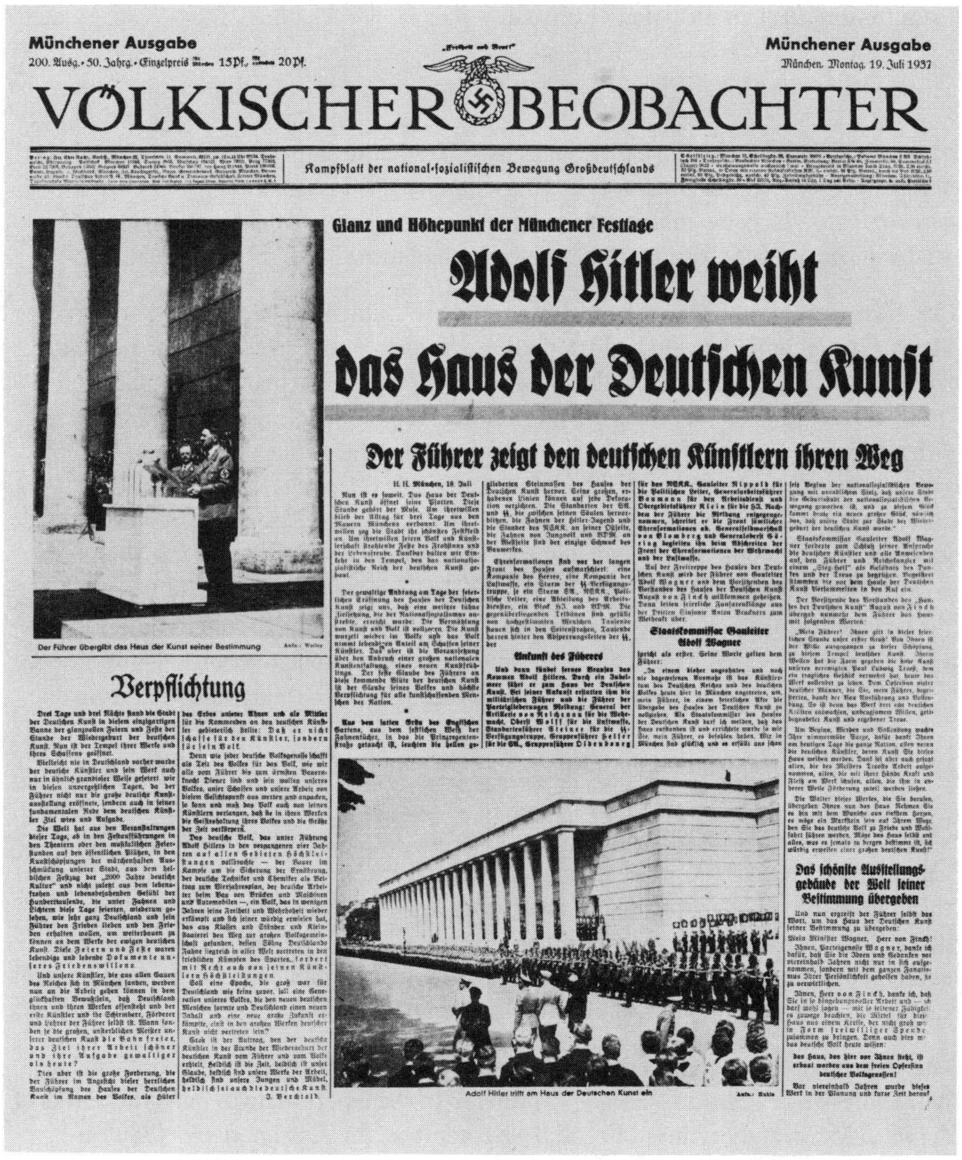

Münchener Ausgabe

200. Ausg. • 50. Jahrg. • Einzelpreis 15 Pf., 20 Pf.

„Freiheit und Brot!"

Münchener Ausgabe

München, Montag, 19. Juli 1937

VÖLKISCHER BEOBACHTER

Kampfblatt der national-sozialistischen Bewegung Großdeutschlands

Glanz und Höhepunkt der Münchener Festtage

Adolf Hitler weiht das Haus der Deutschen Kunst

Der Führer zeigt den deutschen Künstlern ihren Weg

Der Führer übergibt das Haus der Kunst seiner Bestimmung

Verpflichtung

Ankunft des Führers

Staatskommissar Gauleiter Adolf Wagner

Das schönste Ausstellungsgebäude der Welt seiner Bestimmung übergeben

Adolf Hitler trifft am Haus der Deutschen Kunst ein

Figure 84 Opening of the Haus der Deutschen Kunst, Munich 1937, in *Völkischer Beobachter*, 19 July 1937 (Bayerische Staatsbibliothek).

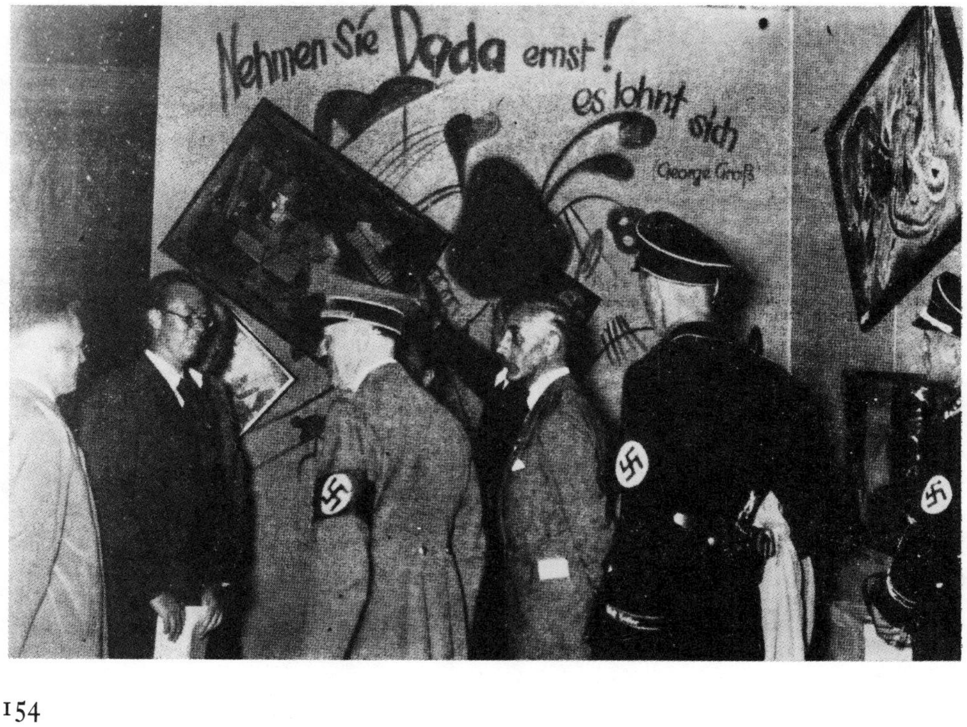

Figure 85 Hitler at the *Entartete Kunst* exhibition, in *Völkischer Beobachter*, 18 July 1937 (Bayerische Staatsbibliothek).

The grand purpose behind Zeigler's collecting was, besides the implied protection of the *Volk* from the perils of modernism, the organisation of an exhibition to be called, with a reference to Nordau, *Entartete Kunst* ('Degenerate Art'). Calculated to abuse modern artists and make their art appear ridiculous, paintings were hung in the new *Haus der Deutschen Kunst* ('House of German Art') (Fig. 84) surrounded by crude, insulting daubs more revealing of their detractors than of themselves.[23] Hitler and Ziegler can be seen enjoying the show in Figure 85.

The precise criteria which Ziegler used in making his collection are not clear, for, in fact, he made a most discriminating exhibition of modern art of the highest quality. Many works by ex-Bauhaus masters were represented there, but none were still in Germany to witness the farce.

It had been almost twenty years since the foundation of the Bauhaus in Weimar. In those years the prospects for art in Germany had changed from its participation in utopian schemes for social reconstruction in a regenerated culture to a base object of amusement for ill-educated bullies. But even if it was dead in Germany, the Bauhaus ideal lived on elsewhere.

Notes

1 'Bauhaus' is an untranslatable German word derived from the words *Bau(en)*, 'to build', and *Haus*, 'house'.

2 *Sturm* is German for 'storm' and is redolent of the *Sturm und Drang* ('Storm and Stress') movement of German Romanticism; the Romantics were a consistent source of inspiration for art in the twentieth century.

3 The Kaiser's objections had been as much concerned with von Tschudi's purchase of pictures by Delacroix as with more recent work.

4 Hess lists few portraits or figure studies by Feininger. See, for instance, *Bildnis eines tragischen Wesens* (*Portrait of a Tragic Being*,) 1920; Hess, 1959, Figure 212.

5 See Unit 8, pp. 90–92, for a summary of Hölzel's life and work.

6 Itten was certainly interested in Chinese culture. He made his pupils read Lao Tse and Chung Tse and it appears that he may have been influenced by an important book on Chinese art, Otto Fischer's *Chinesische Landschafts Malerei* (*Chinese Landscape Painting*).

7 Theosophy was the form of speculative mysticism which had attracted Mondrian and Kandinsky. Feininger appears to be misinformed on the nature of Itten's beliefs; there is nothing to suggest that he was interested in theosophy.

8 Schlemmer's *Triadic Ballet* is his most famous dance piece. Composed for performance at the Bauhaus Week of 1923, it originally had musical accompaniment by Paul Hindemith. The original print of the film is now lost, but the ballet survives in a modern filmed reconstruction.

9 At Dessau the two lived next door to one another in a semidetached pair of masters' houses which Gropius had designed at Burgkühner Allee.

10 In his *Exact Experiments in the Realm of Art* written in 1928, the middle of the Dessau period, Klee had refuted Constructivism.

11 'Art does not reproduce the visible, but makes visible.' This statement would seem to suggest the influence of Konrad Fiedler on Klee's philosophy.

12 A *verst* is a Russian unit of distance approximately equal to 3500 feet.

13 Kandinsky has described his synaesthetic experiences in his *Rückblicke* (*Recollections*), which is reprinted in Herbert, 1964, pp. 19–44.

14 So far from being the intellectual that Kallai describes, Moholy's first wife, Lucia, has recently denied that her husband was an intellectual at all. In her *Marginalien zu Moholy-Nagy* (1972) she claims that Moholy's poor German made theoretical exposition impossible for him and that she herself wrote most of his early books.

15 Far from being a purely scientific interest, it has been suggested that Moholy's concern for light is related to his brief flirtation with the Mazdaznan cult (of which sun worship forms a fundamental part) to which his first wife, Lucia, had introduced him.

16 It is possible, but unlikely, that Moholy may have got the idea of creating the telephone pictures from Richard Huelsenbeck's *Dada Almanack*. In this Huelsenbeck wrote that 'a good painter must be able to order his pictures by telephone and have them carried out by a cabinet maker'.

17 A large part of the responsibility for the perpetuation of the myth must rest with Sybil Moholy-Nagy, Moholy's second wife, whose book, *Moholy-Nagy—Experiment in Totality* (1969), suggests the use of the telephone.

18 In German the name 'Malevich' is usually rendered 'Malewitsch'. I adhere to the conventional English transliteration.

19 Three of Moholy's articles on typography, 'The New Typography', 'Bauhaus and Typography' and 'Contemporary Typography', are translated in Kostelanetz, 1971, pp. 75–80.

20 For instance, Josef Albers and Marcel Breuer (see Hamilton, pp. 342–45).

21 Properly the *NSDAP*, *National Sozialistische Deutsche Arbeiter Partei* ('National Socialist German Workers' Party').

22 Nolde did, in fact, maintain equivocal views regarding Nazism, even though his paintings were proscribed by the party.

23 Hitler's speech inaugurating the Great Exhibition of German Art, which coincided with the *Entartete Kunst* exhibition, is reproduced in Chipp, pp. 474*ff*.

Recommended Reading

The following books should be readily available in most good libraries and provide further discussion and references concerning issues raised in this unit:

Banham, R. (1960 and subsequent editions) *Theory and Design in the First Machine Age*, The Architectural Press.

Dunlop, I. (1972) *The Shock of the New*, Weidenfeld and Nicolson.
Contains a section on the *Entartete Kunst* exhibition of 1937.

Franciscono, M. (1971) *Walter Gropius and the Creation of the Bauhaus in Weimar: The Ideals and Artistic Theories of its Founding Years*, University of Illinois Press.
A scholarly account which is very useful, but overlong and turgid.

Gay, P. (1974) *Weimar Culture: The Outsider as Insider*, Penguin.
An elegant essay on the political background of Germany in the years when the Bauhaus was founded.

Lehmann-Haupt, H. (1954) *Art under Dictatorship*, Oxford University Press, New York.
A brilliant book which is very useful on the fall of advanced art in Nazi Germany.

Naylor, G. (1968) *The Bauhaus*, Studio Vista.
A modest summary.

Neumann, E. (1970) *Bauhaus and Bauhaus People*, Van Nostrand Reinhold, New York.
An intriguing collection of reminiscences by old Bauhaus staff and students.

Pevsner, N. (1937) *Academies of Art, Past and Present*, Cambridge University Press.
A book on the history of art education, long out of print, but not yet superseded.
Pevsner, N. (1972) *Some Architectural Writers of the Nineteenth Century*, Oxford University Press.
A very scholarly and detailed account of the writings of men like Ruskin, Morris, Cole and Semper who helped to form the intellectual environment in which the Bauhaus was created.
Posener, J. (1972) *From Schinkel to the Bauhaus*, Lund Humphries.
An original and stimulating survey of German architecture and attitudes to art.
Roters, E. (1969) *The Painters of the Bauhaus*, Praeger, New York.
The only book devoted exclusively to the painters of the Bauhaus.
Royal Academy (1968) *Fifty Years Bauhaus*, exhibition catalogue, Royal Academy, London.
The best and most convenient summary of all the aspects of the Bauhaus.
Wingler, H. M. (1969) *The Bauhaus—Weimar, Dessau, Berlin, Chicago*, MIT Press.
An enormous compilation of documents by the head of the Bauhaus-Archiv.

Besides these general works there is a massive amount of books available written either by Bauhaus masters or about them:

Beyer, H., Gropius, W. and Gropius, I. (1975) *Bauhaus 1919–1928*, first published 1938, Secker and Warburg.
Bredendieck, H. (1962) 'The legacy of the Bauhaus', *Art Journal*, XXII/1, Fall 1962.
Recollections of a former Bauhaus student now involved in art education in the United States.
Curjel, H. (1957) 'Johannes Itten', *Werk*, 44 no. 10, October 1957, pp. 359–66.
A study of the career of the early Bauhaus master (in German).
Van Doesburg, T. (1969) *Principles of Neo-Plastic Art*, English translation of his *Bauhausbuch*, Lund Humphries.
Geelhaar, E. (1973) *Paul Klee and the Bauhaus*, Adams and Dart, Bath.
Grohmann, W. (1958) *Kandinsky*, Harry N. Abrams, New York.
The standard work on Kandinsky's *oeuvre*.
Grohmann, W. (1967) *Paul Klee*, Harry N. Abrams, New York.
The standard work on Klee's *oeuvre*.
Gropius, W. (ed.) (1961) *The Theater of the Bauhaus*, Middletown, Connecticutt.
With contributions from Schlemmer, Moholy-Nagy and Molnar.
Hess, H. (ed.) (1961) *Lyonel Feininger*, Harry N. Abrams, New York.
The standard work.
Hildebrandt, H. (1952) *Oskar Schlemmer*, Munich.
The standard work.
Hirschfeld-Mack, L. (1963) *The Bauhaus—An Introductory Survey*, Victoria.
Itten, J. (1961) *The Art of Color*, Reinhold, New York.
One of Itten's later works, the summary of a lifetime's investigation into the nature of art.
Itten, J. (1963) *My Preliminary Course at the Bauhaus*, Reinhold, New York.
The literary exposition of Itten's teaching method.
Kandinsky, W. (1948) *Point and Line to Plane*, English translation of *Bauhausbuch*, Guggenheim Museum, New York.
Klee, P. (1953) *Pedagogical Sketchbook*, English translation of *Bauhausbuch*, Praeger, New York.
Kostelanetz, R. (1971) *Moholy-Nagy*, Documentary Monographs in Modern Art, Allen Lane.
Moholy, L. (1972) *Marginalien zu Moholy-Nagy: dokumentarische Ungereimheiten*, Verlag Richard Scherpe, Krefeld (in German and English).
A fascinating, if questionable, correction of history by Moholy-Nagy's first wife.

Moholy-Nagy, L. (1938) *The New Vision*, English translation of Moholy's second *Bauhausbuch*, W. W. Norton, New York.
Moholy-Nagy, L. (1969) *Painting, Photography, Film*, English translation of Moholy's first *Bauhausbuch*, Lund Humphries.
The exposition on his credo of non-objective art.
Moholy-Nagy, S. (1969) *Moholy-Nagy : Experiment in Totality*, first published 1950, MIT Press.
A detailed biography of Moholy by his second wife.
Ness, J. L. (1975) *Lyonel Feininger*, Documentary Monographs in Modern Art, Allen Lane.
Rotzler, W. (1972) *Johannes Itten : Werke und Schriften*, Orell Füssli Verlag, Zurich.
The monograph on Itten's life and work (in German).
Scheidig, W. (1967) *Crafts of the Bauhaus*, Spring Books.
Thwaites, J. A. (1951) 'The Bauhaus painters and the new style epoch', *Art Quarterly*, 14, Spring 1951, pp. 19–32.
A slightly confused article, but unique in its scope.
Wagenfeld, W. (1948) *Wesen und Gestalt der Dinge um Uns*, Potsdam.
A survey, by an ex-Bauhaus student, of the influence and future of the Bauhaus idea (in German).

Additional References

Von Erffa, H. (1957) 'Bauhaus: First Phase', *Architectural Review*, August 1957.
Herbert, R. L. (1964) *Modern Artists on Art*, Prentice-Hall.
Malevich K. (1959) *The Non-Objective World*, English translation of his *Bauhausbuch*, Theobald and Co., Chicago.
Pehnt, W. (1973) *Expressionist Architecture*, Thames and Hudson.

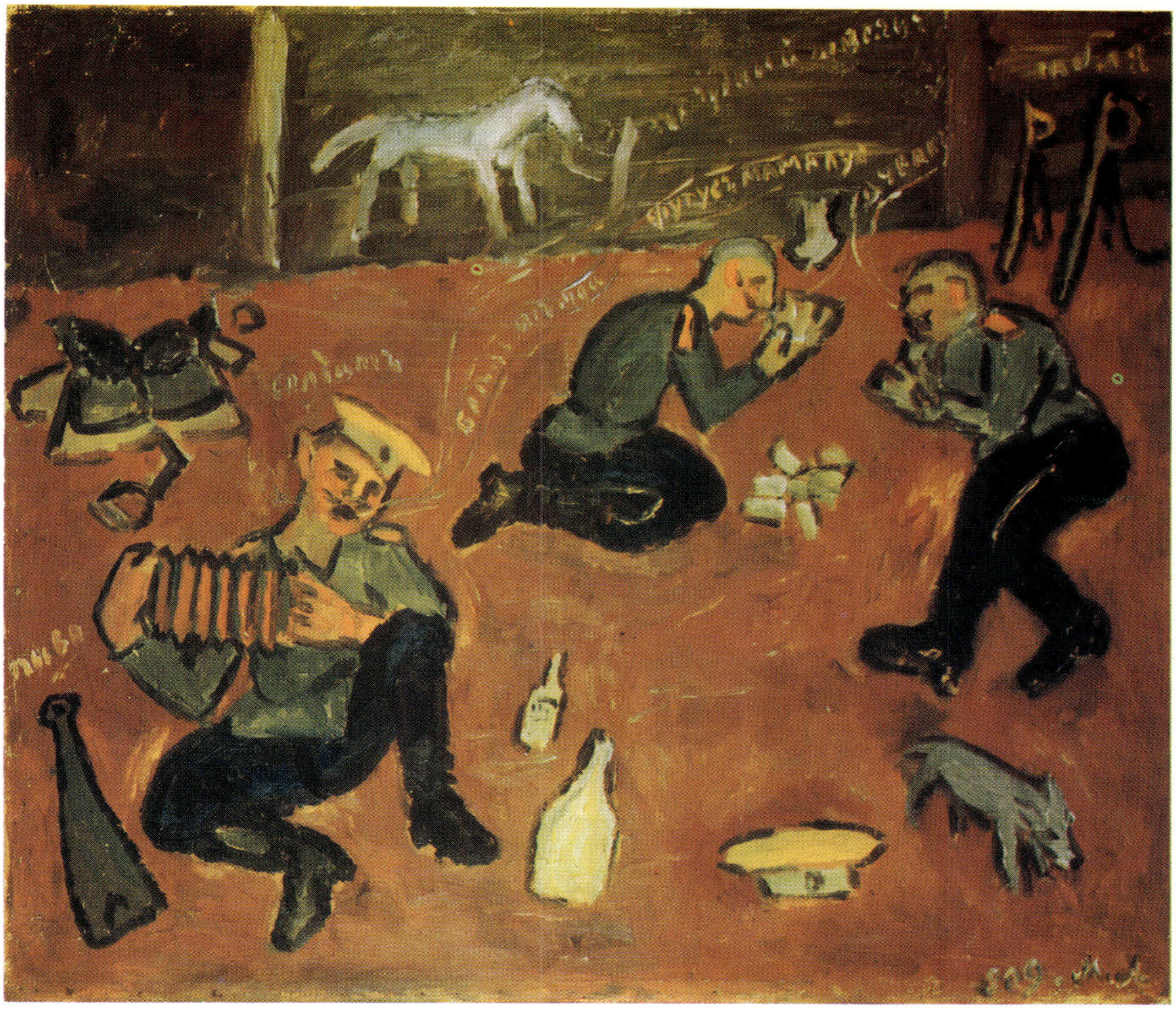

Plate 1 Mikhail Larionov, *Soldiers*, second version, *c.* 1909, oil, $34\frac{5}{8} \times 40\frac{1}{4}$ ins (Private collection, courtesy Madame Larionov; photo: courtesy the estate of Camilla Gray).

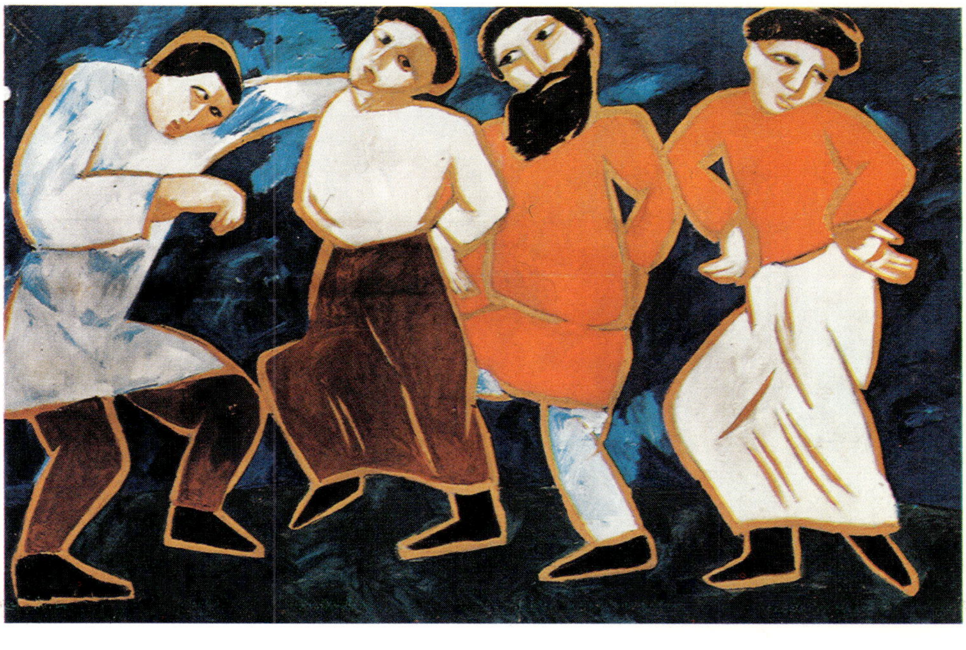

Plate 2 Natalia Goncharova, *Dancing Peasants*, 1911, oil, $36 \times 56\frac{3}{4}$ ins (Private collection, courtesy Madame Larionov).

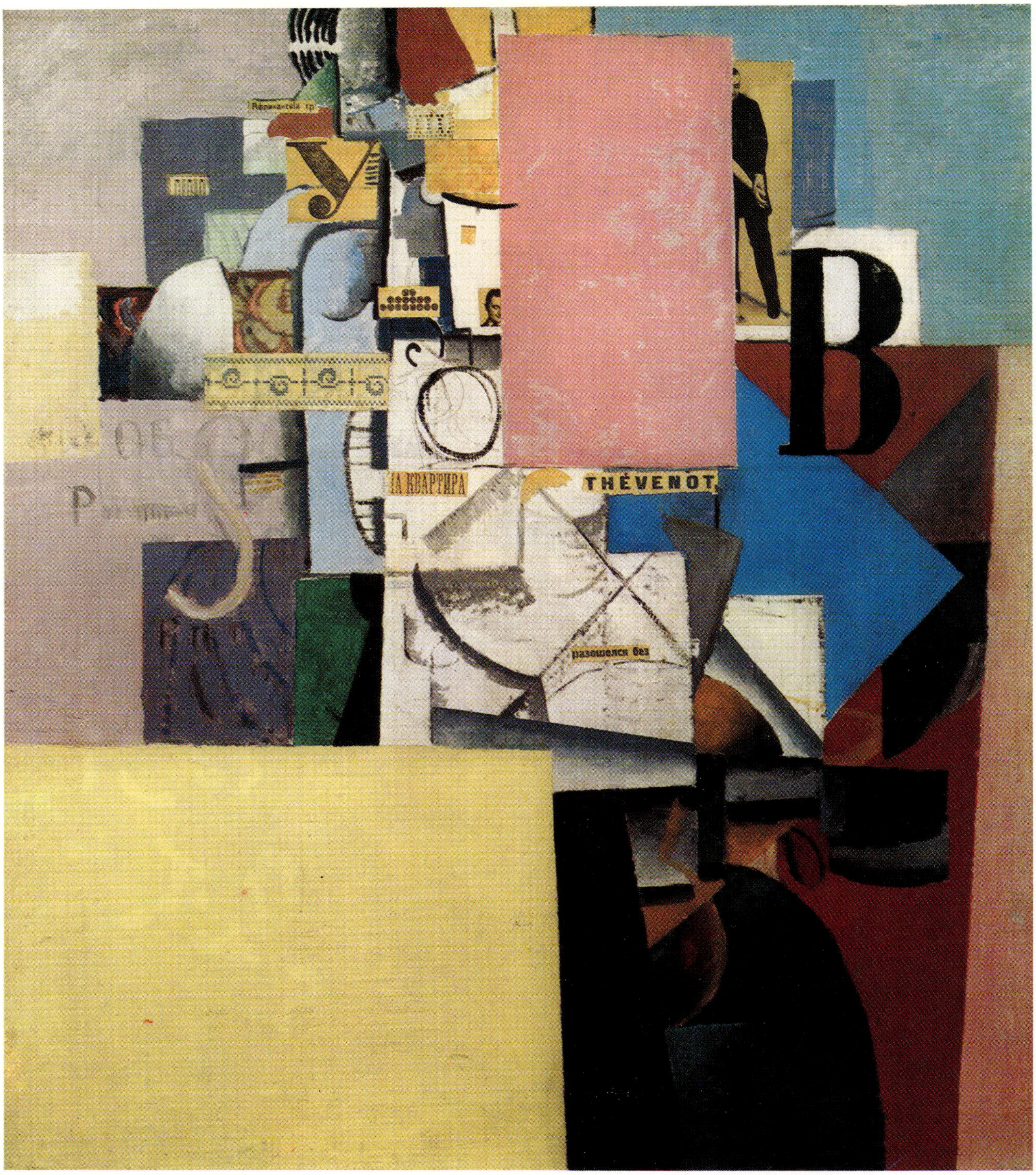

Plate 3 Kazimir Malevich, *Woman at a Poster Column*, 1914, oil on canvas and collage, $27\frac{7}{8} \times 25\frac{1}{8}$ ins (Stedelijk Museum, Amsterdam).

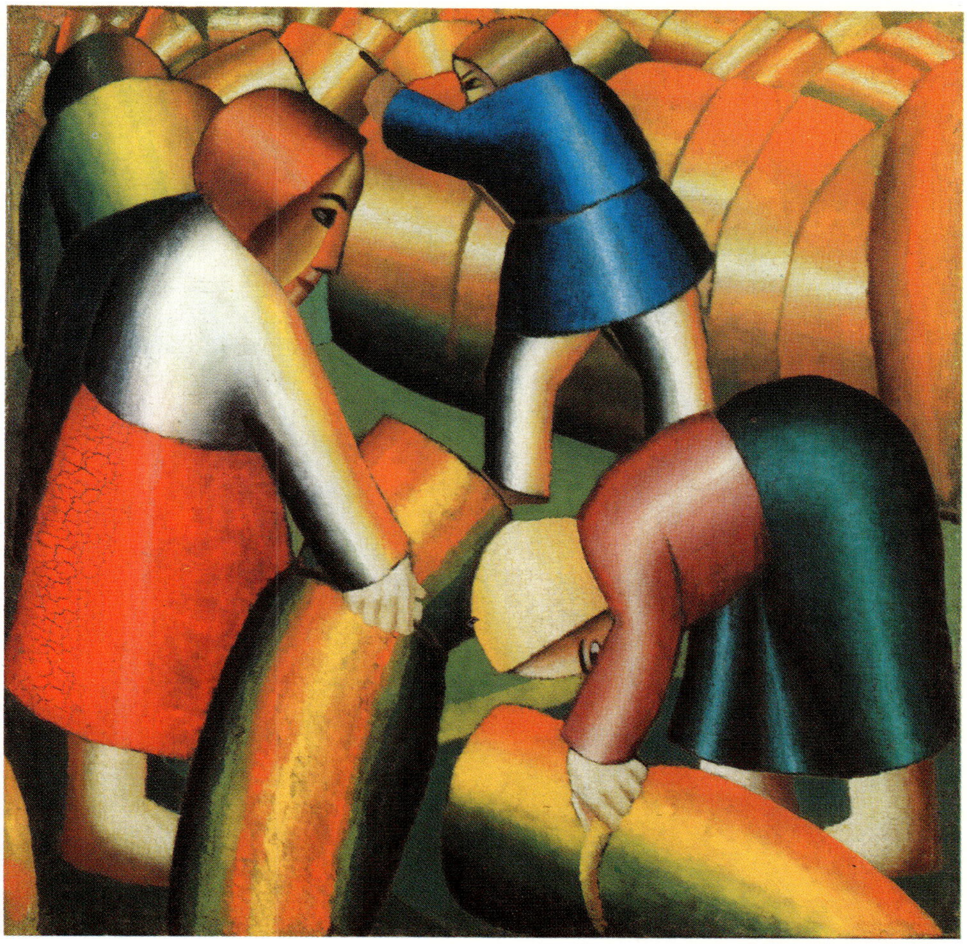

Plate 4 Kazimir Malevich, *Taking in the Rye*, 1912, oil, $28\frac{3}{8} \times 29\frac{3}{8}$ ins (Stedelijk Museum, Amsterdam).

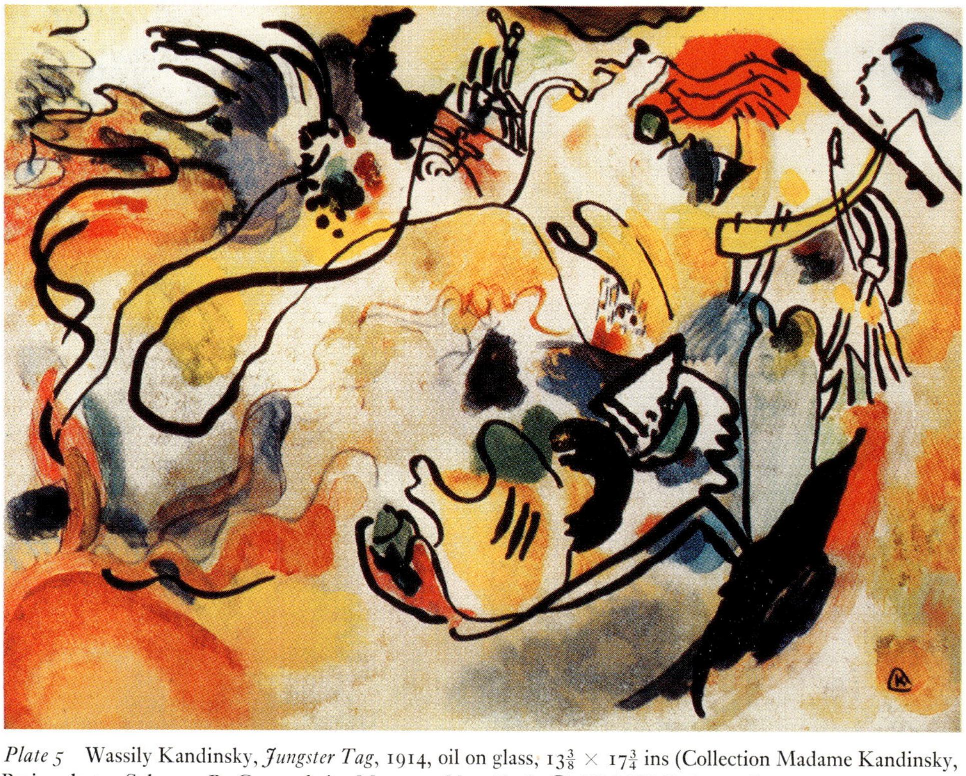

Plate 5 Wassily Kandinsky, *Jungster Tag*, 1914, oil on glass, $13\frac{3}{8} \times 17\frac{3}{4}$ ins (Collection Madame Kandinsky, Paris; photo: Solomon R. Guggenheim Museum, New York © ADAGP Paris 1976).

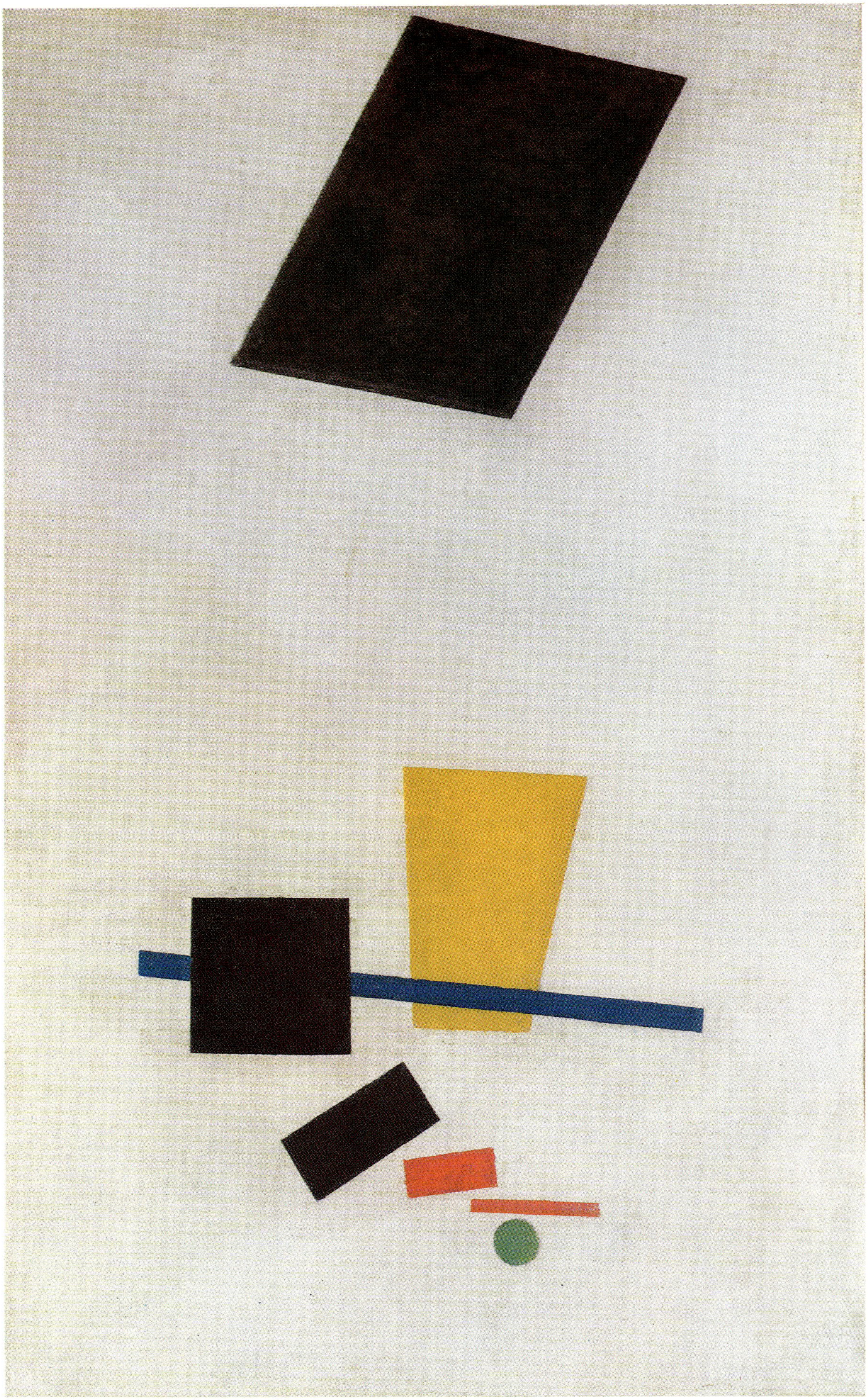

Plate 6 Kazimir Malevich, *Painterly Realism of a Football Player*, *c.* 1915, oil, $27\frac{1}{2} \times 17\frac{1}{4}$ ins (Stedelijk Museum, Amsterdam).

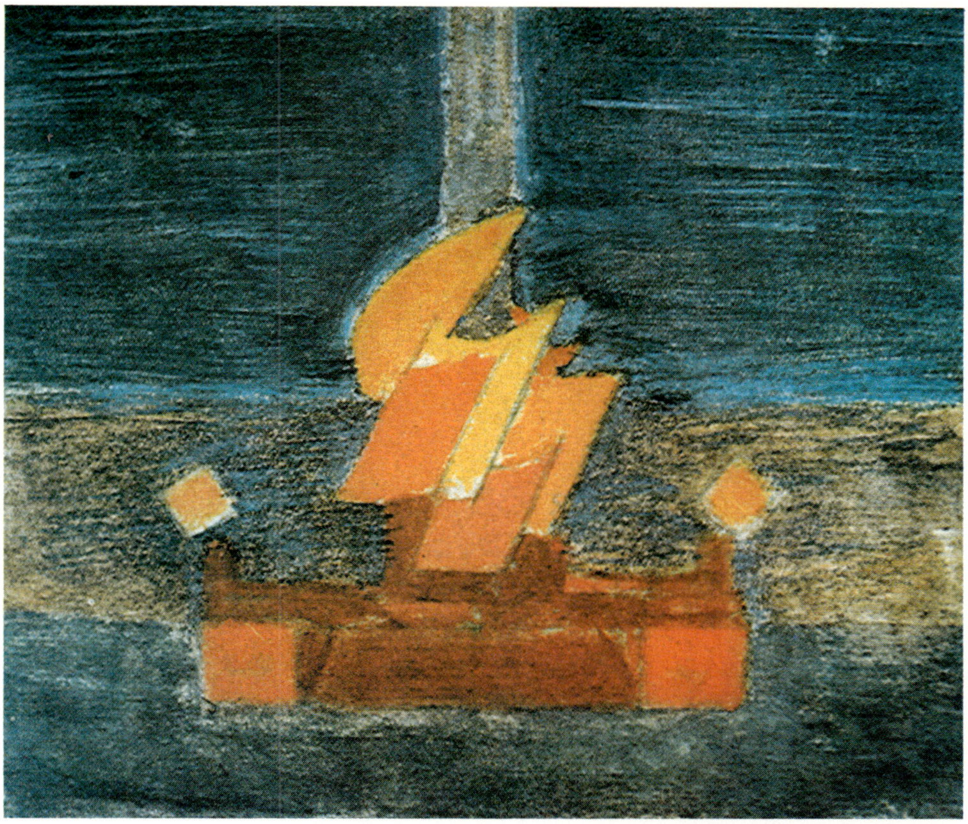

Plate 7 Nathan Altman, Design for decorations to celebrate the first Anniversary of the Revolution, 1918 Leningrad (Original probably lost; taken from *Soyuz Sovetskiy Khudozhnikov, Agitatsionno-Mussorogo Iskusstvo*, 1967, Moscow).

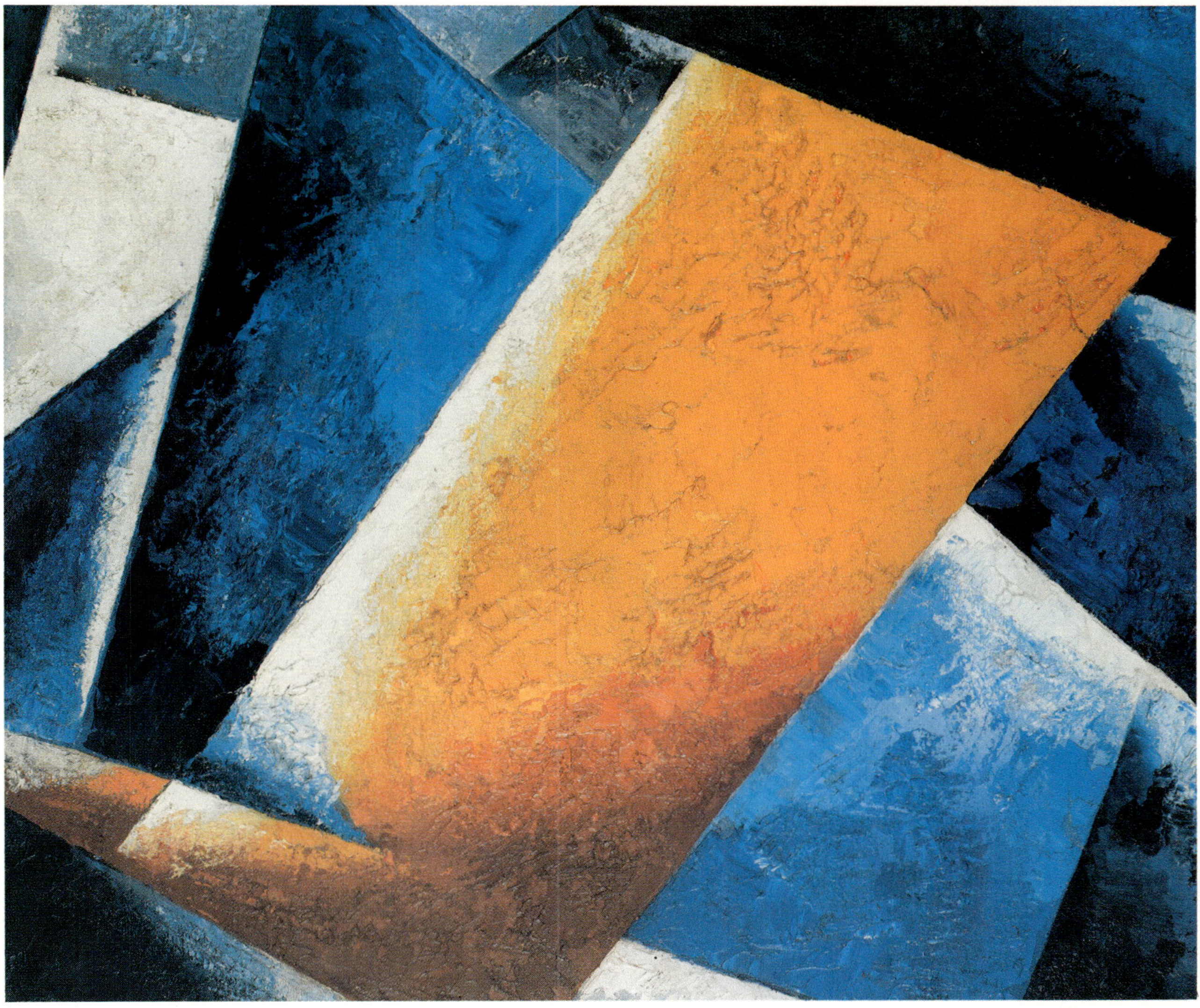

Plate 8 Liubov Popova, *Architectonic Construction*, 1918, oil, $17\frac{3}{4} \times 20\frac{7}{8}$ ins (Annely Juda Gallery, London).

Plate 9 Kazimir Malevich, *Suprematist Painting*, 1917/18, oil, $38\frac{1}{8} \times 27\frac{1}{2}$ ins (Stedelijk Museum, Amsterdam).

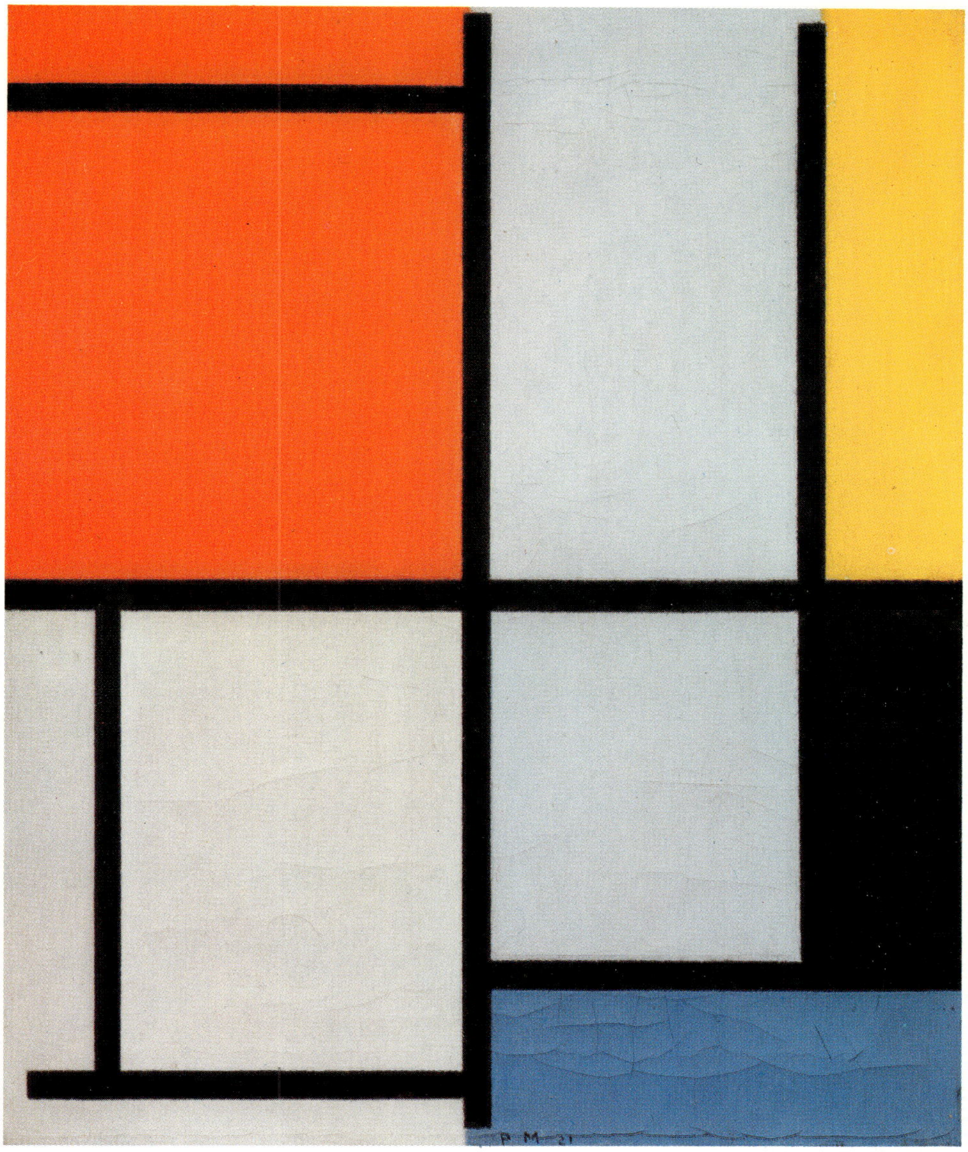

Plate 10 Piet Mondrian, *Composition*, 1921, oil, $19\frac{1}{2} \times 17\frac{5}{8}$ ins (Kunstmuseum Basle, Emanuel Hoffmann Foundation, courtesy Mr Holtzman; colorphoto: Hans Hinz).

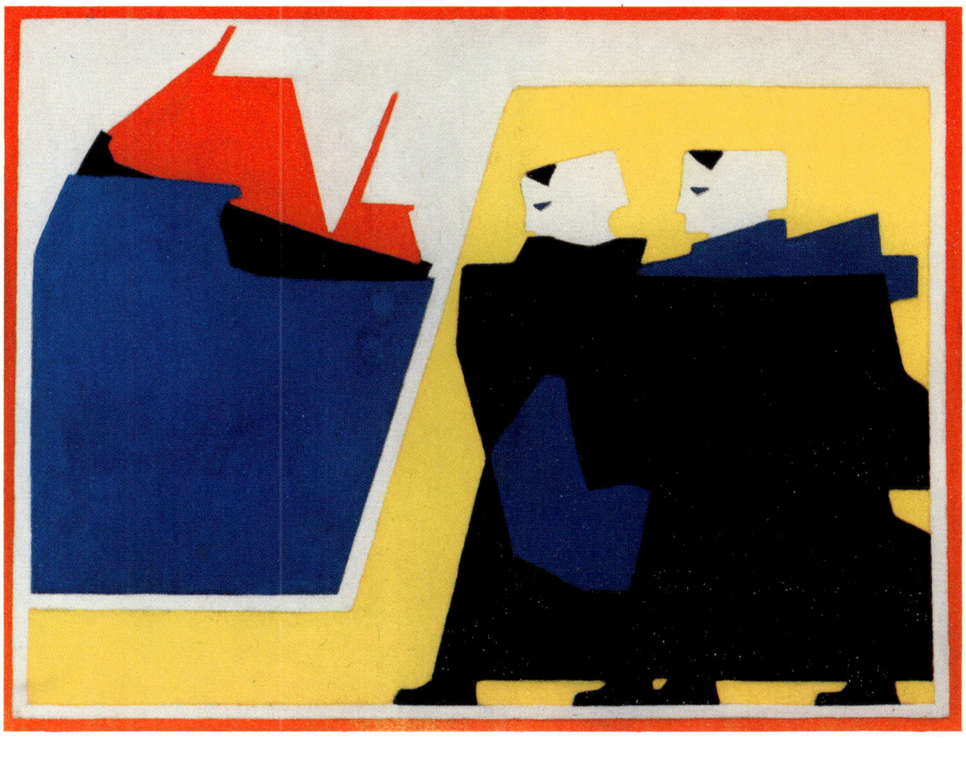

Plate 11 Bart van der Leck, *The Tempest*, 1916, oil, $46\frac{3}{8} \times 62\frac{1}{2}$ ins (Rijksmuseum Kröller-Müller, Otterloo).

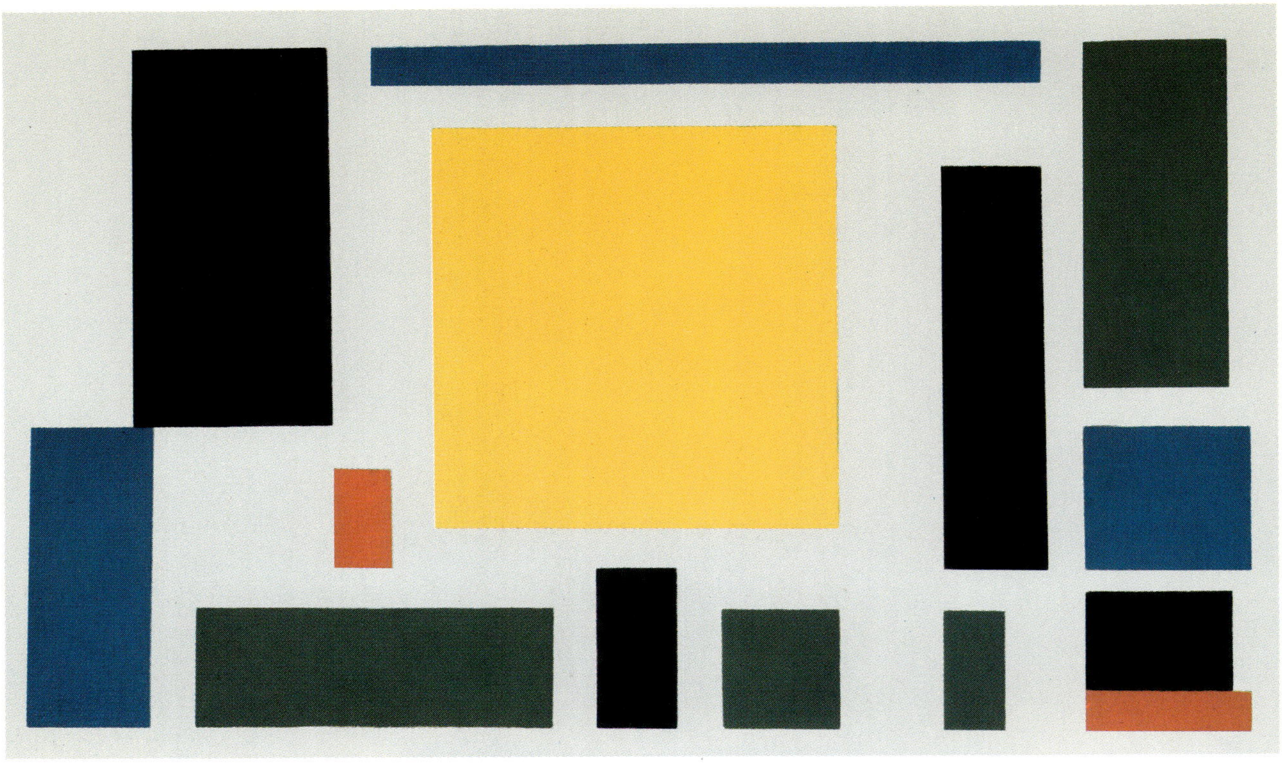

Plate 12 Theo van Doesburg, *Composition VIII: The Cow*, 1916/17, oil, $14\frac{3}{4} \times 25$ ins (Collection Museum of Modern Art, New York).

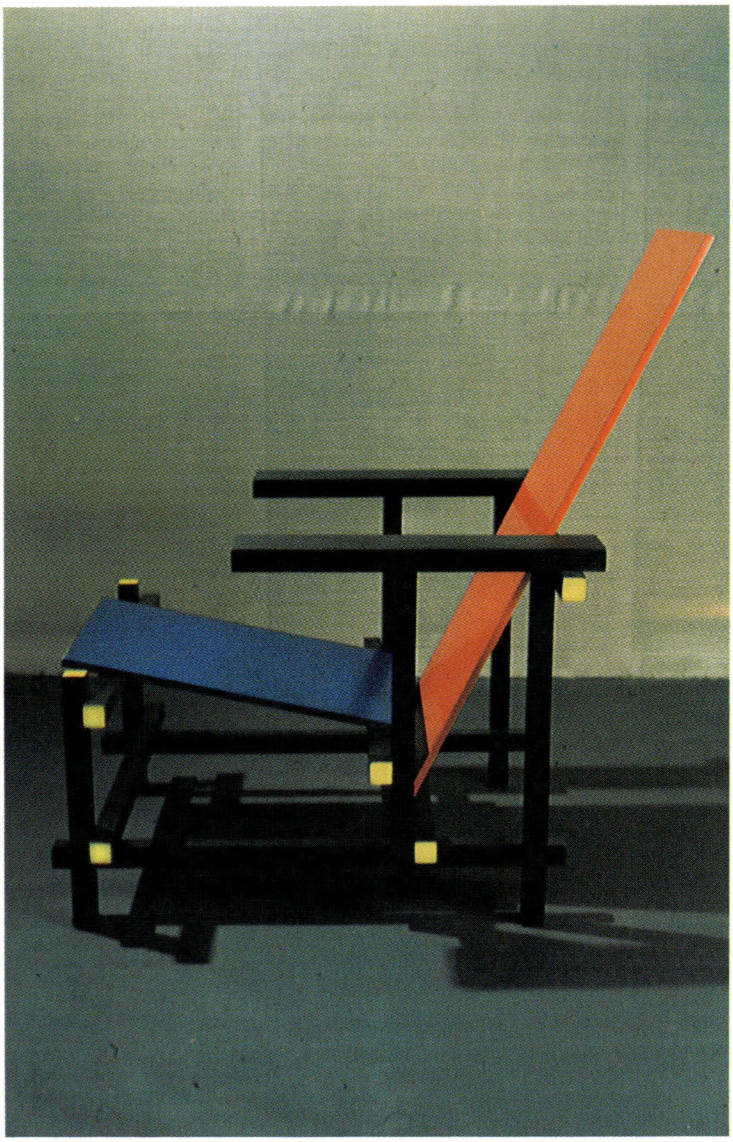

Plate 13 Gerrit Rietveld, *Red Blue Chair*, 1917, manufactured 1918 by Van de Groneken Ltd (Victoria and Albert Museum, London).

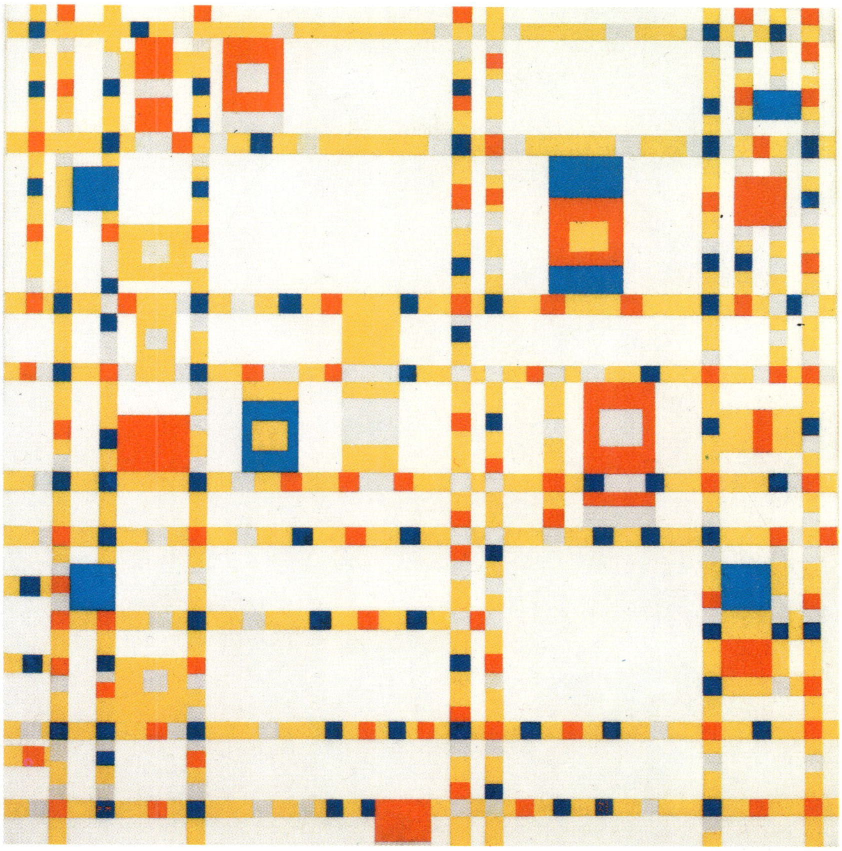

Plate 14 Piet Mondrian, *Broadway Boogie-Woogie*, 1942–43, oil, 50 × 50 ins (Collection Museum of Modern Art, New York).

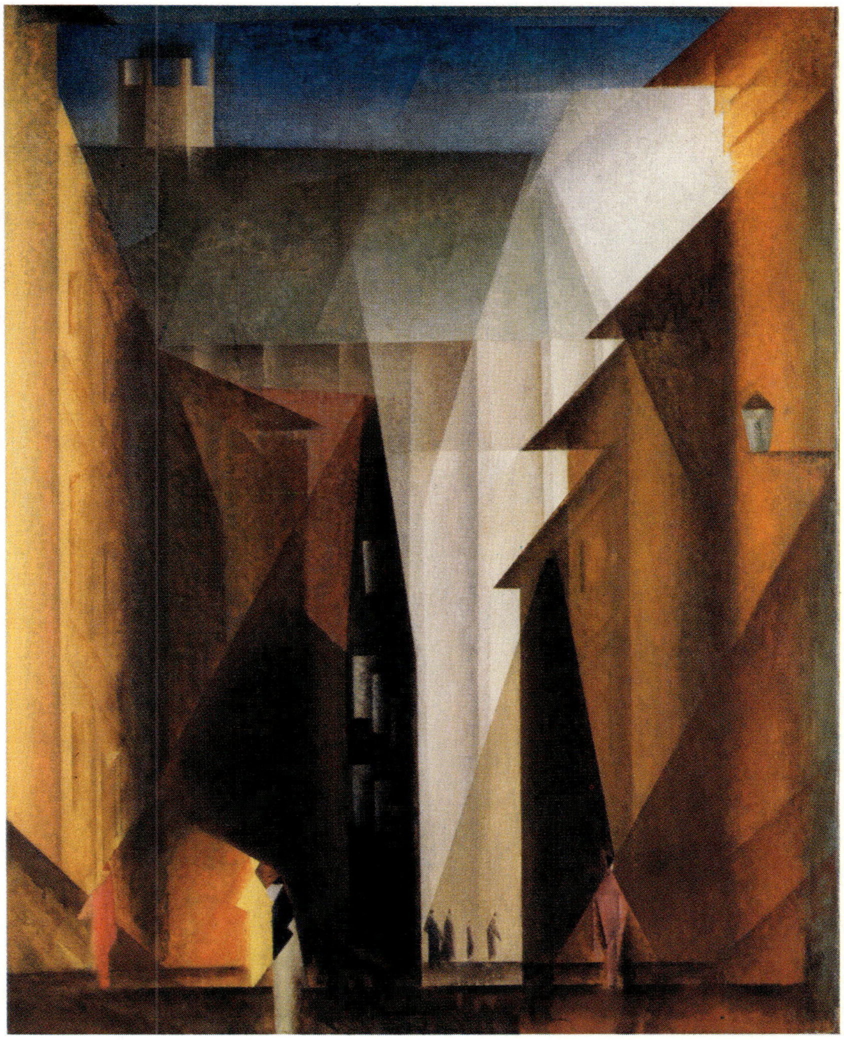

Plate 15 Lyonel Feininger, *Barfusserkirche in Erfurt I*, 1924, oil, 39 × 31½ ins (Staatsgalerie Stuttgart © ADAGP Paris 1976).

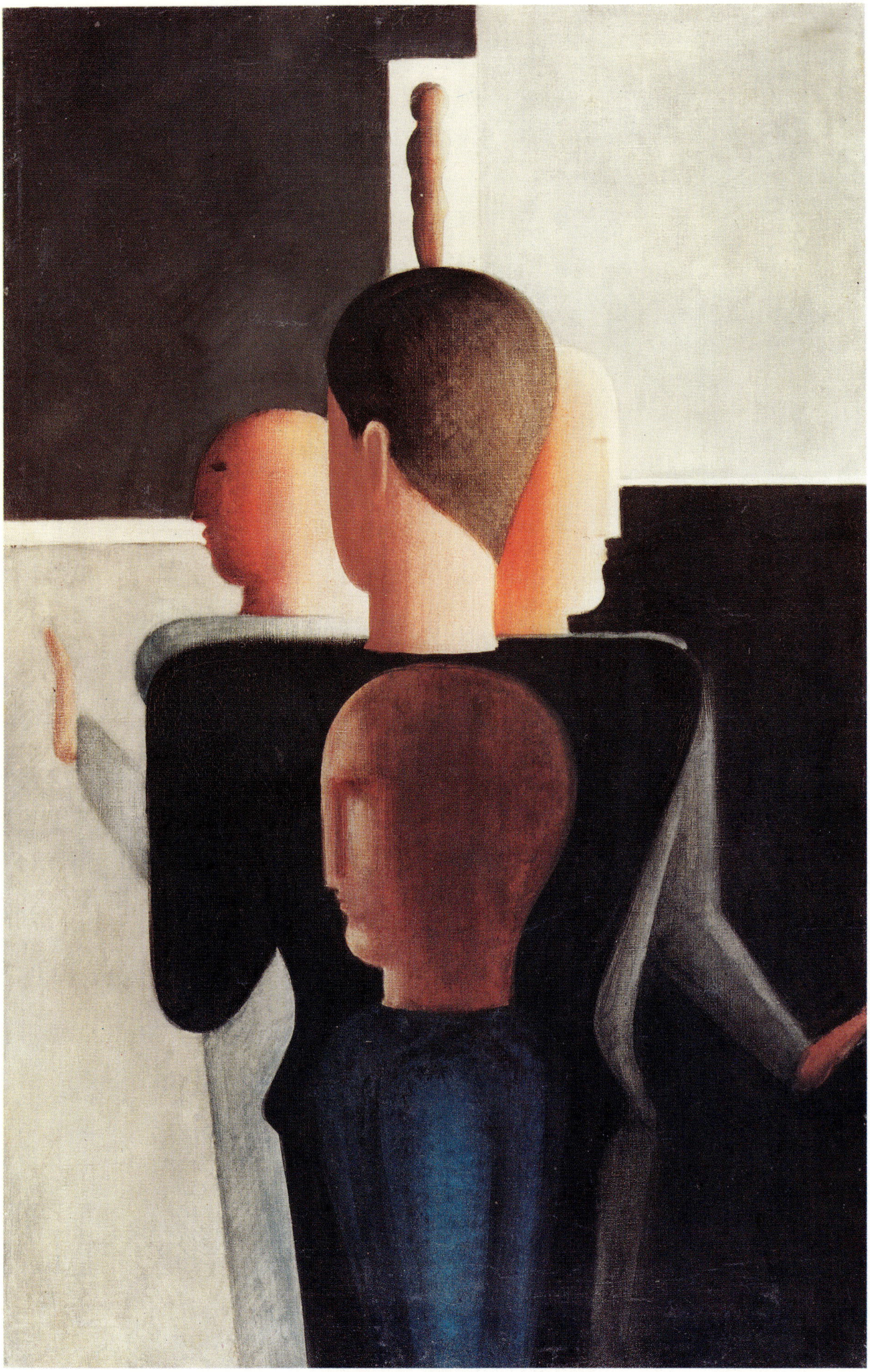

Plate 16 Oskar Schlemmer, *Concentric Group*, 1925, oil, $38\frac{3}{8} \times 24\frac{3}{8}$ ins (Staatsgalerie Stuttgart).

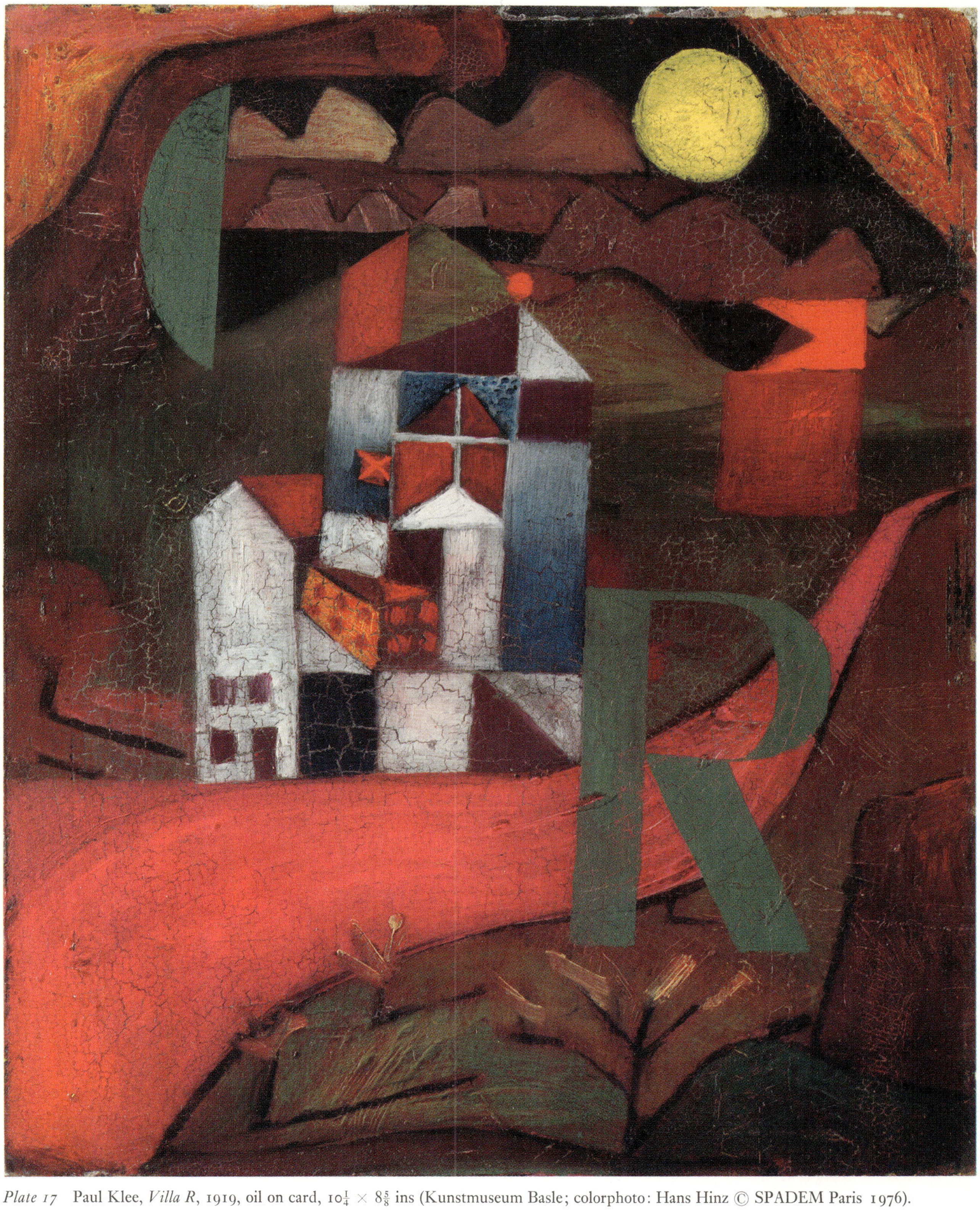

Plate 17 Paul Klee, *Villa R*, 1919, oil on card, $10\frac{1}{4} \times 8\frac{5}{8}$ ins (Kunstmuseum Basle; colorphoto: Hans Hinz © SPADEM Paris 1976).

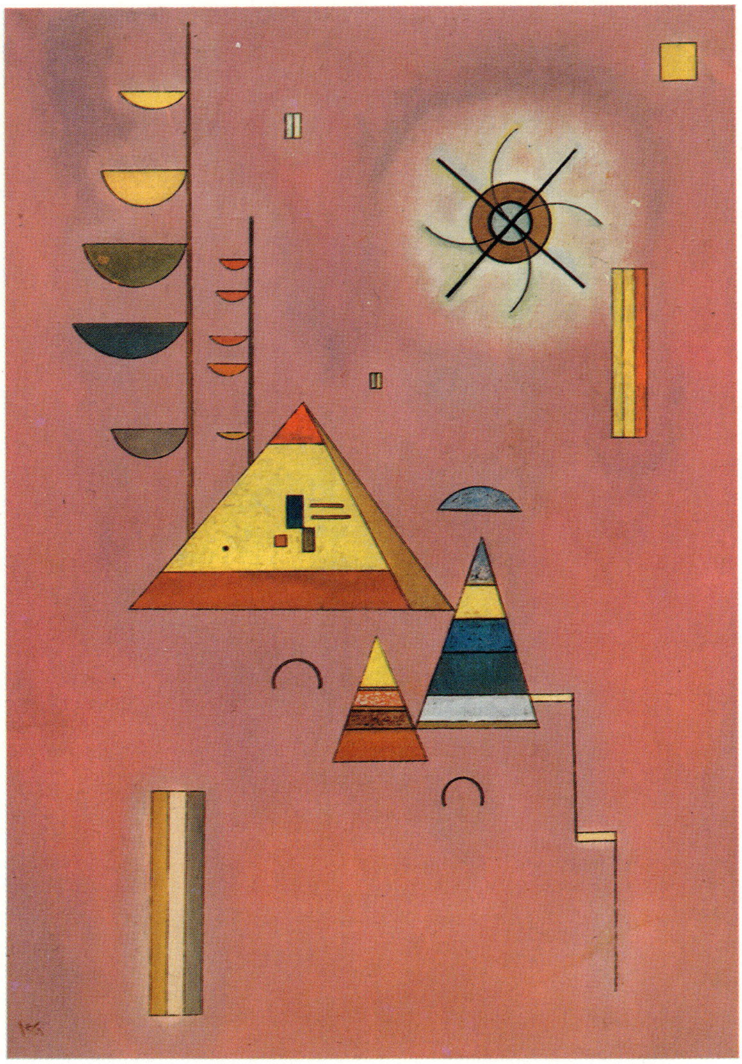

Plate 18 Wassily Kandinsky, *Pink Sweet*, 1929, oil on board, $27\frac{1}{2} \times 19$ ins (Solomon R. Guggenheim Museum, New York, Hilla Rebay Collection © ADAGP Paris 1976).

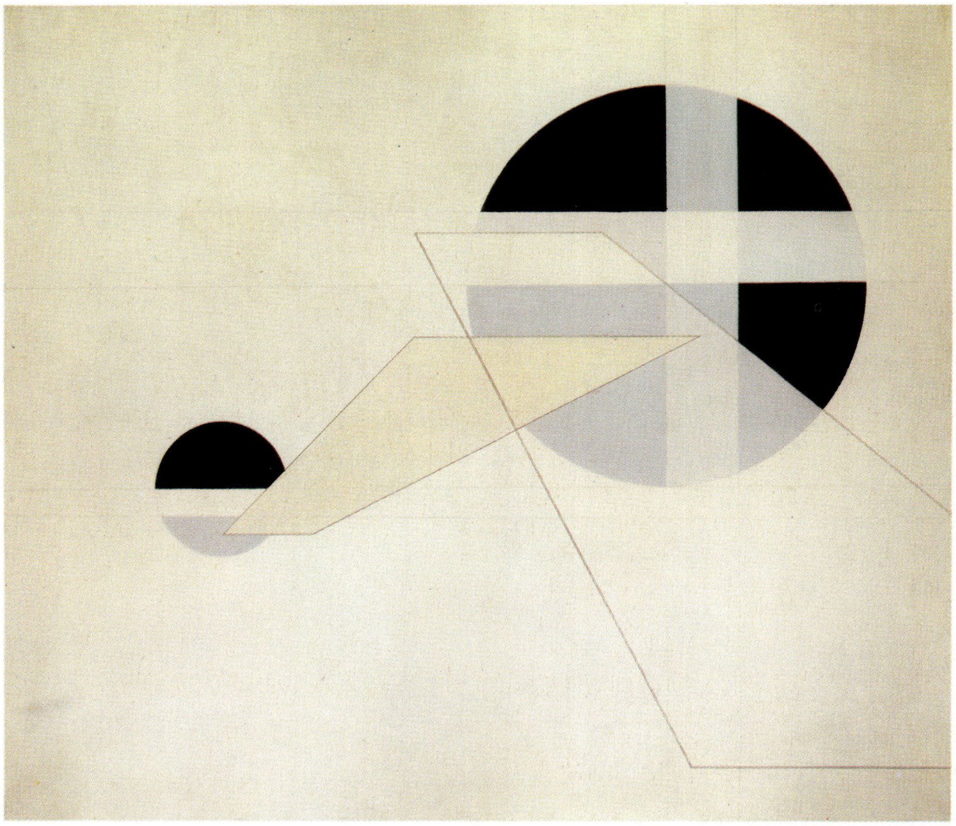

Plate 19 Laszlo Moholy-Nagy, *A XX*, 1924, oil, 46×54 ins (Musée Nationale d'Art Moderne, Paris; photo: AGRACI, courtesy Mrs Hug).